CAVENDISH

PLANT ❦ GUIDES

ROCK GARDEN PLANTS

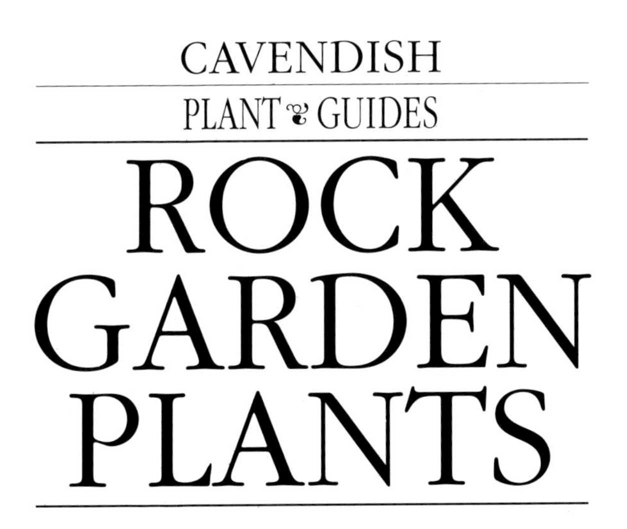

CAVENDISH

PLANT & GUIDES

ROCK GARDEN PLANTS

CAVENDISH BOOKS
VANCOUVER

A DK PUBLISHING BOOK

Produced for DK Publishing by PAGE*One*
Cairn House, Elgiva Lane, Chesham,
Buckinghamshire HP5 2JD

PROJECT DIRECTORS Bob Gordon and Helen Parker
EDITOR Charlotte Stock
DESIGNER Matthew Cook

MANAGING EDITOR Francis Ritter
MANAGING ART EDITOR Derek Coombes
PRODUCTION Martin Croshaw
PICTURE RESEARCH Joanne Beardwell

First American Edition, 1997
2 4 6 8 10 9 7 5 3 1

Published in the United States by
DK Publishing, Inc., 95 Madison Avenue,
New York, New York 10016
Visit us on the World Wide Web at http://www.dk.com

Published in Great Britain by Dorling Kindersley Limited.

Library of Congress Cataloging-in-Publication Data

Rock garden plants. — 1st American ed.
p. cm. — (Eyewitness garden handbooks)
Includes index.
ISBN 0-7894-1455-4
1. Rock plants. I. DK Publishing, Inc. II. Series.
SB421.R73 1997
635.9'672—dc21 96-47941
CIP

Color reproduction by Colourscan, Singapore
Printed and bound by Star Standard Industries, Singapore

CATALOG OF ROCK GARDEN PLANTS

LARGE

SMALL

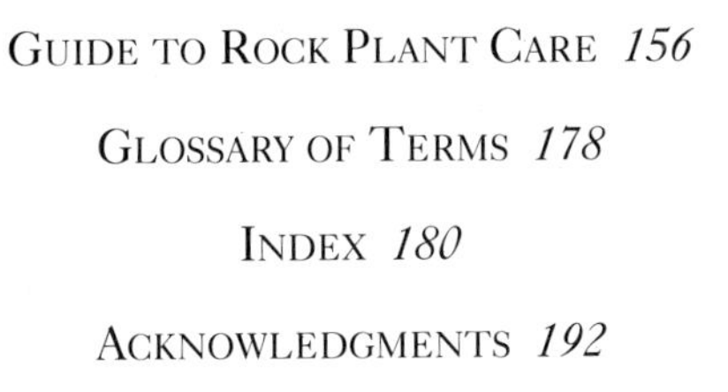

CONTRIBUTORS

CHRISTOPHER GREY-WILSON
Consultant

LINDEN HAWTHORNE
Writer

How to use this Book

This book provides the ideal quick reference guide to selecting and identifying rock plants for the garden.

The Rock Plants in the Garden section is a helpful introduction to rock plants and gives advice on choosing a suitable plant for a particular site or purpose, such as for a border, container, or simply as a specimen.

To choose or identify a plant, turn to the Catalog of Rock Garden Plants, where photographs are accompanied by concise plant descriptions and useful tips on cultivation and propagation. The entries are grouped by size, season of interest, as well as by color (see the color wheel below) to make selection easier.

For additional information on rock plant cultivation, routine care, and propagation, turn to the Guide to Rock Plant Care, where general advice on all aspects of caring for your rock plants can be found.

At the end of the book is a useful two-page glossary, which explains key terms. An index of every rock plant, its synonyms, and common names, together with a brief genus description, allows quick and easy access to the book by plant name.

The Symbols

The symbols below are used throughout the Catalog of Rock Garden Plants to indicate a plant's preferred growing conditions and hardiness. However, both the climate and soil conditions of your particular site should also be taken into account, as they may affect a plant's growth.

Prefers full sun

Prefers partial shade

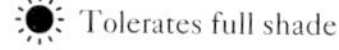

Tolerates full shade

pH Needs acid soil

Prefers well-drained soil

Prefers moist soil

Prefers wet soil

Hardiness

The range of winter temperatures that each plant is able to withstand is shown by the USDA plant hardiness zone numbers that are given in each entry. The temperature ranges for each zone are shown on the endpaper map in this book.

The color wheel

All the rock plants in the book are grouped according to the color of their main feature of interest. They are always arranged in the same order, indicated by the color wheel below. Variegated plants are categorized by the color of their variegation.

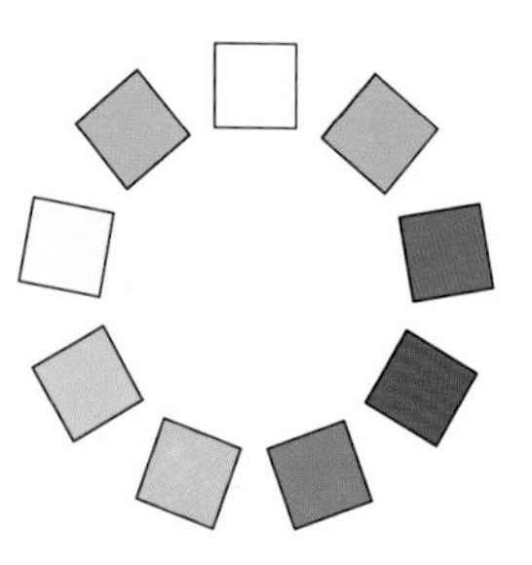

Rock plant size categories

The rock plants featured in the Catalog of Rock Garden Plants are divided according to the average height they attain. However, heights may vary from the ones given, according to site, growing conditions, climate, and age.

The categories are as follows:

Large
Over 6in (15cm)

Small
Up to 6in (15cm)

HOW TO USE THE CATALOG OF ROCK GARDEN PLANTS

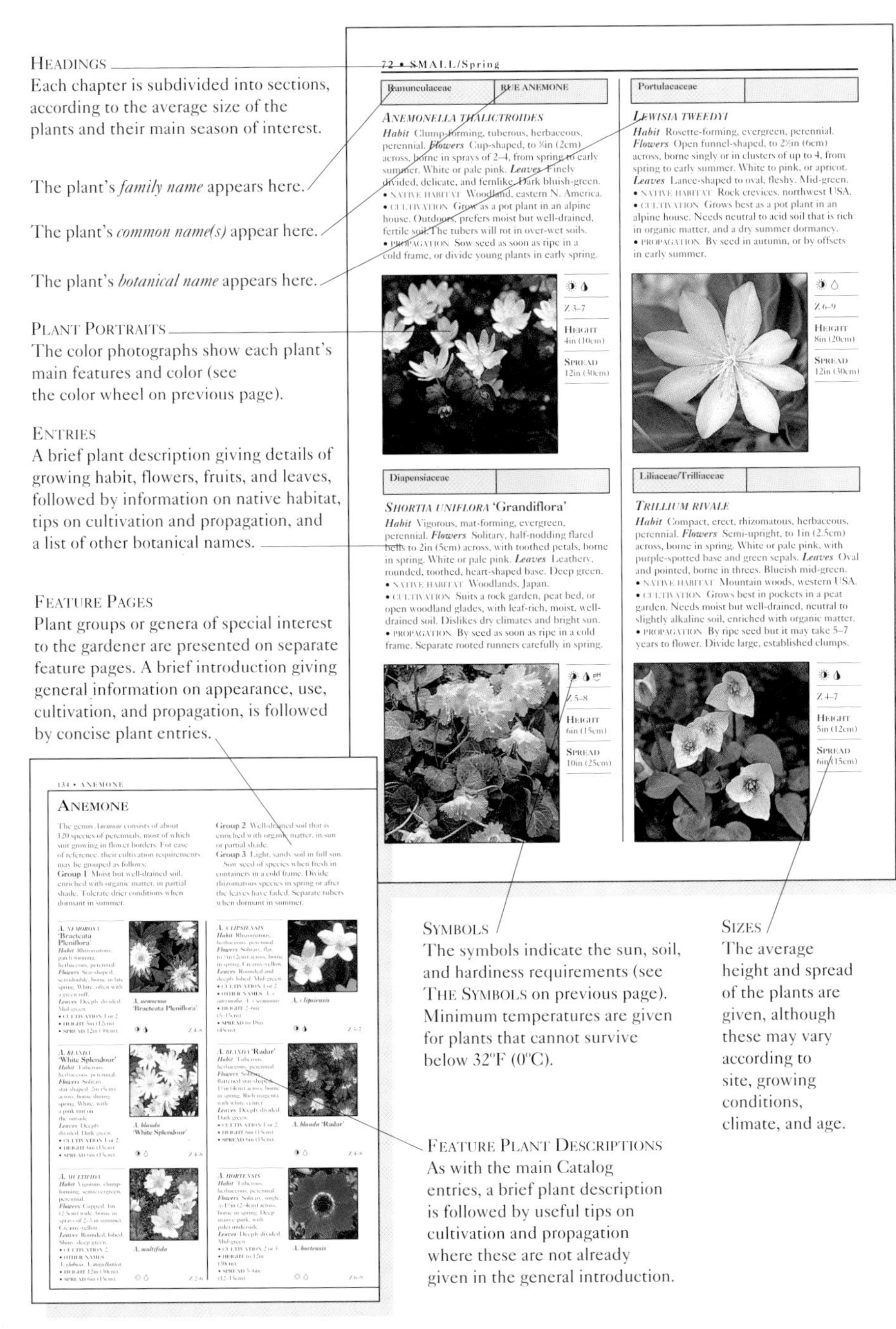

ROCK PLANTS IN THE GARDEN

THE diverse habitats of the world's mountain ranges are home to some of the most attractive plants ever introduced to gardens. True alpines occur at high altitudes above the tree-line, often in specialized habitats, such as rockface crevices, scree slopes, or in sparse, high-alpine turf. They make characteristic adaptations to survive the extremes of climate at high altitudes. A low, creeping habit reduces wind resistance and helps alpines to resist the crushing weight of snow in winter.

A well-constructed rock garden
On a sloping site, a construction that mimics natural rock strata provides perfect drainage and diverse planting niches, from vertical rock crevices to broader terraces.

An extensive root system provides strong anchorage, while searching deeply for water and nutrients in the often poor, sharply drained alpine soils. A reduced leaf size, fleshy leaves, or leathery or hairy leaf surfaces, and a dense, mat- or cushion-forming habit all help the plants to conserve moisture in the face of strong, cold winds and protect them from the burning effects of brilliant sun. Equally, a perennial, woody, or bulbous habit with an underground food-store permits rapid growth in spring to draw the most benefit from the short summer season.

In the wild, alpines are adapted to extremes of temperature but, in winter, high-growing species are insulated with a deep covering of snow, and remain

dormant at around 32°F (0°C). Few of them can withstand the constant wetness at their roots that is often experienced in gardens at lower altitudes in winter. Alpines demand very sharp drainage and protection from winter moisture, and they also dislike warm, humid summers. In the wild, alpines experience fresh, constantly moving air, and often brilliant sunshine during their growing period. While many alpines are quite amenable and undemanding in cultivation, the high-growing alpines have precise requirements. However, they include many beautiful species, with disproportionately large flowers in unrivaled, jewel-bright colors, that will richly reward the extra attention paid to fulfilling these needs.

Rock plants

The term rock plants is used to describe relatively slow-growing plants that are suitable in scale for the rock garden, although they may not necessarily be of alpine origin. These species are usually easier to grow than true alpines and

A blaze of summer color
The brilliant red flowers of Helianthemum *and* Sedum *cascade down a rockface, providing both focus and counterpoint to the gray leaves of* Dianthus *in the background.*

possess several other advantages in the garden. Most true alpines bloom very early in the year, so that they can flower and set seed before the onset of winter snows. Many rock plants, however, bloom well into summer, thus extending the period of interest. For example, helianthemums, which often occur on sunny hills around the Mediterranean, share the need for sharp drainage and bloom from spring into summer. The smaller veronicas, sedums, and phloxes, as well as *Armeria maritima*, a coastal native, also bloom later in the season. Dwarf trees and shrubs, like *Salix*, *Genista*, and *Daphne*, are useful as framework plantings. Native woodlanders, like *Cornus canadensis*, or *Hepatica* species, which prefer moister, shadier conditions, are ideal for niches in a rock garden, where sun-loving rock plants and alpines would fail to thrive.

Planting in the open garden
A free-flowering shrub in bloom, (here, Daphne x burkwoodii *'Somerset'), provides a focal point in a mixed border and acts as a framework for other plantings during the rest of the year.*

Open gardens

Nearly all rock plants and alpines are characterized by a restricted size or neat habit and so are particularly well suited to the confines of a smaller, modern garden. Those that need relatively little cultivation can easily be grown in the open garden, in a scree, or in the crevices of paving and patios.

A sunny, south- or southwest-facing slope that is situated away from any shade cast by large trees or buildings is ideal for a rock garden. In hotter and drier climates, a north-facing slope can be equally effective. A rock garden should try to emulate natural rock formations as closely as possible and provide a diversity of niches to replicate the natural habitats of alpine plants. To achieve this effect and for the greatest visual impact, the rock garden should be constructed on as generous a scale as the site allows.

The arrangement of different-size rocks in natural-looking layers, with terraces and pockets of deeper soil between them, will provide niches that suit a range of plants from various habitats. If sited properly, large rocks provide a deep, moist, and cool root run beneath them, as well as insulating the roots from the worst of the winter cold. Wherever it is positioned, a rock garden will provide different exposures for a wide range of alpines. A series of rocky outcrops with crevices and gullies between them provides ideal conditions for rock-crevice dwellers like the cushion-forming saxifrages or, if given a more northerly exposure, for the shade-loving lewisias. Deep pockets of gritty soil at the base of rocks provide niches for many of the gentians, while wider terraces suit mat-formers like phloxes or *Persicaria affine* 'Donald Lowndes'.

A scree garden is, essentially, a gently sloping bed of loose rock fragments mixed with low-fertility, gritty soil mix. It is a less expensive alternative to a rock garden, and can either be created separately or integrated between or below large rocks to provide a home for natural scree-dwellers such as *Edrainthus serpyllifolius.*

The most natural rock gardens are constructed of local stone, which not only harmonizes better with the surrounding landscape, but also has economic advantages in terms of purchase and transportation costs.

Equally, important conservation issues need to be considered where rock has been extracted from ecologically sensitive rock formations (see p. 157). Where space or expense prohibits the creation of a rock garden, several alternative ways of growing alpines can be considered.

Raised beds and walls

One of the most notable features that makes a raised bed suitable for small gardens is its highly economical use of space. Since drainage is entirely independent of the surrounding soil, a raised bed makes a good option for gardens with heavy, poorly drained clay soils that alpine plants dislike intensely. In addition, dimensions can be planned so that the entire bed can be protected in winter with a cold-frame cover. This is ideal for plants that need unrestricted air movement and protection from winter moisture. A raised bed should be created as an integral part of the overall garden design. A square or rectangular bed offers both sunny and shady sides, and can also be constructed so that the walls incorporate planting niches for crevice-dwelling plants. Larger beds can be designed to provide separate areas with different soil mix types to suit specific cultivation needs. They may even be "landscaped" by bedding rocks into the surface to provide vertical or shaded niches for plants that need

A tapestry of color

The dark foliage of these evergreen shrubs and dwarf conifers provide an attractive backdrop that contrasts with and sets off the jewel-like colors and varied forms of the alpines.

A low raised bed
Here, a low raised bed flanks a narrow stone path and draws the eye to the open garden beyond. The alpines planted in bold and natural drifts thrive in the enhanced drainage offered by a raised bed.

those conditions. When planting raised beds, it is important to consider successional interest as well as the final dimensions of individual species, if they are not to become visually overbearing or to swamp out smaller neighbors.

Given the right exposure, drystone retaining walls can be ideal sites for growing trailing, cushion-, or mat-forming plants. The crevices are almost inevitably sharply drained, and roots can penetrate into the backfill beyond to seek moisture and nutrients and a cool, moist root run. If considering a brick or other type of mortared wall as a planting site, niches should be built in by leaving crevices, cracks, or spaces between the bricks or rocks.

Troughs and sinks

Old stone sinks and troughs provide one of the most attractive ways of growing a collection of alpines, although they are unfortunately both expensive and scarce. Modern facsimiles made of hypertufa, reconstituted stone, or glazed sinks coated with hypertufa are inexpensive alternatives (see p. 163). Filled with a sharply drained, gritty soil mix that is adapted to suit the specific needs of individual plants, sinks and troughs make ideal sites for miniature cushion-formers like *Androsace* or *Saxifraga* species or the small and beautiful *Campanula zoysii*. They are equally effective whether landscaped as miniature gardens or devoted to a collection of a species of a single genus with very similar cultural needs.

The alpine house

An alpine house is a minimally heated greenhouse, usually with raised benches for cultivating alpines under controlled conditions. It differs from an ordinary cold greenhouse mainly in the increased ventilation provided by vents along the sides and roof and, usually, offers the facility to shade plants from the hottest sun in summer. For some gardeners, its primary function is to allow the challenging high-growing alpine plants to be grown under carefully controlled conditions. Alpines that naturally spend their winter dormancy beneath a blanket of snow are insulated from extremes of temperature and shielded from cold winds and excessive rainfall. Often these plants cannot adapt to the variable and very different conditions of low-altitude temperate climates, although some will thrive in the open garden if given the overhead protection of an open cloche or propped pane of glass. The more demanding species, however, will need the finer control offered by an alpine house. While it is commonly associated with plants that do not suit low-altitude climates, an alpine house can also be very rewarding when used to grow to perfection otherwise robust species that flower very early in the year. It protects them from heavy rain or cold damage, and the predations of slugs, snails, and other pests (see p. 176).

An alpine house collection
(below) A variety of alpines, displayed in containers in an alpine house, make an attractive feature.

Spilling over
(above) Part of a hollowed-out, well-drained tree trunk is used for Sedum spathulifolium *'Cape Blanco'.*

Planters' Guide to Rock Plants

For exposed sites
Antennaria dioica
Campanula portenschlagiana
Carlina acaulis
Chiastophyllum oppositifolium
Dryas octopetala
Erigeron karvinskianus
Euphorbia myrsinites
Helianthemum
Limonium bellidifolium
Pterocephalus perennis
Sempervivum

Air-pollution tolerant
Aubrieta
Aurinia saxatilis 'Dudley Nevill'
Campanula garganica
Campanula poscharskyana
Erinus alpinus
Sedum some
Sempervivum

For moist shade
Cassiope
Daphne blagayana
Hepatica nobilis
Hepatica transsilvanica
Meconopsis cambrica
Primula many spp., cvs.
Sanguinaria canadensis
Shortia uniflora
Trillium spp.

For dry shade
Dianthus carthusianorum
Dianthus deltoides
Genista sagittalis
Gypsophila repens
Saponaria ocymoides

Scree gardens
Acantholimon glumaceum
Aethionema 'Warley Rose'
Alyssum montanum
Androsace lanuginosa
Androsace sarmentosa
Dianthus alpinus
Dianthus erinaceus
Edraianthus pumilio
Erinus alpinus
Papaver alpinum
Papaver fauriei
Sempervivum spp.
Silene acaulis

Paving
Campanula cochleariifolia
Geranium sanguineum
Mentha requienii
Pratia pedunculata
Thymus some

Wall crevices
Aubrieta many cvs.
Aurinia saxatilis 'Dudley Nevill'
Aurinia saxatilis 'Citrina'
Campanula portenschlagiana
Erinus alpinus
Globularia cordifolia
Haberlea rhodopensis
Lewisia Cotyledon Hybrids
Lewisia tweedyi
Onosma alborosea
Ramonda myconi
Saxifraga longifolia
Saxifraga 'Southside Seedling'
Scabiosa graminifolia

Planting in tufa
Androsace small spp., cvs.
Campanula zoysii
Physoplexis comosa
Potentilla nitida
Saxifraga

Planting in troughs
Anchusa caespitosa
Androsace many spp.
Arenaria purpurascens
Asperula suberosa
Dianthus alpinus

Dianthus 'Little Jock'
Dianthus 'La Bourboule'
Edraianthus pumilio
Gentiana saxosa
Omphalodes luciliae
Oxalis enneaphylla
Petrophytum hendersonii
Primula marginata
Saxifraga many
Sedum cauticola
Vitaliana primuliflora

Raised beds
Aethionema 'Warley Rose'
Androsace spp.
Armeria juniperifolia
Bolax gummifera
Campanula zoysii
Daphne cneorum
Daphne petraea 'Grandiflora'
Dianthus alpine spp., cvs.
Draba rigida
Erinacea anthyllis
Globularia spp.
Haberlea rhodopensis
Iberis spp.
Leontopodium alpinum
Lewisia some spp., cvs.
Oxalis adenophylla
Oxalis enneaphylla
Papaver faurei
Primula auricula
Primula marginata
Saxifraga some
Sempervivum
Silene acaulis
Verbascum 'Letitia'

CATALOG OF ROCK GARDEN PLANTS

Compositae/Asteraceae	EDELWEISS

LEONTOPODIUM ALPINUM

Habit Clump-forming, perennial. ***Flowers*** Tiny, woolly, leaflike bracts forming a star, 1–1¼in (2½–3cm) across, borne in spring or early summer. White, with gray-white base. ***Leaves*** Linear to narrowly lance-shaped. Gray-green.

• NATIVE HABITAT Grassy and rocky areas, Europe.
• CULTIVATION Grow in a site with gritty, sharply drained soil that is neutral to alkaline, and protect plant from excessive winter moisture.
• PROPAGATION By seed when ripe or by division in spring, but can be slow to reestablish.

Z 4–7

HEIGHT
8in (20cm)

SPREAD
4in (10cm)

Cruciferae/ Brassicaceae	

IBERIS SEMPERVIRENS

Habit Spreading, evergreen, subshrub.
Flowers Tiny, uneven, cross-shaped, 2in (5cm) across, borne in dense, rounded heads in late spring or early summer. White, often flushed pink.
Leaves Paddle- to spoon-shaped. Dark green.

• NATIVE HABITAT Mountains of southern Europe.
• CULTIVATION Needs well-drained, neutral to alkaline soil. Trim after flowering to keep compact.
• PROPAGATION By seed in autumn in a frame, by softwood, or by semiripe cuttings in mid-summer.
• OTHER NAME *I. commutata.*

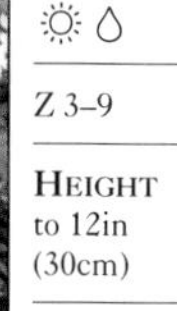

Z 3–9

HEIGHT
to 12in (30cm)

SPREAD
24in (60cm)

Ranunculaceae	ALPINE PASQUE FLOWER

PULSATILLA ALPINA

Habit Tufted, perennial. ***Flowers*** Cup-shaped, fine-haired, 2½in (6cm) across, borne in spring. White, with golden stamens and a blue tint outside. ***Leaves*** Feathery, finely dissected, and hairy. Bright green. ***Fruits*** Silky-haired, spherical seedheads. Silver or gray.

• NATIVE HABITAT Central and southern Europe.
• CULTIVATION Provide moderately fertile soil and good drainage. Dislikes root disturbance.
• PROPAGATION By seed when ripe, or by root cuttings in winter.

Z 5–7

HEIGHT
to 12in (30cm)

SPREAD
8in (20cm)

Ericaceae	

ANDROMEDA POLIFOLIA 'Alba'

Habit Open, semiprostrate, evergreen, shrub.
Flowers Urn-shaped, borne in clusters to 1¼in (3cm) across, in spring and summer. Pure white.
Leaves Narrowly linear and leathery. Dark green.

• NATIVE HABITAT Species found in peat bogs in northern Europe.
• CULTIVATION Prefers leaf-rich, acid soil that stays reliably moist. Tolerates part shade or sun.
• PROPAGATION By softwood cuttings, or by rooted layers in autumn or spring.
• OTHER NAME *A polifolia* 'Compacta Alba'.

Z 2–7

HEIGHT
12in (30cm)

SPREAD
12in (30cm)

Ranunculaceae	

AQUILEGIA FLABELLATA var. *PUMILA* f. *ALBA*

Habit Neat, compact, clump-forming, herbaceous, perennial. ***Flowers*** Semiupright to nodding, bell-shaped, measuring 1¼–2in (3–5cm) across and ¾in (2cm) in length, with 5 incurved spurs. Borne 1–3 per stem in either late spring or early summer. Creamy-white. ***Leaves*** Rounded, slightly fan-shaped, divided, waxy, and heavily textured. Bluish-green.

• NATIVE HABITAT Open woodland and scrub in the mountains of Japan.

• CULTIVATION Ideal for planting in a sheltered niche with partial shade in a rock garden. Grows best in gritty, moist but sharply drained soil, and prefers a site in dappled or partial shade.

• PROPAGATION By seed as soon as ripe, protected by an open frame. May take up to two years before germinating and needs at least one period of frost to induce germination. May self-seed, but is likely to hybridize unless grown in isolation.

• OTHER NAME *A. flabellata* 'Nana Alba'.

Z 4–9

HEIGHT
to 4in
(10cm)

SPREAD
to 4in
(10cm)

Ranunculaceae	

CLEMATIS MARMORARIA

Habit Tufted, spreading, prostrate, often suckering, evergreen, dwarf, shrub. ***Flowers*** Unisexual, upright, saucer-shaped, spanning 1in (2.5cm) across. Borne freely, either solitary or in clusters, on long stalks in early or mid-spring. Greenish-white, becoming creamy-white at maturity. The flowers of the male plant are usually larger and whiter. ***Fruits*** Fluffy, seeded fruitheads produced. Silky-white, turning golden-brown. ***Leaves*** Rigid, parsleylike, finely divided, and glossy. Dark green.

- NATIVE HABITAT High mountains of South Island, New Zealand.
- CULTIVATION Best grown in a trough outdoors, protected by glass in winter. Prefers an alpine house in cold areas. Grow in a sunny site, with fertile, moist but sharply drained soil that is rich in organic matter. Under glass, grow in a mix of equal parts soil, leaf mold, and grit. Water freely when in growth, and keep just moist in winter.
- PROPAGATION By seed as soon as ripe, in a cold frame, by softwood, or by semiripe cuttings.

Z 7–9

HEIGHT
6in (15cm)

SPREAD
10in (25cm)

Compositae/Asteraceae	

Rhodanthemum hosmariense

Habit Bushy, spreading, evergreen, subshrub. ***Flowers*** Solitary, daisylike, 2in (5cm) across, borne in spring to autumn. White, with yellow center. ***Leaves*** Soft-haired, lobed. Silver-green.
- NATIVE HABITAT Atlas Mountains, Morocco.
- CULTIVATION Suitable for growing in a rock garden or raised bed. Needs well-drained soil.
- PROPAGATION By seed in spring, or by taking softwood cuttings.
- OTHER NAMES *Chrysanthemum hosmariense, Leucanthemum hosmariense, Pyrethropsis hosmariense.*

Z 7–9

HEIGHT to 12in (30cm)

SPREAD 12in (30cm)

Ericaceae	

Cassiope 'Muirhead'

Habit Loose, bushy, upright, evergreen, shrub. ***Flowers*** Nodding, bell-shaped, ⅜in (8mm) long, borne on upper parts of stems in spring. White, with red outer petals. ***Leaves*** Tiny, lance-shaped, scalelike, and pressed close to stems. Dark green.
- NATIVE HABITAT Garden origin.
- CULTIVATION Suitable for a rock garden or peat bed. Grow in moist, acid soil that is enriched with organic matter. Prefers a site in partial shade or sun, where the soil remains reliably moist.
- PROPAGATION By semiripe cuttings.

pH

Z 7–9

HEIGHT 8in (20cm)

SPREAD 8in (20cm)

Ranunculaceae	

Pulsatilla vulgaris f. *alba*

Habit Clumping, herbaceous, perennial. ***Flowers*** Upright to nodding bells, silky-haired, 1½–3½in (4–9cm) across, borne in spring. White. ***Fruits*** Round, hairy seedheads. Silver. ***Leaves*** Feathery, with linear lobes, hairy when young. Light green.
- NATIVE HABITAT Short turf and meadows in Britain, and from western France to Ukraine.
- CULTIVATION Grow in well-drained, moderately fertile soil. Dislikes root disturbance.
- PROPAGATION By seed when ripe, or by root cuttings in winter.

Z 5–7

HEIGHT to 8in (20cm)

SPREAD 8in (20cm)

Ericaceae	

Cassiope 'Edinburgh'

Habit Bushy, erect, evergreen, shrub. ***Flowers*** Nodding bells, ⅜in (8mm) long, borne toward the stem tips in spring. White, with small, greenish-brown outer petals. ***Leaves*** Scalelike, lance-shaped, and pressed against stems. Dark green.
- NATIVE HABITAT Garden origin.
- CULTIVATION Suitable for growing in a rock garden or peat bed. Needs a site in partial shade, with moist, acid soil that is rich in organic matter. or sun with soil that remains reliably moist.
- PROPAGATION By semiripe cuttings.

pH

Z 7–9

HEIGHT 10in (25cm)

SPREAD 10in (25cm)

Berberidaceae	RHEUMATISM ROOT, TWIN LEAF

JEFFERSONIA DIPHYLLA

Habit Tuft-forming, herbaceous, perennial. ***Flowers*** Solitary, erect, cupped, 1in (2.5cm) across, borne in late spring and summer. White. ***Leaves*** Cleft into 2 kidney-shaped lobes. Gray-green.

• NATIVE HABITAT Damp woodlands, N. America, from Ontario to Tennessee.

• CULTIVATION Suits a shady niche in a peat bed or rock garden. Needs moist soil enriched with organic matter, and a leaf-mold mulch in summer.

• PROPAGATION By seed as soon as ripe, or by careful division of well-established plants in spring.

Z 5–8

HEIGHT 6in (15cm)

SPREAD 8in (20cm)

Primulaceae	

DODECATHEON MEADIA f. *ALBUM*

Habit Clumping, herbaceous, perennial. ***Flowers*** Drooping, pointed, to ¾in (2cm) long, with reflexed petals, borne in clusters from mid- to late spring. White, with yellow stamens. ***Leaves*** Rosette-forming, toothed and oval. Pale to mid-green.

• NATIVE HABITAT Meadows and open woods, eastern N. America.

• CULTIVATION Suits a woodland or rock garden. Needs leaf-rich, moist soil with organic matter.

• PROPAGATION By ripe seed, or divide in spring.

• OTHER NAME *D. pauciflorum* f. *album*.

Z 5–7

HEIGHT 16in (40cm)

SPREAD 10in (25cm)

Saxifragaceae	FOAM FLOWER

TIARELLA CORDIFOLIA

Habit Rhizomatous, evergreen, perennial. ***Flowers*** Tiny, star-shaped, borne in sprays to 6in (15cm) long, in late spring. White. ***Leaves*** Oval, with 3–5 lobes. Pale green.

• NATIVE HABITAT Woodlands, N. America.

• CULTIVATION Ideal as ground cover in a shady border or woodland garden, but is too vigorous to accompany delicate alpines.Tolerates a range of soils but prefers a cool, moist, leaf-rich site.

• PROPAGATION By seed when ripe or in late winter, or by division in spring.

Z 3–8

HEIGHT 8in (20cm)

SPREAD 12in (30cm) or more

Papaveraceae	

RUPICAPNOS AFRICANA

Habit Short-lived, evergreen, perennial. ***Flowers*** Delicate, tubular, spurred, to ½in (15mm) long, borne in clusters in summer. Pink-purple. ***Leaves*** Fleshy, finely divided and fernlike, forming basal clumps. Bright blue-gray.

• NATIVE HABITAT Sunny cliff faces in the Riff mountains, N. Africa.

• CULTIVATION Grow in sharply drained, gritty soil in an alpine house. Dislikes winter moisture.

• PROPAGATION Collect seed when almost ripe but still green, and sow immediately.

Z 7–9

HEIGHT 6in (15cm)

SPREAD 8in (20cm)

Ericaceae	COMPACT BOG ROSEMARY

ANDROMEDA POLIFOLIA 'Compacta'

Habit Densely twiggy, evergreen, shrub. ***Flowers*** Urn-shaped, borne in clusters to 1¼in (3cm) across, in spring and early summer. Pink. ***Leaves*** Lance-shaped. Dark green, with glaucous underside.

• NATIVE HABITAT Species found in peat bogs in northern Europe.

• CULTIVATION Suits a rock or woodland garden, or a peat bed. Needs leaf-rich, acid soil that remains reliably moist, in a site with partial shade or sun.

• PROPAGATION By softwood cuttings, or by rooted layers, in autumn or spring.

Z 2–7

HEIGHT 6in (15cm)

SPREAD 8in (20cm)

Primulaceae	MOSQUITO BILLS, SAILOR CAPS

DODECATHEON HENDERSONII

Habit Clumping, herbaceous, perennial. ***Flowers*** Drooping, pointed, to 1in (2.5cm) long, borne in early summer. Purple-pink, with darker center and white base. ***Leaves*** Rosette-forming, narrowly oval, and fleshy. Dark green.

• NATIVE HABITAT Grassland, USA.

• CULTIVATION Suitable for a rock garden or alpine house. Keep moist during growth but provide a dry summer dormancy. Grow in leaf-rich soil.

• PROPAGATION By ripe seed or division in spring.

• OTHER NAME *D. latifolium*.

Z 5–7

HEIGHT 16in (40cm)

SPREAD 10in (25cm)

Ericaceae	

PHYLLODOCE × INTERMEDIA 'Drummondii'

Habit Bushy, spreading, evergreen, dwarf shrub. ***Flowers*** Urn-shaped, ¼in (6mm) long, in terminal clusters on slender red stalks, borne in spring and early summer. Deep pink-purple. ***Leaves*** Linear and glossy. Dark green.

• NATIVE HABITAT Garden origin.

• CULTIVATION Suits a peat bed or rock garden, with moist, leaf-rich, acid soil that is rich in organic matter. Trim after flowering to keep compact.

• PROPAGATION By semiripe cuttings.

Z 3–7

HEIGHT 9in (23cm)

SPREAD 9in (23cm)

Ericaceae	

PHYLLODOCE EMPETRIFORMIS

Habit Vigorous, evergreen, mat-forming, shrub. ***Flowers*** Bell-shaped, long-stalked, ¼in (6mm) long, borne in terminal clusters in spring and early summer. Pink-purple. ***Leaves*** Linear, toothed, glossy, with pale, downy underside. Emerald.

• NATIVE HABITAT Alpine and arctic habitats of western N. America, from Alaska to California.

• CULTIVATION Suitable for growing in a peat bed or rock garden. Needs moist, leaf-rich, acid soil.

• PROPAGATION By seed in spring, or by semi-ripe cuttings.

Z 3–7

HEIGHT 12in (30cm)

SPREAD 16in (40cm)

Ranunculaceae	

PULSATILLA VULGARIS var. *RUBRA*

Habit Vigorous, clump-forming, herbaceous, perennial. ***Flowers*** Upright to nodding, bell-shaped, silky-haired, 1½–3½in (4–9cm) across, borne in spring. Red to purple-red. ***Fruits*** Spherical, silky-haired seedheads. Silver. ***Leaves*** Feathery, finely divided into linear lobes, and densely clothed in fine, silky hairs when young. Mid- to dark green with silver hairs.

• NATIVE HABITAT Short turf and meadows, from western France to Ukraine.

• CULTIVATION An easy and reliable species that thrives on a rock garden. It is ideal for growing in gravel plantings or well-drained herbaceous borders. Prefers a site with well-drained, moderately fertile soil. Dislikes root disturbance, and is best planted out when small and left undisturbed. The flowers are particularly attractive when edged with frost, and they remain undamaged by short-lived frosts.

• PROPAGATION By root cuttings in winter, or by just-ripe seed. Self-sows, but may not come true.

☼ ◊

Z 5–7

HEIGHT
8in (20cm) or more

SPREAD
8in (20cm)

Primulaceae	

DODECATHEON PULCHELLUM 'Red Wings'

Habit Tufted, herbaceous, perennial. ***Flowers*** Drooping, pointed, to ¾in (2cm) long, borne in strong-stemmed clusters in mid- to late spring. Magenta-pink, with prominent, deep orange-brown stamens. ***Leaves*** Rosetted, narrowly oval, forming basal clusters. Soft, pale green.
• NATIVE HABITAT Garden origin.
• CULTIVATION Suits a woodland or rock garden. Needs leaf-rich, moist soil with organic matter.
• PROPAGATION By division in spring.

Z 5–7

HEIGHT 8in (20cm)

SPREAD 8in (20cm)

Ericaceae	MOUNTAIN HEATH

PHYLLODOCE CAERULEA

Habit Dwarf, upright, evergreen, shrub. ***Flowers*** Bell-shaped, ½in (1cm) long, borne in terminal clusters in spring and early summer. Pink-purple to rose-red. ***Leaves*** Linear, glossy, and small-toothed, with pale, downy underside. Dark green.
• NATIVE HABITAT Alpine habitats in Europe, Asia, and the USA.
• CULTIVATION Needs moist, leaf-rich, acid soil.
• PROPAGATION Sow seed in spring, or take semiripe cuttings.
• OTHER NAME *P. taxifolia.*

pH

Z 3–7

HEIGHT 12in (30cm)

SPREAD 12in (30cm)

Leguminosae/ Papilionaceae	HEDGEHOG BROOM

ERINACEA ANTHYLLIS

Habit Dense, mound-forming, spiny, evergreen, shrub. ***Flowers*** Pealike, to ¾in (2cm) long, borne in clusters of 2–4 in late spring and early summer. Blue-violet. ***Leaves*** Small, inconspicuous, on tough, green stems. Dark gray-green.
• NATIVE HABITAT Exposed, rocky habitats, from western Mediterranean to eastern Pyrenees.
• CULTIVATION Ideal for a raised bed, scree, or rock garden, with deep, gritty, sharply drained soil.
• PROPAGATION By ripe seed or softwood cuttings.
• OTHER NAME *E. pungens.*

Z 7–9

HEIGHT 12in (30cm)

SPREAD 32in (80cm)

Boraginaceae	

OMPHALODES CAPPADOCICA 'Cherry Ingram'

Habit Carpeting, rhizomatous, evergreen, perennial. ***Flowers*** Resembling forget-me-nots, ¼in (7mm) across, borne in terminal sprays in early spring. Deep azure-blue. ***Leaves*** Oval to heart-shaped, pointed, and fine-haired. Mid-green.
• NATIVE HABITAT Garden origin.
• CULTIVATION Good ground cover for a large border, woodland, or rock garden. Needs a partial- or dapple-shaded site with moist, leaf-rich soil.
• PROPAGATION By seed, or by division in spring.

Z 6–9

HEIGHT
8in (20cm)

SPREAD
24in (60cm)

Ranunculaceae	HALLEN'S PASQUE FLOWER

PULSATILLA HALLERI

Habit Tufted, intensely silver-haired, herbaceous, perennial. ***Flowers*** Erect, goblet-shaped, to 3½in (9cm) across, borne in late spring. Lavender-blue to violet. ***Leaves*** Feathery, finely divided. Light green. ***Fruits*** Round, silky-haired seedheads.
• NATIVE HABITAT Mountain turf, from central and southeast Europe to the Crimea.
• CULTIVATION Needs moderately fertile, sharply drained soil in sun. Dislikes root disturbance.
• PROPAGATION By fresh seed, or by root cuttings in winter.

Z 5–7

HEIGHT
8in (20cm)

SPREAD
6in (15cm)

Ranunculaceae	PASQUE FLOWER

PULSATILLA VULGARIS

Habit Clump-forming, herbaceous, perennial. ***Flowers*** Erect to nodding bells, silky-haired, 2–4in (4–9cm) across, borne in spring. Deep to pale purple. ***Leaves*** Finely divided, hairy when young. Light green. ***Fruits*** Spherical, silky seedheads.
• NATIVE HABITAT Short turf and meadows, in Britain and from western France to Ukraine.
• CULTIVATION Grow in well-drained, moderately fertile soil, and avoid disturbing the roots.
• PROPAGATION By fresh seed, or by root cuttings in winter.

Z 5–7

HEIGHT
16in (40cm) or more

SPREAD
8in (20cm)

Ranunculaceae	ALPINE CLEMATIS

CLEMATIS ALPINA

Habit Deciduous, woody scrambler or leaf-twining climber. ***Flowers*** Solitary, nodding, open bell-shaped, to 3in (7cm) across, borne in spring and, often, again in late summer. Blue, with white center. ***Leaves*** Paired, divided, oval, toothed, with twining leaf stalks. Mid-green. ***Fruits*** Seedheads, becoming fluffy at maturity. Silky-white.

• NATIVE HABITAT Scrub, woodland, occasionally on screes, in the mountains of Europe.

• CULTIVATION Excellent for growing in very cold, exposed sites. As a climber, it is effective in larger rock gardens if allowed to sprawl over rock faces. As a scrambler, the plant will be much lower than the height shown. Choose a site away from small and less vigorous alpines. Grow in fertile, moist but well-drained soil that is rich in organic matter. Prefers a site in sun or dappled shade, with its roots in shade. If necessary, prune plant after flowering, shortening shoots to the allotted space.

• PROPAGATION By seed as soon as ripe, or by softwood or semiripe cuttings in summer.

Z 5–9

HEIGHT
6–10ft
(2–3m)

SPREAD
5ft (1.5m)

Scrophulariaceae	

VERONICA PEDUNCULARIS

Habit Mat-forming, rhizomatous, perennial. ***Flowers*** Saucer-shaped, ⅓in (8mm) span, borne in erect sprays in spring and summer. Deep blue, pink, or white. ***Leaves*** Lance-shaped and glossy. Dark green, tinted purple.

- NATIVE HABITAT Grassy and rocky places in Turkey, Caucasus, and Ukraine.
- CULTIVATION Suits a rock garden or border front, in sun with well-drained, moderately fertile soil.
- PROPAGATION By seed as soon as ripe, or by division in autumn or late winter.

Z 5–8

HEIGHT 4in (10cm)

SPREAD 24in (60cm)

Boraginaceae	CREEPING FORGET-ME-NOT, BLUE-EYED MARY

OMPHALODES VERNA

Habit Carpeting, stoloniferous, semievergreen, perennial. ***Flowers*** Resembling forget-me-nots, to ⅜in (1cm) across, borne in terminal sprays in spring. Deep blue with white eye. ***Leaves*** Hairy, narrowly oval, and pointed. Mid-green.

- NATIVE HABITAT Woodland in Turkey.
- CULTIVATION Good ground cover for a border, woodland, or rock garden. Needs fertile, moist soil with plenty of organic matter, in shady site.
- PROPAGATION By seed, or by division in autumn or late winter.

Z 6–9

HEIGHT 8in (20cm)

SPREAD 12in (30cm) or more

Boraginaceae	

OMPHALODES CAPPADOCICA

Habit Clump-forming, rhizomatous, evergreen, perennial. ***Flowers*** Resembling forget-me-nots, ⅓in (8mm) wide, borne in terminal sprays in early spring. Bright, azure-blue, with white eye. ***Leaves*** Oval, pointed, and fine-haired. Mid-green.

- NATIVE HABITAT Woodland in Turkey.
- CULTIVATION Good ground cover for a border, woodland, or rock garden. Needs fertile, moist soil with plenty of organic matter, in shady site.
- PROPAGATION By seed, or by division in autumn or late winter.

Z 6–9

HEIGHT 8in (20cm)

SPREAD 24in (60cm)

Ranunculaceae	ALPINE COLUMBINE

AQUILEGIA ALPINA

Habit Upright, short-lived, tufted, herbaceous, perennial. ***Flowers*** Nodding, lantern-shaped, to 3½in (9cm) across, with 5 straight or curved spurs measuring up to 1in (2.5cm) long. Borne in nodding heads of 2–3 in late spring. Blue, often with white tips. ***Leaves*** Finely divided, forming basal clumps. Bluish-green.

- NATIVE HABITAT Rocky shade, scrub, and open woodland in the Alps and northern Apennines.
- CULTIVATION Suitable for growing in a herbaceous border, woodland, or rock garden. Grows best in fertile, leaf-rich soil that is moist but well drained, in dappled or partial shade. Prefers climates with cool summers, where it will tolerate sun. In rock gardens, deadhead to prevent self-sowing to the point of nuisance.
- PROPAGATION By seed, as soon as ripe or in spring. Will self-seed freely, hybridizing with other aquilegias in the garden.
- OTHER NAME *A. montana.*

Z 3–8

HEIGHT 18in (45cm)

SPREAD 12in (30cm)

Cruciferae/
Brassicaceae

AURINIA SAXATILIS 'Dudley Nevill'

Habit Mound-forming, evergreen, perennial. ***Flowers*** Cross-shaped, 4-petaled, ⅙–¼in (4–6mm) across, borne in dense clusters in late spring and early summer. Soft buff-yellow. ***Leaves*** Oval, toothed, and hairy. Gray-green.

• NATIVE HABITAT Garden origin.

• CULTIVATION Suitable for growing in any well-drained soil in sun. Trim annually after flowering to maintain the plant's compactness.

• PROPAGATION By softwood cuttings in summer.

• OTHER NAME *Alyssum saxatile* 'Dudley Nevill'.

Z 3–7

HEIGHT
8in (20cm)

SPREAD
12in (30cm)

Cruciferae/
Brassicaceae

AURINIA SAXATILIS 'Citrina'

Habit Mound-forming, evergreen, perennial. ***Flowers*** Cross-shaped, 4-petaled, ⅙–¼in (4–6mm) across, borne in dense clusters in late spring and summer. Soft lemon-yellow. ***Leaves*** Oval, toothed, and hairy. Gray-green.

• NATIVE HABITAT Garden origin.

• CULTIVATION Grow in any well-drained soil in sun. Trim annually after flowering.

• PROPAGATION By softwood cuttings in summer, or by seed in early spring.

• OTHER NAME *Alyssum saxatile* 'Citrina'.

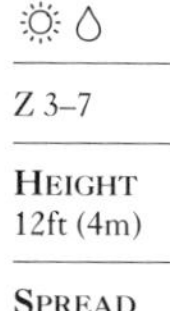

Z 3–7

HEIGHT
12ft (4m)

SPREAD
8ft (2.5m)

Crassulaceae

CHIASTOPHYLLUM OPPOSITIFOLIUM

Habit Tufted, rhizomatous, evergreen, perennial. ***Flowers*** Bell-shaped, ⅕in (5mm) long, borne in spring and early summer. Deep yellow. ***Leaves*** Oval, scalloped, fleshy. Pale green.

• NATIVE HABITAT Shady, rocky sites, Caucasus.

• CULTIVATION Suits rock or wall crevices. Needs moderately fertile, moist but well-drained soil.

• PROPAGATION By seed in autumn, or by cuttings from sideshoots in summer.

• OTHER NAMES *C. simplicifolium*, *Cotyledon simplicifolia*.

Z 5–7

HEIGHT
to 8in (20cm)

SPREAD
6in (15cm)

Leguminosae/
Papilionaceae

CYTISUS x *BEANII*

Habit Deciduous, low-growing, green-stemmed, shrub. ***Flowers*** Pealike, to ½in (15mm) long, in lateral clusters, borne on arching, cylindrical stems in late spring or early summer. Bright yellow. ***Leaves*** Small, simple, linear, hairy. Dark green.

• NATIVE HABITAT Garden origin.

• CULTIVATION Suits a rock garden or raised bed. Will cascade over a retaining wall. Tolerates any well-drained or poor soil, but needs full sun. Trim lightly after flowering, but avoid cutting old wood.

• PROPAGATION By semiripe or ripewood cuttings.

Z 7–8

HEIGHT
24in (60cm)

SPREAD
3ft (1m)

Berberidaceae	

BERBERIS x *STENOPHYLLA* 'Corallina Compacta'

Habit Neat and compact, evergreen, dwarf, shrub. ***Flowers*** Bell-shaped, to ⅜in (1cm) span, borne in profusion in late spring. Red buds, opening to bright orange. ***Fruits*** Rounded berries. Blue-black, with a grayish bloom. ***Leaves*** Linear to narrowly oval, spine-tipped, and ¼–⅜in (6–8mm) long. Dark green.

• NATIVE HABITAT Garden origin. A selection of the hybrid between *B. darwinii* and *B. empetrifolia*.

• CULTIVATION Suitable for growing in a rock garden. Associates well with heathers and dwarf conifers, adding textural and color contrast o both. Tolerates a range of well-drained soils in either sun or dappled shade. Needs little, if any, pruning, but may be trimmed lightly after flowering, if necessary.

• PROPAGATION By semiripe cuttings in summer, but it is difficult to propagate.

☼ ◊

Z 6–9

HEIGHT
12in (30cm)

SPREAD
12in (30cm)

PENSTEMON

The penstemons found mostly in alpine and subalpine habitats in western N. America are valued for their brightly colored, tubular, funnel- or bell-shaped flowers, which are often borne over long periods during summer and autumn. The smaller species are ideal for rock gardens or scree and raised beds, while the taller ones are excellent for growing at the front of a sunny, sheltered border in well-drained soil. The smallest penstemons, like *P. hirsutus* var. *pygmaeus*, are suitable for planting in troughs.

Most of the penstemons described are hardy to about 14°F (-10°C), probably more, if given sharp drainage. However, they experience much lower temperatures in the wild, where cold weather is accompanied by a protective cover of snow or very dry conditions.
This contrasts with the wet, comparatively warm winters that they are subjected to in lowland gardens with maritime climates. For the penstemons described, these less-than-ideal conditions can be improved by adding plenty of sharp grit to the soil to ensure good drainage.

Grow in gritty, well-drained soil in sun, but provide shade from the hottest mid-day sun and shelter from cold, dry winds. Trim after flowering, if necessary, to keep the plant compact. If seed is needed for propagation, leave a few flower spikes in place to allow seed to ripen. Where several species are grown together, hybridiziation sometimes occurs

Propagate by seed sown in late winter or early spring, in pots in a cold frame. Alternatively, take semiripe cuttings of non-flowering shoots in summer and root in a cold frame. Irishman's cuttings (see p. 172), which can often be found on the prostrate creeping species, can be separated and potted up in spring.

P. FRUTICOSUS* var. *SCOULERI ALBUS
Habit Compact, evergreen, subshrub.
Flowers Funnel-shaped, to 2in (5cm) long, borne freely in dense sprays in summer. White.
Leaves Narrowly lance-shaped and glossy. Mid-green.
• OTHER NAME *P. scouleri* 'Albus'.
• HEIGHT 12in (30cm).
• SPREAD 12in (30cm).

P. fruticosus* var. *scouleri albus

☼ ◊ Z 6–8

P. NEWBERRYI
Habit Mat-forming, downy-stemmed, evergreen, sub-shrub.
Flowers Tubular, 1–1¼in (2.5–3cm) long borne in dense sprays in summer. Dark red-pink.
Leaves Elliptic to oval, leathery, with a finely serrated margin. Dark green.
• HEIGHT 10in (25cm).
• SPREAD 12in (30cm).

P. newberryi
Mountain pride

☼ ◊ Z 7–9

P. *RUPICOLA*
Habit Prostrate, evergreen, subshrub.
Flowers Funnel-shaped, to 1⅜in (3.5cm) long, borne in dense, few-flowered sprays in late spring and early summer. Dark red-pink.
Leaves Thick, elliptic to rounded, leathery. Blue-green.
• HEIGHT 4in (10cm).
• SPREAD 18in (45cm).

P. rupicola
Rock penstemon

Z 7–8

P. *NEWBERRYI* f. *HUMILIOR*

Habit Evergreen, subshrub, compact, bushy, mat-forming, with arching, downy branches,
Flowers Tubular, 1in (2.5cm) long, borne in dense sprays in early summer. Dark red-pink.
Leaves Elliptic to oval, leathery, with a finely serrated margin. Dark green.
• HEIGHT 6in (15cm).
• SPREAD 8in (20cm).

P. newberryi* f. *humilior

Z 7–9

P. *PINIFOLIUS*
Habit Spreading, evergreen, subshrub.
Flowers Narrowly tubular, 1in (2.5cm) long, borne in loose spikelike sprays in summer. Bright scarlet.
Leaves Crowded and needlelike. Pale green.
• HEIGHT to 8in (20cm).
• SPREAD to 10in (25cm).

P. pinifolius

Z 8–9

P. *HIRSUTUS* var. *PYGMAEUS*
Habit Mat-forming, rhizomatous, short-lived, evergreen, subshrub.
Flowers Tubular, 1in (2.5cm) long, borne in loose sprays in summer. Violet, with whitish tips.
Leaves Lance-shaped with a toothed margin. Dark green, with purple tint.
• HEIGHT 4in (10cm).
• SPREAD 4in (10cm).

P. hirsutus* var. *pygmaeus

Z 3–7

P. *SERRULATUS*
Habit Spreading, semi-evergreen, subshrub.
Flowers Narrowly bell-shaped, 1in (2.5cm) long, borne in dense, one-sided clusters in late summer. Pink-purple.
Leaves Lance-shaped, tooth-edged. Dark green.
• OTHER NAME *P. diffusus.*
• HEIGHT to 20in (50cm).
• SPREAD 12in (30cm).

P. serrulatus
Cascade penstemon

Z 4–7

Parnassiaceae/ Saxifragaceae	GRASS OF PARNASSUS

PARNASSIA PALUSTRIS

Habit Tufted, semievergreen, perennial. ***Flowers*** Saucer-shaped, solitary, 1in (2.5cm) across, borne on erect stems in early summer. White, with green veins. ***Leaves*** Oval and heart-shaped, forming basal tufts. Pale green.
• NATIVE HABITAT Bogs, northern hemisphere.
• CULTIVATION Suits a bog garden or permanently damp niche in a rock garden. Needs wet, not stagnant soil, that is rich in organic matter, in sun.
• PROPAGATION By seed in autumn, or by division in autumn or early spring.

Z 3–7

HEIGHT
8in (20cm)

SPREAD
4in (10cm)

Plumbaginaceae	

ARMERIA PSEUDARMERIA

Habit Clumping, evergreen, perennial. ***Flowers*** Small, borne in dense round heads, to 1½in (4cm) across, in summer. White or pale pink. ***Leaves*** Lance-shaped, in basal rosettes. Mid-green.
• NATIVE HABITAT Coastal areas, western Portugal.
• CULTIVATION Prefers light, sandy soil that is moderately fertile, in an open site in full sun.
• PROPAGATION By seed in autumn or spring, or by division in early spring.
• OTHER NAMES *A. atrosanguinea* of gardens, *A. latifolia*.

Z 7–9

HEIGHT
to 20in (50cm)

SPREAD
12in (30cm)

Compositae/Asteraceae	

CELMISIA WALKERI

Habit Loose, spreading, evergreen, perennial. ***Flowers*** Daisylike, 1½in (4cm) across, borne on sticky stems in early summer. White, with yellow center. ***Leaves*** Narrowly linear and leathery. Dark green, with hairy, white underside.
• NATIVE HABITAT South Island, New Zealand.
• CULTIVATION Needs slightly acid, fertile, moist but well-drained soil. Prefers cool climates.
• PROPAGATION By seed as soon as ripe, or by rooting leaf rosette cuttings in spring.
• OTHER NAME *C. webbiana*.

pH

Z 6–9

HEIGHT
12in (30cm)

SPREAD
12in (30cm)

Onagraceae	

EPILOBIUM GLABELLUM

Habit Mat- or clump-forming, semievergreen, perennial. ***Flowers*** Solitary, cup-shaped, outward-facing, 1in (2.5cm) across, borne on slender stems in summer. White. ***Leaves*** Narrowly oval. Dark green, tinted bronze, on bristly, red-tinted stems.
• NATIVE HABITAT Riverbeds and mountain grassland, New Zealand.
• CULTIVATION Suitable ground cover for a semi-shaded border. Prefers cool, damp shade.
• PROPAGATION By seed when ripe or in spring, or by division in autumn or early spring.

Z 8–9

HEIGHT
8in (20cm)

SPREAD
8in (20cm)

Leguminosae/ Papilionaceae	

CHAMAECYTISUS PURPUREUS f. *ALBUS*

Habit Dense, semiupright, deciduous, shrub. ***Flowers*** Pealike, 1in (2.5cm) across, borne in lateral clusters in summer. White. ***Leaves*** Small, with 3 oval leaflets. Dark green.
• NATIVE HABITAT Hillsides, southeastern Europe.
• CULTIVATION Suits a rock garden, raised bed, or retaining wall. Tolerates most well-drained, moderately fertile soils, except shallow, chalky ones. Trim after flowering, avoiding old wood.
• PROPAGATION By semiripe or ripewood cuttings.
• OTHER NAME *Cytisus purpureus* f. *albus*.

Z 5–8

HEIGHT
18in (45cm)

SPREAD
24in (60cm)

Geraniaceae	

ERODIUM CHEILANTHIFOLIUM

Habit Compact, mound-forming, evergreen, perennial. ***Flowers*** Flat-faced, to 1in (2.5cm) across, borne in sprays of up to 5 in summer. White with distinct purple marks on top 2 petals. ***Leaves*** Oval, deep-cut, fernlike, crinkled. Gray-green.
• NATIVE HABITAT Southern Spain and N. Africa.
• CULTIVATION Suitable for a raised bed. Grow in gritty, sharply drained, neutral to alkaline soil.
• PROPAGATION By seed when ripe, or by division or basal cuttings in spring.
• OTHER NAME *E. petraeum* subsp. *crispum*.

Z 5–8

HEIGHT
8in (20cm)

SPREAD
12in (30cm)

Cruciferae/ Brassicaceae	PERSIAN STONE CRESS

Aethionema grandiflorum

Habit Loose, short-lived, evergreen or semi-evergreen, subshrub. ***Flowers*** Cross-shaped, 4-petaled, ¼in (6mm) across, borne in loose sprays or clusters in early summer. Pale to deep pink. ***Leaves*** Narrowly lance-shaped. Blue-green.
- NATIVE HABITAT Iran, Iraq, Caucasus, Turkey.
- CULTIVATION Prefers fertile, alkaline soil in sun, but will tolerate poor, slightly acid soils.
- PROPAGATION By softwood cuttings in summer, or by seed in spring. Will hybridize freely.
- OTHER NAME *A. pulchellum.*

Z 5–8

HEIGHT 8–12in (20–30cm)

SPREAD 8–12in (20–30cm)

Boraginaceae	

Onosma alborosea

Habit Low-spreading, clumping, evergreen, perennial. ***Flowers*** Nodding, tubular, 1¼in (3cm) long, borne in congested clusters in summer. White, turning pink, occasionally with violet-blue tips. ***Leaves*** Spoon- to lance-shaped, bristly, and can cause skin irritations. Gray-green.
- NATIVE HABITAT Rock crevices, southwest Asia.
- CULTIVATION Grows best in a scree bed, or planted in vertical crevices of retaining walls. Needs well-drained, very gritty soil.
- PROPAGATION By seed in autumn.

Z 7–9

HEIGHT 10in (25cm)

SPREAD 10in (25cm)

Saxifragaceae	

Astilbe 'Sprite'

Habit Clump-forming, rhizomatous, herbaceous, perennial. ***Flowers*** Tiny, star-shaped, borne in feathery, tapering clusters in summer. Shell-pink. ***Leaves*** Divided into oval leaflets. Mid-green.
- NATIVE HABITAT Garden origin.
- CULTIVATION Grows best in a partially shaded site, with fertile, reliably moist soil that is enriched with organic matter
- PROPAGATION By division in winter or early spring, before new growth begins.
- OTHER NAME *A. simplicifolia* 'Sprite'.

Z 4–8

HEIGHT 20in (50cm)

SPREAD to 3ft (1m)

Leguminosae/Papilionaceae	

Anthyllis montana

Habit Clump- or mat-forming, spreading, woody-based, perennial. ***Flowers*** Tiny, pealike, borne in dense, cloverlike heads, to 1¼in (3cm) across, with 2 lobed, leaflike bracts beneath, in early summer. Pink, red, or purple, sometimes with white tips. ***Leaves*** Small, silky-haired, and finely divided into oval leaflets. Gray-green or silver.

• NATIVE HABITAT Rocky, open places in the Alps, and mountains of southern Europe.

• CULTIVATION Excellent for a scree bed, rock garden, or dry-stone retaining walls. The flowers are attractive to bees and other beneficial insects. Grow in well-drained, poor to moderately fertile soil. Tolerates dry soils, and thrives in climates with long, hot summers.

• PROPAGATION By seed in autumn or winter, or by division of established plants in autumn or spring.

☼ ◊

Z 6–8

HEIGHT
12in (30cm)

SPREAD
24in (60cm)

Ericaceae	

RHODOTHAMNUS CHAMAECISTUS

Habit Dwarf, evergreen, shrub. ***Flowers*** Cup-shaped, 5-petaled, 1¼in (3cm) across, solitary, or in lateral or terminal clusters, borne in early summer. Clear pink. ***Leaves*** Oval to lance-shaped and untoothed. Glossy, lustrous green.

• NATIVE HABITAT Pockets of fertile, acid soil among limestone rocks, eastern Alps.

• CULTIVATION Needs reliably moist but well-drained soil. Tolerates some shade in drier areas.

• PROPAGATION By seed in autumn, or by semi-ripe cuttings in late summer.

Z 5–8

HEIGHT
8in (20cm)

SPREAD
10in (25cm)

Portulacaceae	

LEWISIA 'George Henley'

Habit Clump-forming, evergreen, perennial. ***Flowers*** Cone-shaped, 1in (2.5cm) across, silky, borne in loose clusters from late spring to late summer. Purplish-pink, with magenta veins. ***Leaves*** Narrow, spoon-shaped, fleshy. Dark green.

• NATIVE HABITAT Garden origin.

• CULTIVATION Ideal pot-grown in an alpine house, or suits a scree bed with protection from winter wet. Needs fertile, moist but well-drained soil enriched with organic matter, in partial shade.

• PROPAGATION By root offsets in early summer.

Z 4–7

HEIGHT
6in (15cm)
or more

SPREAD
8in (20cm)

Plumbaginaceae	MATTED SEA LAVENDER

LIMONIUM BELLIDIFOLIUM

Habit Compact, dome-forming, evergreen, perennial. ***Flowers*** Tiny, funnel-shaped, ⅕in (5mm) long, borne in open, wiry-stemmed spikes in early summer. Pale blue-violet. ***Leaves*** Spoon-shaped, leathery, in basal clumps. Dark green.

• NATIVE HABITAT Sandy salt marshes and coastal areas, eastern England, Mediterranean, Black Sea.

• CULTIVATION Suits a trough or scree garden. Grow in light, preferably sandy, well-drained soil.

• PROPAGATION By seed or by division, in spring.

• OTHER NAMES *L. reticulata*, *Statice bellidifolia*.

Z 5–8

HEIGHT
6in (15cm)

SPREAD
6in (15cm)

Labiatae/Lamiaceae	

ORIGANUM 'Kent Beauty'

Habit Prostrate. semievergreen, subshrub, with trailing branches and a suckering, woody rootstock. ***Flowers*** Small, tubular, to ⅝in (15mm) long, borne in whorls in summer. Mauve to pale pink, with darker outer petals. ***Leaves*** Aromatic, and rounded to oval. Bright green.

• NATIVE HABITAT Garden origin.

• CULTIVATION Grows best in a raised bed, on the top of a wall, or other well-drained site in a rock garden. Needs very well-drained, preferably slightly alkaline soil, in a warm, sunny site. Although almost fully cold hardy, to 15°F (-10°C) or slightly lower, it will not withstand excessive moisture combined with low temperatures. In areas with cold, wet winters, protect the crown with an open cloche or propped pane of glass.

• PROPAGATION By division in early spring, or by basal cuttings in spring and summer.

☼ ◊

Z 5–8

HEIGHT
4in (10cm)

SPREAD
8in (20cm)

Saxifragaceae	

Astilbe 'Perkeo'

Habit Compact, erect, clumping, herbaceous, perennial. ***Flowers*** Tiny, star-shaped, borne in feathery, tapering clusters in mid- to late summer. Deep salmon-pink. ***Leaves*** Finely cut. Dark green, with bronze tint on opening.

- NATIVE HABITAT Garden origin.
- CULTIVATION Needs fertile, reliably moist, open soil enriched with organic matter, in part shade.
- PROPAGATION By division in winter or early spring, before new growth begins.
- OTHER NAME *A.* x *crispa* 'Perkeo'.

Z 4–8

HEIGHT to 4in (20cm)

SPREAD to 12in (30cm)

Crassulaceae	

Crassula sarcocaulis

Habit Bushy, evergreen or semievergreen, perennial, with gnarled branches. ***Flowers*** Star-shaped, 1/4in (5mm) wide, borne in late summer. Pink or white. ***Leaves*** Small, fleshy, and oval. Mid-green, with red tints.

- NATIVE HABITAT Lesotho and S. Africa.
- CULTIVATION Suits a warm, sunny rock garden. Needs sharply drained, moderately fertile soil.
- PROPAGATION By seed in spring, or by stem or leaf cuttings in early to mid-summer.
- OTHER NAME *Sedum sarcocaule.*

Z 8–9

HEIGHT to 12in (30cm)

SPREAD 12in (30cm)

Primulaceae	ALPINE BELLS

Cortusa matthioli

Habit Clumping, herbaceous, perennial. ***Flowers*** Bell-shaped, drooping, long-stalked, 3/8in (1cm) long, borne in one-sided clusters in late spring and early summer. Magenta to purple-violet. ***Leaves*** Rounded, lobed, kidney-shaped, and coarsely toothed, in basal rosettes. Dull green, rusty-haired.

- NATIVE HABITAT Mountains, western Europe.
- CULTIVATION Needs a cool site, with moist but well-drained, fertile soil in partial or deep shade.
- PROPAGATION By ripe seed, or by division in early spring or immediately after flowering.

Z 5–8

HEIGHT 8–12in (20–30cm)

SPREAD 6in (15cm)

Labiatae/Lamiaceae	

Origanum laevigatum

Habit Upright, woody-based, wiry-stemmed, suckering, herbaceous, perennial. ***Flowers*** Tubular, 5/8in (15mm) long, borne in loose, airy, whorled clusters throughout summer. Purplish-pink. ***Leaves*** Aromatic and oval. Dark green.

- NATIVE HABITAT Scrub, open woods, grassland and maquis, Turkey and Cyprus.
- CULTIVATION Suits a border front or rock garden. Attracts bees and butterflies. Grows best in well-drained, moderately fertile, preferably alkaline soil.
- PROPAGATION By seed or by division, in spring.

Z 5–9

HEIGHT to 24in (60cm)

SPREAD 18in (45cm)

Geraniaceae	BLOODY CRANESBILL

GERANIUM SANGUINEUM

Habit Dense, rhizomatous, spreading to mound-forming, herbaceous, perennial. ***Flowers*** Upright, cup-shaped, 1½in (4cm) across, borne throughout summer. Magenta, with darker veins and pale eye. ***Leaves*** Deeply cut with lobes. Dark green.

• NATIVE HABITAT Grassy, rocky places, usually on limestone, Europe to northern Turkey.

• CULTIVATION Prefers a site in partial shade, and will tolerate a range of well-drained soils.

• PROPAGATION By seed or by division, in autumn or spring.

Z 4–8

HEIGHT
8in (20cm)

SPREAD
12in (30cm) or more

Portulacaceae	

LEWISIA Cotyledon Hybrids

Habit Tufted, evergreen, perennial. ***Flowers*** Cone-shaped, to 1½in (4cm) span, long-stalked, borne in tight clusters in early summer. Pink or yellow. ***Leaves*** Thick, fleshy, rosetted. Mid-green.

• NATIVE HABITAT Garden origin.

• CULTIVATION Ideal pot-grown in an alpine house or suitable for a scree bed with protection from winter moisture. Needs fertile, moist but well-drained soil rich in organic matter, in partial shade.

• PROPAGATION By offsets in early summer, or by seed in autumn or spring.

pH

Z 4–7

HEIGHT
to 8in (20cm)

SPREAD
6in (15cm) or more

Scrophulariaceae	

MIMULUS 'Whitecroft Scarlet'

Habit Short-lived, spreading, perennial. ***Flowers*** Trumpet-shaped, snapdragonlike, ¾in (2cm) across, borne in sprays throughout summer. Deep scarlet. ***Leaves*** Oval and toothed. Mid-green.

• NATIVE HABITAT Garden origin.

• CULTIVATION Needs reliably moist, fertile soil, enriched with organic matter, in sun or light, dappled shade.

• PROPAGATION By division in spring, or by stem tip cuttings in summer.

• OTHER NAME *M. cupreus* 'Whitecroft Scarlet'.

Z 9–10

HEIGHT
4in (10cm)

SPREAD
8in (20cm)

Ranunculaceae	

AQUILEGIA FORMOSA

Habit Upright, open, herbaceous, perennial, delicate-looking. ***Flowers*** Nodding, lantern-shaped, to 2in (5cm) across, with 5 erect spurs, to ¾in (2cm) long, borne in branched sprays in late spring and early summer. Red, with orange outer sepals and red-orange spurs. ***Leaves*** Finely divided, forming basal clumps. Blue-green.

• NATIVE HABITAT Damp scrub, moist woodland, from sea-level to altitudes of 10,000ft (3,000m) in western N. America, from Alaska to California, Utah, and Montana.

• CULTIVATION Suitable for planting in a rock garden, herbaceous border, or woodland. Where grown on a rock garden, deadhead the flowers to prevent self-sowing to the point of nuisance. Grows best in fertile, leaf-rich soil that contains plenty of organic matter and is moist but well drained. Provide a warm site in sun, or dappled or partial shade.

• PROPAGATION By seed, as soon as ripe or in spring. Self-seeds freely and is likely to hybridize unless grown in isolation from other aquilegias.

Z 3–8

HEIGHT
2–3ft
(60–90cm)

SPREAD
18in (45cm)

Ranunculaceae	

DELPHINIUM NUDICAULE

Habit Slender, short-lived, erect, herbaceous, perennial. ***Flowers*** Hooded, funnel-shaped, ¾in (2cm) span, borne in open sprays in mid-summer. Bright vermilion or scarlet, sometimes yellow. ***Leaves*** Fleshy, long-stalked, lobed. Mid-green.
• NATIVE HABITAT Chaparral, open woodland, and rocky places. Mountains of California..
• CULTIVATION Grow in a warm, sunny site in well-drained, moderately fertile soil.
• PROPAGATION By seed in spring. Flowers in the first season, and is sometimes grown as an annual.

Z 5–7

HEIGHT to 24in (60cm)

SPREAD 8in (20cm)

Compositae/Asteraceae	ALPINE FLEABANE

ERIGERON ALPINUS

Habit Clumping, perennial. ***Flowers*** Slender-stemmed, daisylike, 1½in (3.5cm) across, borne in summer. Lilac-blue to red-purple, with yellow center. ***Leaves*** Oval and hairy. Mid-green.
• NATIVE HABITAT Mountains, central and southern Europe.
• CULTIVATION Suitable for planting in a rock garden. Prefers a sunny site with well-drained soil that does not dry out in summer.
• PROPAGATION By seed in early spring, or by division or basal cuttings in spring.

Z 4–7

HEIGHT 10in (25cm) or more

SPREAD 12in (30cm)

Scrophulariaceae	

CALCEOLARIA ARACHNOIDEA

Habit Rhizomatous, cushion- or mat-forming, evergreen, perennial. ***Flowers*** Pouched, ⅝in (15mm) long, borne in compact clusters in summer and autumn. Dull, deep purple. ***Leaves*** Lance- to spoon-shaped, and densely soft-haired. White.
• NATIVE HABITAT Chile.
• CULTIVATION Needs moist, gritty, well-drained soil. Protect from winter moisture. Under glass, use a mix of equal parts soil, leaf mold and grit.
• PROPAGATION By seed in autumn or spring, or by division in spring.

Z 8–9

HEIGHT to 10in (25cm)

SPREAD to 6in (15cm)

Scrophulariaceae	

WULFENIA CARINTHIACA

Habit Rosette-forming, evergreen, perennial. ***Flowers*** Small, narrowly tubular, two-lipped, borne in one-sided, dense spikes to 4in (10cm) long, in summer. Dark violet-blue. ***Leaves*** Lance-shaped, scalloped margined, rosetted. Dark green.

• NATIVE HABITAT Southeastern Alps and Albania.

• CULTIVATION Suitable for growing on a rock garden or crevice, with gritty, moist but well-drained soil that is rich in organic matter.

• PROPAGATION Sow seed in pots in a cold frame in autumn or spring, or divide after flowering.

Z 6–9

HEIGHT
10in (25cm)

SPREAD
10in (25cm)

Ranunculaceae	FALSE COLUMBINE

SEMIAQUILEGIA ECALCARATA

Habit Slender, short-lived, upright, herbaceous, perennial. ***Flowers*** Drooping, open lantern-shaped, 1in (2.5cm) across, unspurred, borne in clusters in early summer. Dusky pink to deep purple-blue. ***Leaves*** Long-stalked and divided. Mid-green, tinted purple underneath.

• NATIVE HABITAT Mountains of western China.

• CULTIVATION Needs a site in sun, or part or dappled shade with fertile, leaf-rich, well-drained soil that remains reliably moist.

• PROPAGATION By seed in autumn or spring.

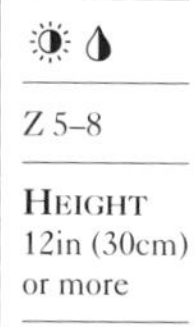

Z 5–8

HEIGHT
12in (30cm) or more

SPREAD
6in (15cm)

Labiatae/Lamiaceae	DRAGON'S MOUTH

HORMINUM PYRENAICUM

Habit Dense, rosette-forming, rhizomatous, evergreen, perennial. ***Flowers*** Tubular, 2-lipped, ¾in (2cm) long, borne in whorls in summer. Dark violet-blue, occasionally pink or white. ***Leaves*** Leathery, toothed, oval, and glossy, forming basal rosettes. Dark green.

• NATIVE HABITAT Pyrenees and Alps.

• CULTIVATION Good for a rock garden or border front. Grow in well-drained, moderately fertile soil.

• PROPAGATION By seed in autumn, or by division in early spring.

Z 6–9

HEIGHT
8in (20cm)

SPREAD
20in (50cm)

Ranunculaceae

AQUILEGIA FLABELLATA

Habit Upright, herbaceous, perennial. ***Flowers*** Semierect to nodding, lantern-shaped, to 2in (5cm) across, with 5 upright, incurved spurs, to ¾in (2cm) long, borne in early summer. Soft blue-purple, with white or cream tips. ***Leaves*** Finely divided, forming basal clumps. Blue-green.

• NATIVE HABITAT Japan, Korea, and Sakhalin.

• CULTIVATION Suitable for growing in open woodland or rock garden. Grows best in climates with cool summers. Prefers a site in dappled or partial shade, with fertile, leaf-rich soil that is moist but well drained. In a rock garden, deadhead the flowers to prevent self-sowing to the point of nuisance.

• PROPAGATION By seed, as soon as ripe or in early spring. Self-seeds freely and is likely to hybridize unless isolated from other species of aquilegia.

• OTHER NAME *A. akitensis.*

Z 4–9

HEIGHT
8–12in
(20–30cm)

SPREAD
to 6in
(15cm)

DAPHNE

The genus *Daphne* includes about 50 species of deciduous, evergreen, and semievergreen shrub, including some smaller species that are ideal for growing in rock gardens, troughs, and raised beds. The species produce 4-lobed, tubular flowers, nearly all of which have a characteristically intense fragrance. Daphnes are valued for their flowers, attractive foliage, bright berries, and neat habit. Most of the smaller species are found in mountain habitats, often cliffs or scree. Careful handling of Daphnes is essential, as all parts of the plant, including the fruits, are highly toxic if ingested, while the sap can cause skin irritation.

Daphnes should be grown in moderately fertile soil that is enriched with leaf mold and is moisture retentive but well drained. Nearly all species prefer slightly acid to slightly alkaline soil, and a site in full sun or dappled shade. *D. arbuscula*, *D. blagayana*, and *D. genkwa* need neutral to acid soil. All daphnes resent being transplanted, so site carefully and leave undisturbed. Mulch with leaf mold or top-dress with grit to keep the root-run cool and evenly moist. Pruning should be kept to a minimum.

Sow seed as soon as ripe in containers in a cold frame. Retain the seed pans for a second year, as germination can be erratic. Semiripe cuttings can be taken between mid- and late summer, but many are very slow to root.

Daphnes are commonly grafted, preferably on rootstock of *D. tangutica* or *D. longilobata* rather than the more traditional *D. mezereum*. Both of these rootstocks make it easier to maintain the characteristically neat and compact habit. The prostrate species can be increased by simple layering in spring or early summer, between 4 and 8 weeks after flowering.

D. ALPINA

Habit Compact, upright, twiggy, deciduous, downy-stemmed, shrub.
Flowers Fragrant, ⅓–⅖in (8–10mm) across, borne in terminal clusters of 4–10, in late spring and early summer. White.
Fruits Oblong berries. Orange-red.
Leaves Lance-shaped and hairy. Gray-green.
• HEIGHT 2ft (60cm).
• SPREAD 2ft (60cm).

D. alpina

Z 4–7

D. JASMINEA

Habit Semi-prostrate, semi-erect, evergreen, shrub.
Flowers Fragrant, ⅓in (8mm) across, borne mostly in pairs in late spring and summer. White or cream, often flushed pink.
Leaves Oblong to oval. Blue- or gray-green.
• HEIGHT 2–12in (5–30cm).
• SPREAD 12in (30cm).

D. jasminea

Z 8–9

D. BLAGAYANA

Habit Spreading, semi-evergreen or evergreen, branched, shrub.
Flowers Fragrant, ⅖in (1cm) across, borne in clusters of 20–30, in spring. Creamy-white.
Fruits Spherical. White or pink.
Leaves Oval and leathery. Dark green.
• HEIGHT to 16in (40cm).
• SPREAD 3ft (90cm).

D. blagayana

Z 7–9

D. GENKWA

Habit Open, upright, deciduous, sparsely branched, shrub.
Flowers Fragrant, ⅘in (2cm) across, borne in clusters of 2–7 in spring, before the leaves. Lilac.
Fruits Small, dry, and egg-shaped. Gray-white.
Leaves Lance-shaped to oval; silky-haired when young. Mid-green.
• HEIGHT 32in (80cm).
• SPREAD 32in (80cm).

D. genkwa

Z 4–7

***D.* CNEORUM**
Habit Low-growing, hummock-forming, evergreen, shrub.
Flowers Fragrant, ⅜in (1cm) across, in heads of 6–20, borne during late spring. Pale to deep pink.
Leaves Lance-shaped. Dark green.
• HEIGHT 12in (30cm).
• SPREAD to 6ft (2m).

D. cneorum
Garland flower

Z 5–8

***D.* PETRAEA 'Grandiflora'**
Habit Compact, slow-growing, evergreen, shrub.
Flowers Fragrant, ⅜in (1cm) across, borne in terminal clusters of 3–5, in late spring. Deep rose-pink.
Leaves Narrowly spoon-shaped, leathery, and glossy. Dark green.
• HEIGHT 4in (10cm).
• SPREAD 10in (25cm).

***D. petraea* 'Grandiflora'**

Z 5–8

***D.* CNEORUM 'Eximia'**
Habit Vigorous, low-growing, spreading, mat- to hummock- forming, evergreen, shrub.
Flowers Fragrant, ⅜in (1cm) across, borne in terminal clusters of 6–20, in late spring. Deep pink.
Leaves Lance-shaped. Dark green.
• HEIGHT 8in (20cm).
• SPREAD to 6ft (2m).

***D. cneorum* 'Eximia'**

Z 5–8

***D.* COLLINA**
Habit Dome-forming. dense, evergreen, shrub.
Flowers Fragrant, ⅓in (8mm) across, silky-haired when young, borne in terminal clusters in late spring. Deep pink.
Fruits Oval. Orange-red.
Leaves Oval and glossy. Mid-green.
• OTHER NAME *D. sericea* Collina Group.
• HEIGHT 20in (50cm).
• SPREAD 20in (50cm).

D. collina

Z 7–8

***D.* ARBUSCULA**
Habit Semiprostrate, dwarf, evergreen, shrub.
Flowers Very fragrant, ⅝in (1.5cm) across, borne in dense clusters in late spring and early summer. Deep pink.
Fruits Dry and egg-shaped. Gray-white.
Leaves Linear to oblong, leathery, glossy. Dark green.
• HEIGHT 6in (15cm).
• SPREAD 18in (45cm).

D. arbuscula

Z 5–8

***D.* JEZOENSIS**
Habit Slow-growing, rounded, upright, shrub, deciduous in summer.
Flowers Fragrant, ⅝in (1.5cm) across, borne in clusters in early spring. Golden-yellow.
Fruits Oval, shiny. Red.
Leaves Lance-shaped and somewhat shiny. Pale then mid-green.
• HEIGHT 2–3ft (60cm–1m).
• SPREAD 12–18in (30–45cm).

D. jezoensis

Z 5–8

HELIANTHEMUM

The genus *Helianthemum* comprises about 110 species of small, evergreen and semievergreen shrub, most of which inhabit stony alpine meadows or open scrub, particularly in the Mediterranean, but also in N. Africa, and N. and S. America, Asia and Europe. The most popular helianthemums (commonly known as rock roses) are the named cultivars derived from crosses between *H. croceum*, *H. apenninum* and *H. nummularium*. They are valued for their neat, spreading to hummock-forming habit, and attractive, usually gray- or silver-green, finely haired foliage. Their often brilliantly colored, saucer-shaped flowers are borne in clusters, over long periods in late spring and summer. Helianthemums are ideal for bringing color into rock gardens and raised beds or, indeed, at the front of flower borders. The smaller species and cultivars, such as *H. lunulatum*, may be used in troughs and suit a dry, sunny border. They are particularly effective as ground cover over a dry, sunny bank, or for crevices of dry-stone retaining walls. Grow in an open, sunny site, in well-drained, moderately fertile soil that is preferably neutral to alkaline. Trim lightly after flowering to keep the plant compact; a second flush of flowers may then be produced in late summer. Sometimes, helianthemums are rather short-lived and often become sparse and leggy at maturity, so it is best to propagate them regularly, replacing leggy specimens.

Take softwood cuttings in late spring or early summer and root in a cold frame. Pinch out the growing tips of young plants to promote a bushy, well-branched habit. Species can be raised from seed sown as soon as ripe or in the early spring. Overwinter young plants in a cold frame, and set them out in in spring.

H. 'Wisley White'
Habit Low, spreading, evergreen, shrub.
Flowers Saucer-shaped, 1in (2.5cm) across, borne in late spring to mid-summer. Creamy-white, with deep yellow center.
Leaves Oblong. Gray-green.
- HEIGHT 12in (30cm).
- SPREAD 18in (45cm).

H. 'Wisley White'

Z 5–7

***H.* APENNINUM**
Habit Low, loosely mound-forming, evergreen, shrub.
Flowers Saucer-shaped, 1in (2.5cm) across, borne from late spring to mid-summer. White, with deep golden-yellow center.
Leaves Oval to linear, and downy. Gray-green.
- HEIGHT to 16in (40cm).
- SPREAD 24in (60cm).

H. apenninum
White rock rose

Z 5–7

H. 'Rhodanthe Carneum'

Habit Spreading, low, evergreen, shrub.
Flowers Saucer-shaped, 1in (2.5cm) across, borne in late spring and mid-summer. Pale pink, with yellow-flushed center.
Leaves Narrowly oblong. Gray-green.
- OTHER NAME *H.* 'Wisley Pink'.
- HEIGHT 12in (30cm).
- SPREAD 18in (45cm).

H. 'Rhodanthe Carneum'

☼ ◊ Z 5–7

H. 'Ben More'

Habit Compact, spreading, twiggy, evergreen, shrub.
Flowers Saucer-shaped, across 1in (2.5cm), borne in loose, terminal clusters from late spring to summer. Deep orange-red.
Leaves Oval to oblong, and glossy. Dark green.
- HEIGHT to 12in (30cm).
- SPREAD 12in (30cm).

H. 'Ben More'

☼ ◊ Z 5–7

H. 'Raspberry Ripple'

Habit Low, spreading, evergreen, shrub.
Flowers Saucer-shaped, 1in (2.5cm) across, borne in summer. White, with deep raspberry-pink center spreading out along the petals.
Leaves Linear to oblong. Dark gray-green.
- HEIGHT 8in (20cm).
- SPREAD 12in (30cm).

H. 'Raspberry Ripple'

☼ ◊ Z 5–7

H. 'Wisley Primrose'

Habit Compact, fast-growing, free-flowering, evergreen, shrub.
Flowers Saucer-shaped, 1in (2.5cm) across, borne over long periods in late spring and summer. Pale primrose-yellow, with golden center.
Leaves Narrowly oblong. Gray-green.
- HEIGHT 12in (30cm).
- SPREAD 18in (45cm).

H. 'Wisley Primrose'

☼ ◊ Z 5–7

H. 'Fire Dragon'

Habit Spreading, evergreen, shrub.
Flowers Saucer-shaped, 1in (2.5cm) across, borne in profusion in late spring and summer. Bright orange-red.
Leaves Elliptic to oblong. Gray-green.
- OTHER NAME *H.* 'Mrs Clay'.
- HEIGHT to 12in (30cm).
- SPREAD 12in (30cm).

H. 'Fire Dragon'

☼ ◊ Z 5–7

H. LUNULATUM

Habit Compact, upright then spreading, dwarf, evergreen, shrub.
Flowers Saucer-shaped, ⅝in (15mm) across, borne in late spring and early summer. Clear yellow, with prominent orange stamens.
Leaves Lance-shaped to elliptical, and hairy. Gray-green.
- HEIGHT 6in (15cm).
- SPREAD 10in (25cm).

H. lunulatum
Shrubby rock rose

☼ ◊ Z 5–7

Campanulaceae	

CODONOPSIS VINCIFLORA

Habit Slender, fragile, twining, tuberous, herbaceous, perennial. ***Flowers*** Saucer-shaped, to 1¾in (4.5cm) across, borne singly on terminal or lateral shoots from mid-summer to autumn. Blue to blue-lilac. ***Leaves*** Lance-shaped to oval. Mid-green, with blue-green underside.
- NATIVE HABITAT Western China.
- CULTIVATION Needs fertile, light, moist but well-drained soil, in a site with sun or dappled shade. Stake plant or allow to climb small shrubs.
- PROPAGATION By seed in autumn or spring.

Z 5–8

HEIGHT
3ft (1m)

SPREAD
24in (60cm)

Iridaceae	

SISYRINCHIUM 'E.K. Balls'

Habit Semievergreen, clump-forming, perennial. ***Flowers*** Star-shaped, ¾in (2cm) across, borne in succession on upright stems in summer. Mauve. ***Leaves*** Sword-shaped, in basal fans. Mid-green.
- NATIVE HABITAT Garden origin.
- CULTIVATION Suitable for growing in a rock garden scree or gravel plantings. Needs a site in full sun with well-drained, moderately fertile soil that is neutral to slightly alkaline.
- PROPAGATION By division in spring.
- OTHER NAME *S.* 'Balls' Mauve'.

Z 8–9

HEIGHT
10in (25cm)

SPREAD
6in (15cm)

Scrophulariaceae	

PARAHEBE CATARRACTAE

Habit Spreading or erect, evergreen, subshrub. ***Flowers*** Saucer-shaped, ⅜in (1cm) across, borne in sprays in summer. White, heavily veined purple. ***Leaves*** Oval to lance-shaped and sharp-toothed. Dark green, tinted purple when young.
- NATIVE HABITAT Lowland and mountain meadows, New Zealand.
- CULTIVATION Needs well-drained, moderately fertile soil, in sun. Shelter from cold, dry winds.
- PROPAGATION By seed when ripe or in spring, or by semiripe cuttings in summer.

Z 8–9

HEIGHT
12in (30cm)

SPREAD
12in (30cm)

Iridaceae	BLUE-EYED GRASS

SISYRINCHIUM GRAMINOIDES

Habit Slender, clump-forming, semievergreen, perennial. ***Flowers*** Starlike, ¾in (2cm) across, borne throughout summer. Deep blue, with yellow throat. ***Leaves*** Linear, grasslike. Mid-green.
• NATIVE HABITAT Damp grassland, N. America.
• CULTIVATION Suits a rock or scree garden, with neutral to slightly alkaline, moderately fertile soil.
• PROPAGATION By seed in autumn or spring. Self-seeds very freely.
• OTHER NAMES *S. angustifolium*, *S. bermudiana*, *S. birameum* of gardens.

Z 8–9

HEIGHT to 12in (30cm)

SPREAD 6in (15cm)

Dipsacaceae	

SCABIOSA GRAMINIFOLIA

Habit Clump-forming, evergreen, perennial. ***Flowers*** Solitary, spherical, pincushionlike, to 1½in (4cm) across, borne on slender stems in summer. Lilac to violet. ***Leaves*** Linear to lance-shaped, grasslike, hairy, in basal tufts. Mid-green.
• NATIVE HABITAT Mountains, southern Europe.
• CULTIVATION Suits a rock garden or border front. Needs dry, well-drained, moderately fertile soil that is neutral to alkaline, preferably in hot sun.
• PROPAGATION By seed in autumn or spring, or by division in spring.

Z 7–9

HEIGHT 10in (25cm)

SPREAD 12in (30cm)

Asteraceae/Compositae	PYRENEAN ASTER

ASTER PYRENAEUS

Habit Upright or ascending, clump-forming, perennial. ***Flowers*** Daisylike, to 2in (5cm) across, borne from mid- to late summer. Violet or purple, with golden center. ***Leaves*** Broadly lance-shaped and slightly toothed. Mid-green.
• NATIVE HABITAT Damp pasture, subalpine meadows, and rocky places, Pyrenees.
• CULTIVATION Suitable for growing in borders. Needs moist but well-drained, fertile soil.
• PROPAGATION By seed in autumn, or by division in spring.

Z 5–8

HEIGHT 16–36in (40–90cm)

SPREAD 12in (30cm)

Campanulaceae	

CODONOPSIS CLEMATIDEA

Habit Tufted, tuberous, herbaceous, perennial. ***Flowers*** Nodding, bell-shaped, 1in (2.5cm) long; borne in early to mid-summer. Greenish-blue. ***Leaves*** Oval and lightly toothed. Gray-green.

• NATIVE HABITAT Grassy and rocky mountain slopes, central Asia.

• CULTIVATION Needs light, fertile, moist but well-drained soil, in sun or dappled shade. Provide light, twiggy support and shelter from wind.

• PROPAGATION By seed in autumn or spring, or by division in early spring. Often self-sows.

Z 5–8

HEIGHT
28in (70cm)

SPREAD
28in (70cm)

Boraginaceae	SHRUBBY CROMWELL

LITHODORA OLEIFOLIA

Habit Semierect, suckering, evergreen, subshrub. ***Flowers*** Funnel-shaped, ⅜in (9mm) long, borne in clusters of 3–7 in early summer. Sky-blue, with pale pink bud. ***Leaves*** Narrowly oval,with silky-haired underside. Dull, dark green.

• NATIVE HABITAT Eastern Spanish Pyrenees.

• CULTIVATION Grow in any well-drained soil in sun. Trim after flowering to keep plant compact.

• PROPAGATION By rooted suckers in spring, or by cuttings in mid-summer.

• OTHER NAME *Lithospermum oleifolium.*

Z 6–8

HEIGHT
8in (20cm)

SPREAD
12in (30cm)

Campanulaceae	HORNED RAMPION

PHYTEUMA SCHEUCHZERI

Habit Tuft-forming, herbaceous, perennial. ***Flowers*** Tubular, 1in (2.5cm) span, borne in rounded, spidery heads in summer. Violet-blue. ***Leaves*** Lance-shaped and sparse-toothed, forming basal clumps. Mid-green.

• NATIVE HABITAT Meadows, European Alps.

• CULTIVATION Suits a rock garden or border front. Tolerates any well-drained, moderately fertile soil in sun, but dislikes excessive winter moisture.

• PROPAGATION By seed in autumn, or by division in autumn or early spring. Self-seeds freely.

Z 5–8

HEIGHT
to 16in
(40cm)

SPREAD
12in (30cm)

Papaveraceae	PRICKLY BLUE POPPY

MECONOPSIS HORRIDULA

Habit Monocarpic, rosette-forming, perennial. ***Flowers*** Cup-shaped, semidrooping, long-stalked, to 3in (8cm) across, borne in sprays on spiny stems in early and mid-summer. Pale to deep blue, mauve, or reddish-blue. ***Leaves*** Oval to narrowly lance-shaped, bristly, with wavy margins. Gray-green, clothed in straw-colored to purple bristles.

• NATIVE HABITAT High altitudes, Himalaya and Tibet.

• CULTIVATION Ideal for woodland or rock gardens and peat terraces. Grow in leaf-rich, moist but well-drained, neutral to acid, open-textured soil. Needs a cool, humid site in dappled shade, and shelter from cold, dry winds. Prefers areas with cool, damp summers.

• PROPAGATION Sow seed as soon as ripe or in spring, in soilless seed mix but uncovered as the light is needed for germination. Keep seedlings from autumn sowings in a cold greenhouse or frame. Will self-sow in favored gardens.

pH

Z 7–8

HEIGHT
8–28in
(20–70cm)

SPREAD
18in (45cm)

Campanulaceae	RING BELLFLOWER

SYMPHYANDRA WANNERI

Habit Upright, rosette-forming, monocarpic, evergreen, perennial. ***Flowers*** Drooping, narrowly bell-shaped, to 1½in (3.5cm) long, borne in clusters in summer. Deep violet-blue. ***Leaves*** Lance-shaped, toothed, rough-haired. Mid-green.

- NATIVE HABITAT Southeastern Europe.
- CULTIVATION Needs a site in sun or softly dappled shade, with light, well-drained, fertile soil. Usually dies after flowering, but may self-seed.
- PROPAGATION By seed in autumn or early spring.
- OTHER NAME *Campanula wanneri.*

Z 6–8

HEIGHT to 20in (50cm)

SPREAD 12in (30cm)

Boraginaceae	

MOLTKIA SUFFRUTICOSA

Habit Upright, loosely branched, deciduous, subshrub. ***Flowers*** Tubular, ¾in (17mm) long, borne in short, dense clusters in summer. Intense, bright blue. ***Leaves*** Linear and bristly. Dark green.

- NATIVE HABITAT Mountain grass, northern Italy.
- CULTIVATION Suitable for planting in a rock garden or crevice of rock or a retaining wall. Grow in sharply drained, preferably alkaline soil.
- PROPAGATION By seed in autumn, or by softwood cuttings in mid-summer.
- OTHER NAME *Lithospermum graminifolium.*

Z 7–9

HEIGHT to 16in (40cm)

SPREAD 12in (30cm)

Scrophulariaceae	

VERONICA AUSTRIACA subsp. *TEUCRIUM* 'Kapitän'

Habit Mat-forming, evergreen, perennial. ***Flowers*** Saucer-shaped, ½in (13mm) across, borne in dense spikes during summer. Gentian-blue. ***Leaves*** Narrowly oval and toothed. Bright green.

- NATIVE HABITAT Garden origin.
- CULTIVATION Suitable for growing in a rock garden or at the front of a border. Grow in well-drained, moderately fertile soil.
- PROPAGATION By division in autumn or spring.
- OTHER NAME *V. teucrium* 'Kapitän'.

Z 5–8

HEIGHT 12in (30cm)

SPREAD 20in (50cm)

Boraginaceae	

LITHODORA DIFFUSA 'Heavenly Blue'

Habit Prostrate, hummock-forming, evergreen, shrub. ***Flowers*** Funnel-shaped, ½in (1cm) across, borne in terminal clusters from late spring to summer. Deep azure-blue. ***Leaves*** Oval to narrowly paddle-shaped and bristly. Dark green.

- NATIVE HABITAT Garden origin.
- CULTIVATION Needs fertile, acid soil.
- PROPAGATION By semiripe cuttings in summer, with gentle heat underneath.
- OTHER NAME *Lithospermum diffusum* 'Heavenly Blue'.

Z 6–8

HEIGHT 6in (15cm)

SPREAD 24in (60cm) or more

Scrophulariaceae

VERONICA PROSTRATA 'Trehane'

Habit Mat-forming, evergreen, perennial. ***Flowers*** Saucer-shaped, ¼–⅜in (6–10mm) across, borne in dense, upright spikes in early or mid-summer. Deep blue. ***Leaves*** Narrowly oval and toothed. Yellow-green to gold.

- NATIVE HABITAT Garden origin.
- CULTIVATION Suitable for rock gardens, gravel-path edges, or at the front of a herbaceous or mixed border. Grow in full sun, in a site with well-drained, moderately fertile soil.
- PROPAGATION Divide in autumn or early spring.

Z 5–8

HEIGHT 6in (15cm)

SPREAD 16in (40cm) or more

Boraginaceae

MERTENSIA ECHIOIDES

Habit Clumping, perennial. ***Flowers*** Funnel-shaped, ¼in (7mm) long, borne in curving clusters on erect stems, in summer. Deep blue. ***Leaves*** Spoon- or lance-shaped, hairy. Dark blue-green.

- NATIVE HABITAT High altitudes, Himalaya.
- CULTIVATION Prefers a site in sun or dappled shade with gritty, moist but sharply drained soil enriched with organic matter.
- PROPAGATION By seed in autumn, keeping seedlings moist and shaded. Divide carefully as growth begins in early spring.

Z 6–8

HEIGHT 8in (20cm)

SPREAD 6in (15cm)

Scrophulariaceae

VERONICA AUSTRIACA subsp. *TEUCRIUM*

Habit Mat- or cushion-forming, evergreen, perennial. ***Flowers*** Saucer-shaped, outward-facing, ½in (13mm) across, borne in paired sprays in summer. Deep, bright blue. ***Leaves*** Narrowly oval and toothed. Bright green.

- NATIVE HABITAT Grassy and rocky habitats, in the mountains of temperate northern Europe.
- CULTIVATION Needs well-drained soil.
- PROPAGATION By seed as soon as ripe, or by division in autumn or spring.
- OTHER NAME *V. teucrium.*

Z 5–8

HEIGHT to 12in (30cm)

SPREAD 16in (40cm)

Rosaceae	ALPINE LADY'S MANTLE

ALCHEMILLA ALPINA

Habit Mat-forming or tufted, rhizomatous, perennial. ***Flowers*** Tiny, star-shaped, ⅛in (3mm) across, borne in loose clusters in summer. Yellow-green. ***Leaves*** Divided into 5–7 lance-shaped leaflets. Green, with silver, silky-haired underside.
• NATIVE HABITAT Alpine turf and mountain habitats in Europe and Greenland.
• CULTIVATION Thrives in sun or light shade, with moist but well-drained, gritty, fertile soil.
• PROPAGATION By seed in autumn, or by division in early spring or autumn.

Z 3–7

HEIGHT to 5in (12cm)

SPREAD to 20in (50cm)

Geraniaceae	YELLOW ERODIUM

ERODIUM CHRYSANTHUM

Habit Compact, tufted, mound-forming, evergreen, perennial. ***Flowers*** Saucer-shaped, ¾in (2cm) across, borne in clusters in summer. Pale sulfur-yellow. ***Leaves*** Finely dissected, fern-like, paddle- to lance-shaped. Silvery-green.
• NATIVE HABITAT Mountains, Greece.
• CULTIVATION Suits a raised bed or rock garden. Grow in sharply drained, neutral to alkaline soil.
• PROPAGATION By seed when ripe, or by division or basal cuttings in spring. Male and female flowers borne on separate plants; both are needed for seed.

Z 7–8

HEIGHT 6in (15cm)

SPREAD 16in (40cm)

Labiatae/Lamiaceae	

ORIGANUM ROTUNDIFOLIUM

Habit Woody-based, rhizomatous, herbaceous or semievergreen, perennial. ***Flowers*** Tubular, ⅝in (15mm) long, borne in nodding whorls in summer. Pale pink, dominated by overlapping, large apple-green bracts. ***Leaves*** Rounded to heart-shaped and aromatic. Blue-gray.
• NATIVE HABITAT Turkey, Armenia, and Georgia.
• CULTIVATION Ideal pot-grown in an alpine house. Needs sharply drained, alkaline soil, in sun.
• PROPAGATION By seed in autumn or spring, by division in spring, or by cuttings in mid-summer.

Z 5–8

HEIGHT 4–12in (10–30cm)

SPREAD 12in (30cm)

Guttiferae/Clusiaceae	

HYPERICUM OLYMPICUM f. *UNIFLORUM* 'Citrinum'

Habit Upright, deciduous, subshrub. ***Flowers*** Saucer-shaped, 2½in (6cm) across, borne in summer. Pale lemon-yellow. ***Leaves*** Broadly oval. Gray-green, with glaucous underside.
• NATIVE HABITAT Garden origin.
• CULTIVATION Ideal for a rock garden, a raised bed, or gravel plantings. Needs sun or light shade, with sharply drained, moderately fertile soil.
• PROPAGATION By softwood or semiripe cuttings. Self-sown seedlings may come true.

Z 6–8

HEIGHT 10in (25cm)

SPREAD 12in (30cm)

Linaceae	

LINUM ARBOREUM

Habit Dwarf, evergreen, shrub. ***Flowers*** Funnel-shaped, to 1¼in (3cm) across, in compact, terminal clusters, opening from pointed buds; individually short-lived, but borne in succession throughout summer. Rich, deep yellow. ***Leaves*** Thick and oval, often crowded into rosettes. Dark blue-green.

• NATIVE HABITAT Rocky habitats, southern Aegean to Crete and western Turkey. Plants in the wild are often larger than dimensions given.

• CULTIVATION Excellent for growing on a rock garden, a raised bed, or crevices of dry, retaining walls. Also suits planting in large troughs or pans in an alpine house. Grow in a warm site, in full sun, with light, sharply drained, moderately fertile soil. The flowers open fully in warm, sunny weather.

• PROPAGATION By seed in spring or autumn, or by semiripe cuttings in summer in a cold frame.

☼ ◊

Z 3–8

HEIGHT
12in (30cm)

SPREAD
12in (30cm)

Scrophulariaceae	

VERBASCUM 'Letitia'

Habit Dense, rounded, stiff-branched, evergreen, subshrub. ***Flowers*** Outward-facing, saucer-shaped, ⅝in (15mm) across, borne in short spikes throughout summer. Bright yellow, with reddish-orange center. ***Leaves*** Lance-shaped and irregularly toothed. Gray-green.

• NATIVE HABITAT Garden origin.

• CULTIVATION Suits a rock garden, raised bed, or crevice of a dry, retaining wall. Needs sharply drained, moderately fertile soil in warm sun.

• PROPAGATION By semiripe cuttings in summer.

Z 8–9

HEIGHT 10in (25cm)

SPREAD 20in (50cm)

Ranunculaceae	

TROLLIUS ACAULIS

Habit Clumping, herbaceous, perennial. ***Flowers*** Bowl-shaped, terminal, usually solitary, to 2in (5cm) across, borne in summer. Golden-yellow. ***Leaves*** Rounded, segmented into narrowly lance-shaped lobes. Mid-green.

• NATIVE HABITAT Moist, grassy slopes, Himalaya.

• CULTIVATION Needs leaf- or peat-rich, moist soil that is acid or alkaline, in sun or partial shade.

• PROPAGATION By seed when ripe or in spring (may take 2 years to germinate), or by division as new growth begins or after flowering.

Z 5–8

HEIGHT 4–12in (10–30cm)

SPREAD 6in (15cm)

Cruciferae/ Brassicaceae	MOUNTAIN ALISON

ALYSSUM MONTANUM

Habit Prostrate, mat-forming, evergreen, perennial. ***Flowers*** Scented, cross-shaped, 4-petaled, ⅕in (5mm) across, borne in spikes in early summer. Golden-yellow. ***Leaves*** Paddle-shaped to oval, forming rosettes. Gray.

• NATIVE HABITAT Rocky and stony sites, Europe.

• CULTIVATION Suitable for a rock garden and raised beds. Needs sunny site, with well-drained, preferably gritty, moderately fertile soil.

• PROPAGATION By seed in autumn or spring, or by greenwood cuttings in mid-summer.

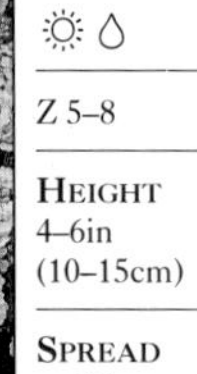

Z 5–8

HEIGHT 4–6in (10–15cm)

SPREAD to 20in (50cm)

Onagraceae	SUNDROPS

OENOTHERA PERENNIS

Habit Tufted, clumping, evergreen, perennial. ***Flowers*** Funnel-shaped, ¾in (2cm) across, opening from nodding buds, borne in loose, erect spikes in summer. Yellow. ***Leaves*** Narrowly spoon-shaped, forming rosettes. Mid-green.

• NATIVE HABITAT Mountains, eastern N. America.

• CULTIVATION Needs well-drained, moderately fertile, gritty or stony soil, in a warm, sunny site.

• PROPAGATION By seed in autumn or early spring, or by careful division in spring.

• OTHER NAME *O. pumila.*

Z 3–9

HEIGHT 8in (20cm)

SPREAD 8in (20cm)

Guttiferae/Clusiaceae	

HYPERICUM CERASTOIDES

Habit Erect, then arching, evergreen, subshrub. ***Flowers*** Star-shaped, to 1¾in (4.5cm) across, borne in clusters of 5 in early summer. Deep yellow. ***Leaves*** Oval or narrow, downy. Gray-green.

• NATIVE HABITAT Woods and rocks, southern Bulgaria, northeast Greece, and northwest Turkey.

• CULTIVATION Needs moderately fertile, sharply drained, ideally sandy and slightly acid soil, in sun.

• PROPAGATION By seed or by division, in spring or autumn.

• OTHER NAME *H. rhodoppeum.*

Z 5–8

HEIGHT 6in (15cm)

SPREAD to 16in (40cm)

Compositae/Asteraceae	

EURYOPS ACRAEUS

Habit Dense, dome-forming, evergreen, shrub. ***Flowers*** Daisylike, 1in (2.5cm) across, borne singly or in 2–3 in summer. Clear, citrus yellow. ***Leaves*** Leathery, waxy, linear and flattened, with toothed tips. Bright silver-gray.

• NATIVE HABITAT Rocky areas, S. Africa.

• CULTIVATION Grow in sharply drained soil, in warm, sheltered site. Dislikes excessive moisture.

• PROPAGATION By seed in spring, or by softwood or semiripe cuttings in summer.

• OTHER NAME *E. evansii* of gardens.

Z 9–10

HEIGHT 20in (50cm)

SPREAD 20in (50cm)

Polygonaceae	SULFUR FLOWER

ERIOGONUM UMBELLATUM

Habit Mat-forming, evergreen, perennial. ***Flowers*** Tiny, borne in dense clusters to 2½in (6cm) across, in summer. Cream to sulfur-yellow, with copper tints at maturity. ***Leaves*** Spoon-shaped to oval. Mid-green, with woolly, white undersides.

• NATIVE HABITAT Southwestern Canada to western USA.

• CULTIVATION Grow in poor to moderately fertile, gritty, sharply drained soil in sun.

• PROPAGATION By seed in autumn, or by rooting rosette cuttings in spring and early summer.

Z 6–8

HEIGHT 12in (30cm)

SPREAD to 36in (90cm)

Scrophulariaceae	

VERBASCUM DUMULOSUM

Habit Forms large, spreading domes, downy-stemmed, evergreen, subshrub. ***Flowers*** Outward-facing, saucer-shaped, ⅝in (15mm) across, borne in short spikes, to 6in (15cm) high, during summer. Bright yellow, with red eye. ***Leaves*** Oval, often scalloped, and densely felted. Gray or gray-green.

• NATIVE HABITAT Dry, stony hillsides, southwestern Turkey.

• CULTIVATION Suitable for a rock garden or raised bed, with overhead protection from winter moisture. Best planted on its side in a vertical rock or wall crevice. Needs a warm, sunny site, with gritty or stony, sharply drained, moderately fertile, and preferably alkaline soil. Although quite hardy, it will not tolerate cold in combination with winter moisture. May also be grown in an alpine house in a mix of equal parts soil-based potting mix and grit.

• PROPAGATION By seed in late spring in a cold frame, or by semiripe cuttings in summer.

☼ ◊

Z 8–9

HEIGHT
to 10in
(25cm)

SPREAD
to 28in
(70cm)

Ranunculaceae	GRASS-LEAVED BUTTERCUP

RANUNCULUS GRAMINEUS

Habit Slender, upright, clumping, herbaceous, perennial. ***Flowers*** Cup-shaped, ¾in (2cm) across, borne on upright, branched stems in late spring and early summer. Lemon-yellow. ***Leaves*** Grasslike and linear to lance-shaped. Blue-green.
• NATIVE HABITAT Mountain pastures, southern Europe.
• CULTIVATION Tolerates any moist but well-drained soil in a sunny or partially shaded site.
• PROPAGATION By division in early spring or autumn, or by seed as soon as ripe.

Z 6–8

HEIGHT to 12in (30cm)

SPREAD 6in (15cm)

Leguminosae/ Papilionaceae	

GENISTA PILOSA 'Procumbens'

Habit Prostrate, free-flowering, deciduous, shrub, with downy branches. ***Flowers*** Pealike, ⅜in (1cm) long, borne in spikes in early summer. Yellow. ***Leaves*** Lance-shaped. Dark green.
• NATIVE HABITAT Garden origin. Species occurs in heath, open woods, and rocky places.
• CULTIVATION Suitable for a raised bed or rock garden, and will trail over a large rock or bank. Needs a sunny site with light, well-drained, moderately fertile soil. Tolerates poor, dry soils.
• PROPAGATION By semiripe cuttings in summer.

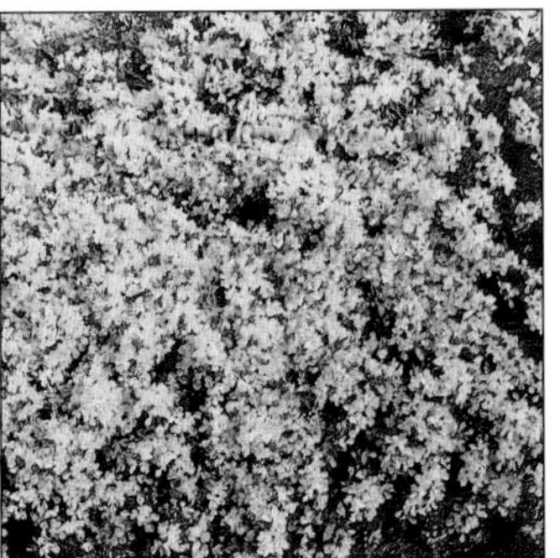

Z 6–8

HEIGHT 8in (20cm)

SPREAD 20in (50cm) or more

Leguminosae/ Papilionaceae	

GENISTA LYDIA

Habit Mound-forming, free-flowering, deciduous, shrub, with arching, prickle-tipped branches. ***Flowers*** Pealike, ⅝in (15mm) long, borne in small clusters in early summer. Yellow. ***Leaves*** Small, narrowly oval. Blue-green.
• NATIVE HABITAT Rocky sites, eastern Balkans.
• CULTIVATION Suitable for a large rock garden or raised bed. Needs a warm, sunny site, with light, well-drained, moderately fertile soil.
• PROPAGATION By seed in autumn or spring, or by semiripe cuttings in summer.

Z 7–9

HEIGHT to 24in (60cm)

SPREAD 36in (90cm)

Crassulaceae	ROSEROOT

Rhodiola rosea

Habit Clumping, herbaceous, with succulent, thick stems, perennial. ***Flowers*** Tiny, star-shaped, ¼in (6mm) across, borne in dense, terminal heads in summer. Pink bud, opening to yellow-green. ***Leaves*** Fleshy and oval. Gray-green, with red tips.
• NATIVE HABITAT Rocks, sea cliffs, screes, from sea level to high altitudes, northern hemisphere.
• CULTIVATION Best grown in gritty compost.
• PROPAGATION By seed in spring or autumn, or by division in spring.
• OTHER NAMES *Sedum roseum, S. rhodiola.*

Z 2–8

HEIGHT 8–12in (20–30cm)

SPREAD 12in (30cm)

Papaveraceae	ALPINE POPPY

Papaver alpinum

Habit Short-lived, tufted, evergreeen, perennial. ***Flowers*** Cup-shaped, solitary, 1½in (4cm) across, borne in summer. White, orange, or yellow. ***Leaves*** Hairy, and finely divided into linear segments. Gray-green.
• NATIVE HABITAT Alps and Pyrenees.
• CULTIVATION Grows best in a sunny site, with low-fertility, stony, free-draining soils.
• PROPAGATION By seed in spring. Often self-seeds, but seldom to the point of nuisance. Needs to be propagated regularly.

Z 5–8

HEIGHT 6–8in (15–20cm)

SPREAD 4in (10cm)

Compositae/Asteraceae	GOLDEN HAWKSBEARD

Crepis aurea

Habit Tap-rooted, rosette-forming, perennial. ***Flowers*** Dandelion-like, 1¼in (3cm) across, borne on stems covered in black and white hairs, during summer. Bright orange-yellow. ***Leaves*** Oval to lance-shaped and deep-toothed. Light green.
• NATIVE HABITAT Rocky places and mountains, in Italy and the Balkans.
• CULTIVATION Good for wall plantings or rocky places. Tolerates any well-drained soil in sun.
• PROPAGATION By seed as soon as ripe. Self-seeds freely, and can become a nuisance.

Z 5–8

HEIGHT 4–12in (10–30cm)

SPREAD to 12in (30cm)

Ericaceae	

GAULTHERIA CUNEATA

Habit Dwarf, densely branched, evergreen, shrub. ***Flowers*** Urn-shaped, ¼in (6mm) across, borne in lateral spikes in late spring. White. ***Leaves*** Pointed, oval, toothed, and leathery. Mid-green. ***Fruits*** Globose berries, ¼in (6mm) across. White.
- NATIVE HABITAT Western China.
- CULTIVATION Excellent for growing in a rock or woodland garden, or a peat bed. Needs moist but well-drained, leaf-rich, neutral to acid soil.
- PROPAGATION By seed as soon as ripe, or by semiripe cuttings in mid- to late summer.

Z 5–8

HEIGHT
12in (30cm)

SPREAD
36in (90cm)

Labiatae/Lamiaceae	

ORIGANUM AMANUM

Habit Spreading, wiry-stemmed, semi-herbaceous, subshrub. ***Flowers*** Tubular, slightly curved, 1½in (4cm) long, borne in terminal whorls in autumn. Bright pink, with green base. ***Leaves*** Aromatic and oval. Bright green.
- NATIVE HABITAT Mountain rocks, Turkey.
- CULTIVATION Under glass, grow in equal parts soil, leaf mold, and grit. Needs sharply drained, gritty, alkaline soil. Dislikes winter moisture.
- PROPAGATION By seed in spring, or by cuttings of basal shoots in mid-summer.

Z 5–8

HEIGHT
3in (8cm)

SPREAD
12in (30cm)

Rosaceae	

SORBUS REDUCTA

Habit Suckering, thicket-forming, deciduous, shrub. ***Flowers*** Small, saucer-shaped, borne in clusters 3in (8cm) across, in spring. White. ***Leaves*** Pinnate and glossy. Dark green; rich red in autumn. ***Fruits*** Round berries, ½in (1cm) span. White, flushed crimson.
- NATIVE HABITAT Mountains, western China.
- CULTIVATION Grow in an open site in full sun, with moderately fertile, well-drained soil.
- PROPAGATION By seed in autumn or spring, or by softwood cuttings in early summer.

Z 5–7

HEIGHT
12–24in
(30–60cm)

SPREAD
3–6ft
(1–2m)
or more

Compositae/Asteraceae	

Celmisia semicordata

Habit Clump-forming, somewhat rhizomatous, evergreen, perennial. ***Flowers*** Daisylike, 3in (8cm), borne on upright, green-white stems in early and mid-summer. White, with yellow center. ***Leaves*** Erect, then recurved, sword- to lance-shaped, leathery, with fine, silky hair. Silver-green, white underneath.

• NATIVE HABITAT Alpine and subalpine pastures, at high altitudes, South Island, New Zealand.

• CULTIVATION Excellent for planting in a raised bed or rock garden, but grows best in cool, moist climates. Needs a sunny or partially shaded site, with slightly acid, moist but well-drained soil that is rich in organic matter.

• PROPAGATION By seed as soon as ripe, or by careful division in spring. Offspring may be hybrids unless isolated, and few viable seeds generally are produced.

• OTHER NAME *C. coriacea* of gardens.

Z 6–9

HEIGHT
to 20in (50cm)

SPREAD
12in (30cm)

Ranunculaceae

RANUNCULUS CALANDRINIOIDES

Habit Clumping, fleshy-rooted, semi-evergreen, perennial. ***Flowers*** Cup-shaped, 2in (5cm) across, borne in loose cluster of up to 3 in late winter and early spring. White, flushed pink. ***Leaves*** Smooth and oval, dying back in summer. Blue-green.
• NATIVE HABITAT Atlas mountains, N. Africa.
• CULTIVATION Needs gritty, sharply drained soil that is rich in organic matter. Under glass, use equal parts of soil, leaf mold, and sharp sand.
• PROPAGATION By seed when ripe but still green, or by division in autumn or after flowering.

Z 7–8

HEIGHT
8in (20cm)

SPREAD
6in (15cm)

Asteraceae/Compositae

OZOTHAMNUS SELAGO

Habit Upright, evergreen, hebe-like, subshrub. ***Flowers*** Solitary, cylindrical, borne in summer. Cream. ***Leaves*** Aromatic, oval to triangular, scale-like. Dark green, with woolly, white underside.
• NATIVE HABITAT South Island, New Zealand.
• CULTIVATION Suitable for growing in a trough, a scree bed, or an alpine house. Needs gritty, sharply drained soil, and protection from winter moisture.
• PROPAGATION By seed when ripe, or by semi-ripe cuttings in summer.
• OTHER NAME *Helichrysum selago.*

Z 7–9

HEIGHT
to 16in (40cm)

SPREAD
10in (25cm)

Compositae/Asteraceae

OZOTHAMNUS CORALLOIDES

Habit Erect, dome-forming, evergreen, subshrub. ***Flowers*** Solitary, cylindrical, borne in summer. Pale yellow. ***Leaves*** Leathery, diamond-shaped, scalelike. Dark green, woolly-white underneath.
• NATIVE HABITAT New Zealand.
• CULTIVATION Suitable for a trough, a scree bed, or an alpine house. Grow in gritty, sharply drained soil, and protect from winter moisture.
• PROPAGATION By seed when ripe, or by semi-ripe cuttings in mid- to late summer.
• OTHER NAME *Helichrysum coralloides.*

Z 7–9

HEIGHT
6in (15cm)

SPREAD
6in (15cm)

Salicaceae

SALIX x *BOYDII*

Habit Very slow-growing, erect, deciduous, shrub, with gnarled branches. ***Flowers*** Insignificant female catkins borne occasionally on bare branches in spring. ***Leaves*** Almost circular, rough-textured, prominently veined, and untoothed. Gray-green.
• NATIVE HABITAT Angus mountains, Scotland.
• CULTIVATION Suitable for planting in a trough or rock garden. Grows best in gritty, moist but sharply drained soil.
• PROPAGATION By hardwood cuttings in winter.
• OTHER NAME *S.* 'Boydii'.

Z 4–7

HEIGHT
12in (30cm)

SPREAD
to 40in (1m)

Cruciferae/ Brassicaceae	TRIFOLIATE BITTERCRESS

CARDAMINE TRIFOLIA

Habit Creeping, rhizomatous, evergreen, patch-forming, perennial. ***Flowers*** Cross-shaped, to ⅝in (15mm) across, borne in congested sprays in late spring. White, sometimes pink, with yellow anthers. ***Leaves*** Divided into 3 rounded to diamond-shaped leaflets. Dark green.

• NATIVE HABITAT Central and southern Europe.

• CULTIVATION Ideal for a shady corner of a rock garden in moist, fertile soil. Tolerates deep shade.

• PROPAGATION By seed in autumn or spring, or by division in autumn or after flowering.

Z 5–7

HEIGHT to 6in (15cm)

SPREAD 12in (30cm) or more

Cruciferae/ Brassicaceae	

ARABIS CAUCASICA 'Variegata'

Habit Mat-forming, evergreen, perennial. ***Flowers*** Fragrant, cross-shaped, to ⅜in (1cm) across, borne in loose sprays in spring. White. ***Leaves*** Oval, toothed, rosetted. Mid-green, edged pale-yellow.

• NATIVE HABITAT Garden origin.

• CULTIVATION Suitable for planting in a rock garden, on a dry bank, or on the top of a retaining wall. Thrives in any well-drained soil in full sun, and will tolerate hot, dry conditions and poor soils. Trim plant after flowering.

• PROPAGATION By softwood cuttings in summer.

Z 4–7

HEIGHT 6in (15cm)

SPREAD 20in (50cm)

Caryophyllaceae	CORSICAN SANDWORT

ARENARIA BALEARICA

Habit Prostrate, mat-forming, mosslike, evergreen, perennial. ***Flowers*** Solitary, saucer-shaped, ¼–⅜in (6–10mm) across, borne in late spring to summer. White. ***Leaves*** Tiny and broadly oval. Bright, shining green.

• NATIVE HABITAT Western Mediterranean islands.

• CULTIVATION Will cling tightly to a shady, porous sandstone rock face or damp wall, forming a dense mat of foliage. Needs a moist, shaded site.

• PROPAGATION By seed in autumn, or take rooted cuttings.

Z 4–7

HEIGHT ⅜–¾in (1–2cm)

SPREAD 12in (30cm or more)

Portulacaceae	

Lewisia brachycalyx

Habit Dwarf, tufted, herbaceous, perennial. ***Flowers*** Solitary, funnel-shaped, to 2in (5cm) across, borne in profusion from late spring to early summer. White or pale pink. ***Leaves*** Lance-shaped, fleshy, in basal rosettes. Dark green.

• NATIVE HABITAT Stony, open meadows and grassland, southern California and Arizona, USA.

• CULTIVATION Needs sharply drained, neutral to acid soil. Best in an alpine house to protect from excessive wet when dormant in summer.

• PROPAGATION By seed in autumn in a cold frame.

Z 4–7

HEIGHT 3in (8cm)

SPREAD 3in (8cm)

Fumariaceae/ Papaveraceae	DUTCHMAN'S BREECHES

Dicentra cucullaria

Habit Tuberous, clump-forming, herbaceous, perennial. ***Flowers*** Drooping, heart-shaped, to ¾in (2cm) long, borne on arching stems in early spring. White, tipped yellow. ***Leaves*** Fernlike and finely divided. Blue-green.

• NATIVE HABITAT Woods, eastern N. America.

• CULTIVATION Suits a woodland or rock garden, in gritty, fertile soil. Dies back soon after flowering and needs a dry summer dormancy.

• PROPAGATION By seed as soon as ripe or in spring. Divide after the leaves have died down.

Z 4–7

HEIGHT 8in (20cm)

SPREAD 10in (25cm)

Rosaceae	ROCK SPIRAEA

Petrophytum hendersonii

Habit Mat-forming, evergreen, subshrub. ***Flowers*** Tiny, borne in conical, spikelike sprays to 3in (8cm) long, in summer. White. ***Leaves*** Spoon-shaped, hairy. Blue-green.

• NATIVE HABITAT Scree and rock crevices, mountains of western N. America.

• CULTIVATION Excellent for a scree or raised bed. Needs gritty, sharply drained, preferably slightly alkaline soil that is not too fertile.

• PROPAGATION By seed in autumn, or by softwood or semiripe cuttings in summer.

Z 6–9

HEIGHT 4in (10cm)

SPREAD 8in (20cm)

Portulacaceae	

Lewisia columbiana

Habit Evergreen, perennial. ***Flowers*** Open funnel-shaped, 1in (2.5cm) across, borne in lax clusters from spring to summer. Deep to pale pink, with darker veins. ***Leaves*** Lance-shaped or linear, in fleshy rosettes. Dark green.

• NATIVE HABITAT Western N. America.

• CULTIVATION Excellent for growing as a pot plant in an alpine house. Can be grown in troughs outdoors but protect from winter moisture.

• PROPAGATION By seed in autumn, or by offsets in early summer.

Z 4–7

HEIGHT 6in (15cm)

SPREAD 6in (15cm)

Caryophyllaceae	

SAGINA SUBULATA 'Aurea'

Habit Mat-forming, stem-rooting, mosslike, evergreen, perennial. ***Flowers*** Solitary, tiny, 5-petaled, ⅙in (4mm) across, borne in summer. White. ***Leaves*** Linear, pointed. Yellow-green.
• NATIVE HABITAT Garden origin.
• CULTIVATION Suits a rock garden or paving crevices, where it forms a spreading mat. Needs moist but well-drained, neutral to acid soil. Prefers some midday shade but dislikes hot, dry weather.
• PROPAGATION Divide in spring or summer.
• OTHER NAME *S. glabra* 'Aurea'.

Z 6–8

HEIGHT
⅜in (1cm)

SPREAD
8in (20cm)

Liliaceae/Trilliaceae	SNOW TRILLIUM

TRILLIUM NIVALE

Habit Compact, clump-forming, rhizomatous, herbaceous, perennial. ***Flowers*** Upright, to 1½in (4cm) across, borne in early spring. Pure white, with green sepals. ***Leaves*** Oval and pointed, in threes. Dark blue-green.
• NATIVE HABITAT Southeastern USA.
• CULTIVATION Quite difficult to grow, but suits a rock garden or an alpine house. Needs moist, well-drained, fertile, neutral to slightly alkaline soil.
• PROPAGATION By seed as soon as ripe, but may take 5–7 years to flower. Divide after flowering.

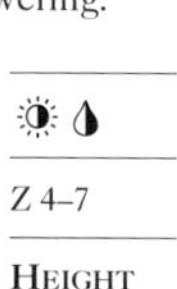

Z 4–7

HEIGHT
5in (12cm)

SPREAD
4in (10cm)

Papaveraceae	DOUBLE BLOOD ROOT

SANGUINARIA CANADENSIS 'Plena'

Habit Rhizomatous, herbaceous, patch-forming, perennial. ***Flowers*** Solitary, cup-shaped, double, 3in (7cm) across, borne in spring. Glistening white. ***Leaves*** Kidney-shaped, lobed. Bluish gray-green.
• NATIVE HABITAT Garden origin.
• CULTIVATION Suits a woodland, rock garden, or peat bed. Needs reliably moist, well-drained fertile soil in partial or dappled shade. Tolerates part-day sun in moist soils, but dislikes being disturbed.
• PROPAGATION Divide after flowering in spring.
• OTHER NAME *S.c.* 'Flore Plena'.

Z 3–7

HEIGHT
6in (15cm)

SPREAD
12in (30cm)

Papaveraceae	BLOOD ROOT, RED PUCCOON

SANGUINARIA CANADENSIS

Habit Rhizomatous, herbaceous, patch-forming, perennial. ***Flowers*** Solitary, cup-shaped, single, to 2in (5cm) across, borne in spring with the leaves. White. ***Leaves*** Kidney-shaped. Bluish gray-green.
• NATIVE HABITAT Woodlands, eastern N. America.
• CULTIVATION Excellent for a woodland, rock garden, or peat bed. Needs fertile, reliably moist but well-drained soil, in partial or dappled shade. Will tolerate part-day sun in moist soils.
• PROPAGATION Divide after flowering in spring, or sow seed in autumn in a cold frame.

Z 3–7

HEIGHT
6in (15cm)

SPREAD
12in (30cm)

Ranunculaceae	SPRING PASQUE FLOWER

PULSATILLA VERNALIS

Habit Tufted, rosette-forming, evergreen, perennial. ***Flowers*** Bell-shaped, erect, silky-haired, to 2½in (6cm) across, borne from drooping buds in spring. White, flushed blue-violet. ***Leaves*** Finely cut, sparsely haired, leathery. Deep green.
• NATIVE HABITAT Alpine turf, from Spain to Scandinavia, and from Bulgaria to Siberia.
• CULTIVATION Grow in moist, sharply drained soil in a scree or an alpine house. Protect from winter wet.
• PROPAGATION By seed as soon as ripe.

Z 3–7

HEIGHT
4in (10cm)

SPREAD
4in (10cm)

Ranunculaceae	ALPINE BUTTERCUP

RANUNCULUS ALPESTRIS

Habit Short-lived, fibrous-rooted, evergreen, perennial. ***Flowers*** Cupped, to ¾in (2cm) across, borne from late spring to mid-summer. White. ***Leaves*** Kidney-shaped, lobed. Dark, glossy green.
• NATIVE HABITAT Mountains, central and southern Europe.
• CULTIVATION Suits an alpine house or a scree bed, in gritty, fertile, moist, sharply drained soil.
• PROPAGATION By seed, when still slightly green, in an open frame, but germination is erratic. Otherwise, by division in early spring or autumn.

Z 4–7

HEIGHT
4in (10cm)

SPREAD
4in (10cm)

Ericaceae	

CASSIOPE LYCOPODIOIDES

Habit Mat-forming, evergreen, shrub. ***Flowers*** Bell-shaped, ¼in (6mm) long, borne from the upper leaf axils in late spring. White, with red sepals. ***Leaves*** Tiny, scalelike, and closely overlapping on the slender stems. Dark green.
• NATIVE HABITAT Northwest N. America, Japan.
• CULTIVATION Suits a sheltered site on a rock garden, in acid soil that is rich in organic matter.
• PROPAGATION By seed in autumn, or by semiripe cuttings in summer, preferably in a propagating frame with a misting unit.

Z 3–7

HEIGHT
3in (8cm)

SPREAD
10in (25cm)

Ranunculaceae	WHITE LESSER CELANDINE

RANUNCULUS FICARIA f. *ALBUS*

Habit Tufted, tuberous, herbaceous, perennial. ***Flowers*** Solitary, saucer-shaped, ⅘–1⅕in (2–3cm) across, borne in late winter and early spring. Cream, fading to white at maturity. ***Leaves*** Basal, broadly heart-shaped, dying back soon after flowering. Dark glossy green.

• NATIVE HABITAT Garden origin. The white-flowered form occurs naturally in wild populations, in hedgerows, deciduous woodland, and damp grassy habitats. It has been selected and propagated vegetatively in cultivation.

• CULTIVATION Spreads rapidly and, like the yellow-flowered species, is too invasive for the rock garden. More suitable for naturalizing in turf, or for growing in a wild or woodland garden. Grow in moist soil that is enriched with organic matter, in partial or deep shade.

• PROPAGATION Divide in spring or autumn.

Z 4–7

HEIGHT
6in (15cm)

SPREAD
12in (30cm) or more

Ericaceae	

CASSIOPE MERTENSIANA

Habit Dense, upright, evergreen, subshrub. ***Flowers*** Bell-shaped, to ⅓in (8mm) long, borne from the upper leaf axils in spring. Creamy-white, with red or green sepals. ***Leaves*** Tiny, oval to lance-shaped, overlapping along stem. Dark green.
- NATIVE HABITAT Arctic and N. America.
- CULTIVATION Suits a sheltered site in a rock garden, in acid soil that is rich in organic matter.
- PROPAGATION By seed in autumn, or by semiripe cuttings in summer, preferably in a propagating frame with a misting unit.

Z 4–7

HEIGHT
6in (15cm)

SPREAD
10in (25cm)

Saxifragaceae	FOAMFLOWER

TIARELLA WHERRYI

Habit Compact, clumping, evergreen, perennial. ***Flowers*** Small, star-shaped, borne in spikelike sprays 5–14in (15–35cm) long, on upright brown stems, in spring. White or pink-tinted. ***Leaves*** Triangular, 3-lobed. Pale green, tinted red.
- NATIVE HABITAT Appalachian Mountains, USA.
- CULTIVATION Suitable for a rock or woodland garden, in cool, moist soil. Tolerates a shady site.
- PROPAGATION By seed when ripe or in spring, or by division in spring or early summer.
- OTHER NAME *T. cordifolia* var. *collina*.

Z 3–8

HEIGHT
8in (20cm)

SPREAD
12in (30cm)

Diapensiaceae	OCONEE BELLS

SHORTIA GALACIFOLIA

Habit Clump-forming, stoloniferous, evergreen, perennial. ***Flowers*** Solitary, half-nodding, funnel-shaped, to 1in (2.5cm) across, with toothed petals, borne in late spring. White. ***Leaves*** Leathery, rounded, and sharply toothed. Dark green.
- NATIVE HABITAT Woodlands, eastern USA.
- CULTIVATION Good for a rock garden, peat bed, or open woodland glades, in leaf-rich, acid, moist, well-drained soil. Needs semi- or deep shade.
- PROPAGATION By seed as soon as ripe in a cold frame. Separate rooted runners carefully in spring.

Z 4–7

HEIGHT
6in (15cm)

SPREAD
10in (25cm)

Caryophyllaceae	HIMALAYAN GYPSOPHILA

GYPSOPHILA CERASTIOIDES

Habit Mat-forming, semievergreen, perennial. ***Flowers*** Shallow funnel-shaped, to ⅝in (15mm) across, borne in loose clusters in late spring. White, with pink veins or tint. ***Leaves*** Spoon-shaped or broadly oval, almost stalkless. Mid-green.
- NATIVE HABITAT Western Himalaya.
- CULTIVATION Good for a raised bed, dry-stone retaining wall, or rock garden. Needs light, sharply drained, preferably slightly alkaline soil, in full sun.
- PROPAGATION By seed in winter, or by division in spring.

Z 4–7

HEIGHT
2in (5cm)

SPREAD
6in (15cm)

Ranunculaceae	RUE ANEMONE

ANEMONELLA THALICTROIDES

Habit Clump-forming, tuberous, herbaceous, perennial. ***Flowers*** Cup-shaped, to ⅘in (2cm) across, borne in sprays of 2–4, from spring to early summer. White or pale pink. ***Leaves*** Finely divided, delicate, and fernlike. Dark bluish-green.
• NATIVE HABITAT Woodland, eastern N. America.
• CULTIVATION Grow as a pot plant in an alpine house. Outdoors, prefers moist but well-drained, fertile soil. The tubers will rot in over-wet soils.
• PROPAGATION Sow seed as soon as ripe in a cold frame, or divide young plants in early spring.

Z 3–7

HEIGHT
4in (10cm)

SPREAD
12in (30cm)

Diapensiaceae	

SHORTIA UNIFLORA 'Grandiflora'

Habit Vigorous, mat-forming, evergreen, perennial. ***Flowers*** Solitary, half-nodding flared bells to 2in (5cm) across, with toothed petals, borne in spring. White or pale pink. ***Leaves*** Leathery, rounded, toothed, heart-shaped base. Deep green.
• NATIVE HABITAT Woodlands, Japan.
• CULTIVATION Suits a rock garden, peat bed, or open woodland glades, with leaf-rich, moist, well-drained soil. Dislikes dry climates and bright sun.
• PROPAGATION By seed as soon as ripe in a cold frame. Separate rooted runners carefully in spring.

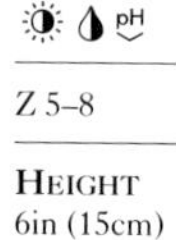

Z 5–8

HEIGHT
6in (15cm)

SPREAD
10in (25cm)

Portulacaceae	

LEWISIA TWEEDYI

Habit Rosette-forming, evergreen, perennial. ***Flowers*** Open funnel-shaped, to 2½in (6cm) across, borne singly or in clusters of up to 4, from spring to early summer. White to pink, or apricot. ***Leaves*** Lance-shaped to oval, fleshy. Mid-green.
• NATIVE HABITAT Rock crevices. northwest USA.
• CULTIVATION Grows best as a pot plant in an alpine house. Needs neutral to acid soil that is rich in organic matter, and a dry summer dormancy.
• PROPAGATION By seed in autumn, or by offsets in early summer.

Z 6–9

HEIGHT
8in (20cm)

SPREAD
12in (30cm)

Liliaceae/Trilliaceae	

TRILLIUM RIVALE

Habit Compact, erect, rhizomatous, herbaceous, perennial. ***Flowers*** Semi-upright, to 1in (2.5cm) across, borne in spring. White or pale pink, with purple-spotted base and green sepals. ***Leaves*** Oval and pointed, borne in threes. Bluish mid-green.
• NATIVE HABITAT Mountain woods, western USA.
• CULTIVATION Grows best in pockets in a peat garden. Needs moist but well-drained, neutral to slightly alkaline soil, enriched with organic matter.
• PROPAGATION By ripe seed but it may take 5–7 years to flower. Divide large, established clumps.

Z 4–7

HEIGHT
5in (12cm)

SPREAD
6in (15cm)

Caryophyllaceae	PINK SANDWORT

ARENARIA PURPURASCENS

Habit Mat- or cushion-forming, evergreen, perennial. ***Flowers*** Star-shaped, to ⅝in (15mm) across, in clusters of 2–4, borne in profusion from late spring to mid-summer. Deep pink. ***Leaves*** Paired, sharp-pointed, oval to lance-shaped, hairy at the margins. Glossy, dark green.

• NATIVE HABITAT Pyrenees and mountains of northern Spain.

• CULTIVATION Suitable for growing in a rock garden, trough, or scree bed, or for planting in crevices in rock work, walls, and paving. It is especially valued for its flowering period that extends well into summer, when many true alpines are past their flowering peak. Grow in low-fertility, sandy, moist but well-drained soil in sun, with some shade from hot summer sun.

• PROPAGATION Sow seed as soon as ripe or in autumn, in containers under an open frame. Divide in spring.

Z 4–7

HEIGHT
⅘–2in
(2–5cm)

SPREAD
8in (20cm)

Primulaceae	

DIONYSIA CURVIFLORA

Habit Compact, cushion-forming, evergreen, perennial. ***Flowers*** Salver-shaped, ¼in (6mm) across, borne in spring. Pink, with yellow eye. ***Leaves*** Tiny, spoon-shaped to oblong, hairy above, forming small rosettes. Gray-green.

- NATIVE HABITAT Mountains, southwestern Iran.
- CULTIVATION Suitable for growing in an alpine house, in very gritty soil and a deep collar of grit. Keep plant barely moist in winter.
- PROPAGATION By seed as soon as ripe. Root single rosettes in summer; water only from below.

Z 6–8

HEIGHT 2in (5cm)

SPREAD 10in (25cm)

Cruciferae/ Brassicaceae	

THLASPI CEPIFOLIUM subsp. *ROTUNDIFOLIUM*

Habit Tuft-forming, short-lived, evergreen, perennial. ***Flowers*** Cross-shaped, ⅜in (1cm) across, borne in clusters in spring. Deep lilac-pink. ***Leaves*** Broadly oval to rounded. Dark green.

- NATIVE HABITAT Rocks, screes, Alps, Apennines.
- CULTIVATION Grow in an alpine house, in a mix of equal parts soil, leaf-mold, and grit, or in a scree bed with protection from winter moisture.
- PROPAGATION By ripe seed under a cold frame
- OTHER NAME *T. rotundifolium.*

Z 5–8

HEIGHT 4in (10cm)

SPREAD 6in (15cm)

Caryophyllaceae	MOSS CAMPION

SILENE ACAULIS

Habit Cushion- or mat-forming, mosslike, evergreen, perennial. ***Flowers*** Solitary, almost stemless, star-shaped, to ⅜in (1cm) across, borne in spring. Often not freely borne in cultivation. Deep pink. ***Leaves*** Tiny and linear. Bright green.

- NATIVE HABITAT Europe and N. America.
- CULTIVATION Suitable for a scree bed or trough in gritty, sharply drained soil. Grows well in an alpine house in a mix of equal parts soil and grit.
- PROPAGATION By seed in autumn, placed in a cold frame.

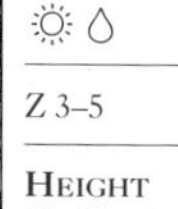

Z 3–5

HEIGHT 2in (5cm)

SPREAD 8in (20cm)

Primulaceae	

DIONYSIA INVOLUCRATA

Habit Dense, cushion-forming, evergreen, perennial. ***Flowers*** Salver-shaped, ¼–⅝in (7–15mm) across, borne in late spring and early summer. Violet, with a white or red eye. ***Leaves*** Oval, finely toothed. Dark green.

- NATIVE HABITAT Shady cliffs, Pamir Mountains.
- CULTIVATION Grow in an alpine house or in tufa, with protection from excessive overhead wet. Needs very gritty soil and a deep collar of grit.
- PROPAGATION By ripe seed in summer. Water sparingly from below in winter.

Z 6–8

HEIGHT 9ft (2.8m)

SPREAD 7ft (2.2m)

Portulacaceae	

Lewisia 'Pinkie'

Habit Dwarf, rosette-forming, free-flowering, evergreen, perennial. ***Flowers*** Open funnel-shaped, ¾–1½in (2–4cm) across, borne in compact clusters from spring to summer. Shades of pink. ***Leaves*** Narrowly spoon- to lance-shaped, fleshy, forming clusters of rosettes. Dark green.

- NATIVE HABITAT Garden origin.
- CULTIVATION Best grown as a pot plant in an alpine house. Outdoors, suits a trough with neutral to acid soil. Protect from winter moisture.
- PROPAGATION By offset cuttings in early summer.

Z 5–7

HEIGHT 6in (15cm)

SPREAD 8in (20cm)

Portulacaceae	

Lewisia cotyledon 'Rose Splendour'

Habit Rosette-forming, free-flowering, evergreen, perennial. ***Flowers*** Open funnel-shaped, 1½in (4cm) across, borne in compact clusters from spring to summer. Clear rose-pink. ***Leaves*** Spoon- to lance-shaped, fleshy, forming rosettes. Dark green.

- NATIVE HABITAT Garden origin.
- CULTIVATION Best grown as a pot plant in an alpine house. Outdoors, suits a trough with neutral to acid soil. Protect from winter moisture.
- PROPAGATION By offsets in early summer, or by seed in autumn. Seedlings may vary.

Z 4–7

HEIGHT 8in (20cm)

SPREAD 8in (20cm)

Cruciferae/ Brassicaceae	

Aubrieta × *cultorum* 'Joy'

Habit Vigorous, mat-forming, evergreen, perennial. ***Flowers*** Short-stemmed, double, to ½in (15mm) across, borne in spring. Mauve. ***Leaves*** Oval and slightly toothed. Soft mid-green.

- NATIVE HABITAT Garden origin.
- CULTIVATION Good for growing on rock gardens, sunny banks, and walls. Needs neutral to alkaline, well-drained soil in sun. Trim lightly after flowers.
- PROPAGATION By softwood cuttings in early summer, or by semiripe cuttings in mid-summer.
- OTHER NAMES *A. deltoidea* 'Joy', *A.* 'Joy'.

Z 5–8

HEIGHT 2in (10cm)

SPREAD 8in (20cm)

Plumbaginaceae	

Armeria juniperifolia

Habit Cushion-forming, evergreen, subshrub. ***Flowers*** Cupped, ⅝in (15mm) across, borne in rounded heads in late spring. Purple-pink. ***Leaves*** Hairy, linear, stiff, and rosetted. Gray-green.

- NATIVE HABITAT Alpine pasture and rock crevices, mountains of central Spain.
- CULTIVATION Suits a rock garden or trough in well-drained, moderately fertile soil, in sun.
- PROPAGATION By seed in autumn or spring, or by semiripe cuttings in summer.
- OTHER NAME *A. caespitosa*.

Z 4–8

HEIGHT 2–3in (5–8cm)

SPREAD 6in (15cm)

Cruciferae/ Brassicaceae	

ARABIS x *ARENDSII* 'Rosabella'

Habit Compact, mat-forming, evergreen, perennial. ***Flowers*** Cross-shaped, to ⅝in (15mm) across, borne in short clusters in late spring and early summer. Deep rose-pink. ***Leaves*** Elliptic, hairy, forming rosettes. Gray-green.
• NATIVE HABITAT Garden origin.
• CULTIVATION Good for a dry bank or in wall crevices. Prefers well-drained soil in sun but will tolerate hot, dry conditions and low-fertility soils.
• PROPAGATION By softwood cuttings in summer.
• OTHER NAME *A. caucasica* 'Rosabella'.

Z 4–7

HEIGHT 2–4in (5–10cm)

SPREAD 8–12in (20–30cm)

Diapensiaceae	

SHORTIA SOLDANELLOIDES

Habit Mat-forming, stoloniferous, evergreen, perennial. ***Flowers*** Broad, flared bells to 1in (2.5cm) across, with fringed petals, borne in late spring. Deep pink. ***Leaves*** Oval to rounded, with a heart-shaped base, toothed, leathery. Glossy green.
• NATIVE HABITAT Woodlands, Japan.
• CULTIVATION Good for growing in a rock garden, peat bed, or open woodland glades, in moist, well-drained, leaf-rich, acid soil. Dislikes dry climates.
• PROPAGATION By seed as soon as ripe in a cold frame. Separate rooted runners carefully in spring.

pH

Z 6–9

HEIGHT 4–12in (10–30cm)

SPREAD 10in (25cm)

Scrophulariaceae	FAIRY FOXGLOVE

ERINUS ALPINUS

Habit Tufted, short-lived, evergreen, perennial. ***Flowers*** Five-lobed, to ⅖in (1cm) across, borne in short spikes in late spring and summer. Pink, purple, or white. ***Leaves*** Soft, sticky, lance- to wedge-shaped, lobed, mostly rosetted. Mid-green.
• NATIVE HABITAT Southern and central Europe.
• CULTIVATION Needs light, well-drained soil that is moderately fertile. Tolerates partial shade.
• PROPAGATION Sow seed in autumn in a cold frame, or root rosettes as cuttings in spring. Generally, will self-sow in the garden.

Z 4–7

HEIGHT 3in (8cm)

SPREAD 4in (10cm)

Portulacaceae	

LEWISIA 'Trevosia'

Habit Rosette-forming, free-flowering, evergreen, perennial. ***Flowers*** Open funnel-shaped, to ⅝in (4cm) across, borne in long sprays from spring to summer. Salmon-pink. ***Leaves*** Spoon- to lance-shaped, fleshy, borne in rosettes. Dark green.
- NATIVE HABITAT Garden origin.
- CULTIVATION Best grown as a plant pot in an alpine house. Outdoors, suits a trough with neutral to acid soil. Protect from winter moisture.
- PROPAGATION By offsets in early summer, or by seed in autumn. Seedlings may vary.

Z 5–7

HEIGHT 8in (20cm)

SPREAD 8in (20cm)

Portulacaceae	PURSLANE, SPRING BEAUTY

CLAYTONIA MEGARHIZA var. *NIVALIS*

Habit Short-lived, tap-rooted, evergreen, perennial. ***Flowers*** Cup-shaped, ⅘–1⅕in (2–3cm) across, borne in dense clusters in early summer. Deep rose-pink. ***Leaves*** Fleshy, spoon-shaped, in rosettes. Dark to gray-green.
- NATIVE HABITAT Rocky Mountains, USA.
- CULTIVATION Suits an alpine house. Needs gritty, sharply drained, fertile soil in a sunny site.
- PROPAGATION By seed in autumn in a cold frame. Propagate regularly.
- OTHER NAME *Calandrinia megarhiza* var. *nivalis*.

Z 3–7

HEIGHT 2in (5cm)

SPREAD 6in (15cm)

Primulaceae	

ANAGALLIS TENELLA 'Studland'

Habit Mat-forming, evergreen, perennial. ***Flowers*** Solitary, honey-scented, upright, bell-shaped, ¼–⅜in (6–10mm) across, borne in late spring and early summer. Deep pink. ***Leaves*** Small, rounded to oval. Bright green.
- NATIVE HABITAT Cool climates in Europe.
- CULTIVATION Thrives in damp sites in a rock garden. Needs moist but well-drained soil. Excellent for growing in shallow pots in an alpine house.
- PROPAGATION Stems self-root freely.

Z 6–9

HEIGHT to 4in (10cm)

SPREAD to 16in (40cm)

Cruciferae/ Brassicaceae	

ARABIS BLEPHAROPHYLLA 'Frühlingszauber'

Habit Mat-forming, evergreen, perennial. ***Flowers*** Scented, ⅕in (5mm) across, borne in short sprays in late spring and early summer. Deep pink-purple. ***Leaves*** Oval, toothed, hairy margins. Dark green.

• NATIVE HABITAT Garden origin.
• CULTIVATION Suitable for growing in a rock garden, on a dry bank, or in wall crevices. Will tolerate hot, dry conditions and low-fertility soils.
• PROPAGATION By softwood cuttings in summer
• OTHER NAME *A. blepharophylla* 'Spring Charm'.

Z 4–7

HEIGHT 4in (10cm)

SPREAD 8in (20cm)

Compositae	

ANTENNARIA DIOICA 'Rosea'

Habit Stoloniferous, mat-forming, semi-evergreen, perennial. ***Flowers*** Small, fluffy, to ¾in (2cm) long, clustered in terminal heads, borne on stems in late spring and early summer. Deep rose-pink. ***Leaves*** Spoon-shaped. Gray-green, with densely white-felted underside.

• NATIVE HABITAT Garden selection.
• CULTIVATION Good as low ground cover, in a rock garden, gravel plantings, and wall crevices. Grow in any moderately fertile, well-drained soil.
• PROPAGATION Separate rooted stems in spring.

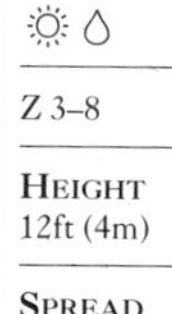

Z 3–8

HEIGHT 12ft (4m)

SPREAD 8ft (2.5m)

Ericaceae	ROCK OR MOUNTAIN CRANBERRY

VACCINIUM VITIS-IDAEA subsp. *MINUS*

Habit Creeping, rhizomatous, mat-forming, evergreen, shrub. ***Flowers*** Bell-shaped, ¼in (6mm) long, borne in nodding sprays in late spring and early summer. Deep pink. ***Leaves*** Oval and glossy. Dark green.

• NATIVE HABITAT Arctic and alpine habitats, N. America.
• CULTIVATION Suits a rock garden or peat bed, in moist but well-drained, leaf-rich or sandy, acid soil.
• PROPAGATION By seed in a cold frame in autumn, or by semiripe cuttings in mid- to late summer.

pH

Z 4–7

HEIGHT 4–8in (10–20cm)

SPREAD indefinite

Compositae/Asteraceae	

LEPTINELLA ATRATA subsp. *LUTEOLA*

Habit Tufted, creeping, evergreen, perennial. ***Flowers*** Conical, ⅝in (15mm) across, borne in late spring and early summer. Dark red-brown, with creamy-white stigmas at maturity. ***Leaves*** Fern-like and finely divided. Gray-green, tinted purple.

• NATIVE HABITAT Alpine habitats, New Zealand.
• CULTIVATION Suitable for growing in a scree bed, with gritty, sharply drained soil.
• PROPAGATION By seed in an open frame when ripe, or by division in spring.
• OTHER NAME *Cotula atrata* var. *luteola*.

Z 7–9

HEIGHT 6in (15cm)

SPREAD 8in (20cm)

ANDROSACE

Androsaces, commonly known as rock jasmines, are found in alpine turf, screes, and rock crevices in the mountains of the northern hemisphere. Although androsaces are quite hardy, they need sharp drainage to be able to thrive in areas with wet winters. Those described thrive in scree and raised beds or in troughs. They also suit pot culture in an alpine house.

All androsaces need moist but gritty and sharply drained soil in full sun. In an alpine house, pot them up in a mix of equal parts grit and soil-based potting mix. In areas with wet winters, protect plant with a sheet of glass or place under a cloche.

Propagate by seed sown as soon as ripe in an open frame, or root single rosettes as cuttings in early or mid-summer.

A. *VILLOSA*
Habit Cushion-forming, evergreen, perennial.
Flowers Flat, ¼–½in (6–10mm) across, borne in headlike clusters in spring. White, with yellow eye that matures to red.
Leaves Linear to oval, in tightly packed rosettes, silky-haired underside. Gray-green.
• HEIGHT 1½in (4cm).
• SPREAD 8in (20cm).

A. *villosa*

☼ ◊ Z 4–7

A. *CARNEA*
Habit Tufted to loose cushion-forming, evergreen, perennial.
Flowers Cupped, ¼–⅜in (5–8mm) across, borne in compact headlike clusters in spring. Pink, with yellow eye.
Leaves Linear, pointed, hairy-margined, fleshy, in rosettes. Deep green.
• HEIGHT 2in (5cm).
• SPREAD 3–6in (8–15cm).

A. *carnea*
Pink rock jasmine

☼ ◊ Z 4–7

A. *LANUGINOSA*
Habit Mat-forming, with trailing, red-tinted stems.
Flowers Flat, ⅓–½in (8–12mm) across, borne in headlike clusters in summer. Pale pink.
Leaves Elliptic, silky-hairy, rosetted or alternate. Gray-green.
• HEIGHT 4in (10cm), occasionally more.
• SPREAD 12in (30cm) or more .

A. *lanuginosa*

☼ ◊ Z 4–5

A. *CARNEA* subsp. *LAGGERI*
Habit Densely tufted, evergreen, perennial.
Flowers Up to ⅓in (8mm) across, borne in loose heads in spring. Deep pink.
Leaves Linear, pointed and fleshy. Mid-green.
• OTHER NAME *A. laggeri*.
• HEIGHT 2in (5cm).
• SPREAD 3–6in (8–15cm).

A. *carnea* subsp. *laggeri*

☼ ◊ Z 4–7

A. *VILLOSA* var. *JACQUEMONTII*
Habit Mat-forming, stoloniferous, rosetted.
Flowers Flat, ¼–⅜in (6–10mm) across, borne in heads in spring. Deep pink, with lime eye.
Leaves Oval to linear. Silvery-green, with silky hairs below.
• OTHER NAME *A. jacquemontii*.
• HEIGHT 1½in (4cm).
• SPREAD 8in (20cm).

A. *villosa* var. *jacquemontii*

☼ ◊ Z 4–7

A. *SARMENTOSA*
Habit Stoloniferous, mat-forming, evergreen, perennial.
Flowers Flat, ¼–⅜in (7–9mm) across, borne in compact heads in late spring. Deep rose-pink, with yellow-green eye.
Leaves Oval and white-haired. Pale gray-green.
• HEIGHT 2–4in (5–10cm).
• SPREAD 12in (30cm) or more.

A. *sarmentosa*

☼ ◊ Z 4–7

PRIMULA

The genus *Primula* comprises about 400 species, some evergreen, including popular cottage-garden favorites, such as cowslips, primroses, and auriculas. All have basal rosettes of leaves and tubular, bell-shaped, or flat (primroselike) flowers. Nearly all of the alpine and rock garden species thrive best in climates with cool, moist summers. Most of these come from the mountains of the northern hemisphere (almost half of all primulas are from western China and the Himalaya) growing in alpine turf, stony pastures, shaded cliffs, or rock crevices.

For ease of reference, their cultivation requirements may be grouped as follows.

Group 1 Sun or partial shade, in moist but well-drained soil, rich in organic matter.

Group 2 Partial shade, in deep, moist, neutral to acid soil, rich in organic matter.

Group 3 Partial or deep shade, in peat-rich, gritty, moist but sharply drained soil, with protection from winter wet.

Group 4 In an alpine house or cold frame, in equal parts soil leaf mold, and grit. Do not wet the foliage of those with white-mealy leaves when watering. *P. allionii* needs alkaline soil and suits alpine-house culture.

Group 5 Partial shade, or full sun with some midday shade, in moist but sharply drained, gritty, slightly alkaline soil.

Some true alpine species, such as *P. marginata* and *P. auricula* and their cultivars, are quite hardy and suit rock gardens. However, their early flowers and mealy leaves can be spoiled by excessive rain, so they are often grown in an alpine house or protected cloches. Propagate by seed as soon as ripe or in late winter and early spring, in a cold frame; by division from autumn to early spring; or by offsets in autumn or early spring. Some, like *P. denticulata* var. *alba*, can be increased by root cuttings in winter.

P. *DENTICULATA* var. *ALBA*

Habit Sturdy, rosette-forming, herbaceous, perennial.
Flowers Flat, up to ¾in (2cm) across, borne in dense, spherical heads on stout, erect stems, in spring. White, with yellow eye.
Leaves Mainly oval to spoon-shaped. Green, with white underside.
- CULTIVATION 1 or 2.
- HEIGHT 18in (45cm).
- SPREAD 18in (45cm).

P. denticulata var. *alba*

Z 6–8

P. *MARGINATA* 'Linda Pope'

Habit Vigorous, evergreen, perennial.
Flowers Flat, to 1¼in (3cm) across, borne in heads of 4–16, in spring. Mauve-blue, with small, white center.
Leaves Oval, toothed, and smooth. Mid-green, white-farinose.
- CULTIVATION 4 or 5.
- OTHER NAME *P.* 'Linda Pope'.
- HEIGHT 6in (15cm).
- SPREAD 6–9in (15–23cm).

P. marginata 'Linda Pope'

Z 6–8

P. GRACILIPES
Habit Rosette-forming, evergreen, perennial.
Flowers Short-stemmed, funnel-shaped, to 1in (2.5cm) across, borne in late winter to late spring. Purple-pink, with white-edged, orange eye.
Leaves Toothed, oblong to spoon-shaped or oval. Mid-green.
• CULTIVATION 3 or 4.
• HEIGHT 4in (10cm).
• SPREAD 8in (20cm).

P. gracilipes

Z 4–7

P. ALLIONII
Habit Evergreen, tufted to cushion-forming, perennial.
Flowers Tubular, flat-faced, to 1¼in (3cm) across, borne in clusters of 1–5, in spring. White, or pink to red-purple.
Leaves Lance-shaped, scalloped or fine-toothed, and hairy. Gray-green.
• CULTIVATION 4.
• HEIGHT 4in (10cm).
• SPREAD 8in (20cm).

P. allionii

Z 6–8

P. JULIAE
Habit Stoloniferous, herbaceous, perennial.
Flowers Solitary, long-stalked, saucer-shaped, to 1¼in (3cm) across, in spring. Magenta, with yellow eye.
Leaves Rounded and scalloped. Dark green.
• CULTIVATION 1, 2, or 4.
• HEIGHT 3in (7cm).
• SPREAD 10in (25cm) or more .

P. juliae

Z 4–7

P. ROSEA
Habit Herbaceous, perennial.
Flowers Flat, to 1¼in (3cm) across, borne in clusters of 4–12, in spring. Deep rose-pink, with yellow eye.
Leaves Smooth, oval to lance-shaped, scalloped or fine-toothed. Mid-green.
• CULTIVATION 2.
• HEIGHT 8in (20cm).
• SPREAD 8in (20cm).

P. rosea

Z 6–8

P. POLYNEURA
Habit Herbaceous, perennial.
Flowers To 1in (2.5cm) across, borne in loose, long-stalked clusters in late spring and early summer. Purple-pink, with yellow eye.
Leaves Hairy, oval to rounded, lobed, forming basal rosettes. Mid-green.
• CULTIVATION 2.
• HEIGHT 18in (45cm).
• SPREAD 18in (45cm).

P. polyneura

Z 6–8

P. 'Wanda'
Habit Very vigorous, evergreen, perennial.
Flowers Flat, to 1⅜in (3.5cm) across, borne in basal clusters over long periods in spring. Deep, claret-red.
Leaves Oval, toothed, and slightly hairy. Purple-green.
• CULTIVATION 1 or 2.
• HEIGHT 4in (10cm).
• SPREAD 12in (30cm).

P. 'Wanda'

Z 5–8

P. marginata 'Pritchard's Variety'

Habit Virtually evergreen, perennial.
Flowers Shallow, flat, 1¼in (3cm) across, borne in long-stalked clusters in spring. Deep lavender-blue.
Leaves Toothed and oval. Mid-green, with white farinose margins.

- CULTIVATION 4 or 5.
- HEIGHT 6in (15cm).
- SPREAD 12in (30cm).

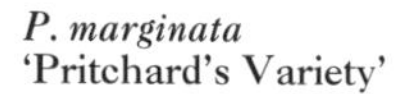

P. marginata
'Pritchard's Variety'

Z 6–8

P. capitata

Habit Virtually herbaceous, perennial.
Flowers Funnel-shaped, ⅜in (1cm) across, fragrant, borne in rounded clusters on white-mealy stems, in summer. Purple.
Leaves Oblong to lance-shaped and mealy. Pale to mid-green.

- CULTIVATION 2.
- HEIGHT 16in (40cm).
- SPREAD 16in (40cm).

P. capitata

Z 4–7

P. vulgaris 'Double Sulphur'

Habit Vigorous, evergreen, perennial.
Flowers Funnel-shaped, double, to 1–1¾in (2.5–4cm) across, borne in spring. Pale yellow.
Leaves Lance-shaped to oval, scalloped to toothed, deeply veined and quilted. Bright green.

- CULTIVATION 2.
- HEIGHT 8in (20cm).
- SPREAD 10in (25cm).

P. vulgaris
'Double Sulphur'

Z 5–8

P. AURICULA

Habit Evergreen, often white-mealy, perennial.
Flowers Fragrant, flat, to 1in (2.5cm) across, borne in long-stalked clusters of 2–30, during spring. Deep yellow.
Leaves Fleshy, smooth, oval to spoon-shaped or rounded. Pale to gray-green, often mealy.
• CULTIVATION 4 or 5.
• HEIGHT 8in (20cm).
• SPREAD 10in (25cm).

P. auricula
Auricula

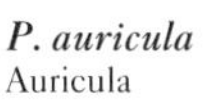

Z 3–7

P. ELATIOR

Habit Clump-forming, perennial.
Flowers Funnel-shaped, fragrant, to 1in (2.5cm) across, borne in one-sided clusters on upright stalks, in spring. Yellow.
Leaves Oval to oblong, scalloped, hairy, in basal rosettes. Bright-green.
• CULTIVATION 1 or 2.
• HEIGHT 8–12in (20–30cm).
• SPREAD 6–10in (15–25cm).

P. elatior
Oxlip

Z 4–7

P. VERIS

Habit Clump-forming, perennial.
Flowers Funnel-shaped, fragrant, ⅝–1in (1.5–2.5cm) long, borne in one-sided clusters of 2–16 on upright stems, in spring. Deep yellow.
Leaves Oblong to oval, crinkled, hairy, and often scalloped or toothed. Mid-green.
• CULTIVATION 1 or 3.
• HEIGHT 6–10in (15–25cm).
• SPREAD 6–10in (15–25cm).

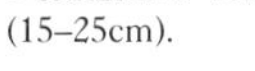

P. veris
Cowslip

Z 4–7

Convallariaceae/ Liliaceae	

POLYGONATUM HOOKERI

Habit Slow-growing, creeping, rhizomatous, herbaceous, perennial. ***Flowers*** Solitary, upright, bell-shaped, to ⅝in (15mm) across, borne in late spring and early summer. Pale to deep pink. ***Leaves*** Narrowly elliptic. Mid- to dark green.

• NATIVE HABITAT Woodland, Eastern Himalaya.

• CULTIVATION Suitable for growing in a peat bed or trough. Needs moist but well-drained soil that is rich in organic matter.

• PROPAGATION Sow seed in autumn in a cold frame, or divide in spring or after flowering.

Z 5–8

HEIGHT 2–4in (5–10cm)

SPREAD 12in (30cm)

Cruciferae/ Brassicaceae	

AUBRIETA x *CULTORUM* 'Argenteovariegata'

Habit Mat-forming, evergreen, perennial. ***Flowers*** Single, to ⅝in (15mm) across, borne in spring. Pinkish-mauve. ***Leaves*** Oval and slightly toothed. Soft mid-green, with silver-white margins.

• NATIVE HABITAT Garden origin.

• CULTIVATION Needs neutral to alkaline, well-drained soil in sun. Trim lightly after flowering.

• PROPAGATION By softwood cuttings in early summer, or by semiripe cuttings in mid-summer.

• OTHER NAME *A. deltoidea* 'Argenteovariegata'.

Z 5–8

HEIGHT 2in (5cm)

SPREAD 20in (50cm)

Scrophulariaceae	

MAZUS REPTANS

Habit Creeping, mat-forming, evergreen, perennial. ***Flowers*** Solitary, 2-lipped, ⅜–⅝in (10–15mm) across, borne in late spring and summer. Purple-blue, with white-, red-, and yellow-spotted lips. ***Leaves*** Lance-shaped to oval and coarsely toothed. Shiny, mid-green.

• NATIVE HABITAT Damp habitats, Himalaya.

• CULTIVATION Grows best in a sheltered site in sun, with moist but well-drained soil .

• PROPAGATION By seed in spring or autumn in a cold frame, or by division in spring.

Z 5–9

HEIGHT 2in (5cm)

SPREAD 12in (30cm)

Primulaceae	HAIRY SNOWBELL

SOLDANELLA VILLOSA

Habit Vigorous, clump-forming, evergreen, perennial. ***Flowers*** Nodding, bell-shaped, ⅝in (15mm) long, with fringed petals, borne on long, hairy stalks in mid-spring. Violet. ***Leaves*** Kidney-shaped. Mid-green, with paler underside.

• NATIVE HABITAT Alpine rocks, western Pyrenees.

• CULTIVATION Ideal for a peat bed. Needs fertile, moist but sharply drained soil in sun but with shade from hottest sun. Top-dress with grit.

• PROPAGATION By seed as soon as ripe in a cold frame. Divide after flowering.

Z 4–7

HEIGHT to 8in (20cm)

SPREAD 8in (20cm)

Cruciferae/ Brassicaceae	

AUBRIETA x *CULTORUM* 'J.S. Baker'

Habit Vigorous, mat-forming, evergreen, perennial. ***Flowers*** Single, to ⅝in (15mm) across, borne in clusters in spring. Purple, with white eye. ***Leaves*** Oval and slightly toothed. Soft mid-green.
• NATIVE HABITAT Garden origin.
• CULTIVATION Suitable for rock gardens, sunny banks, and walls. Grow in well-drained, neutral to alkaline soil in sun. Trim plant after flowering.
• PROPAGATION By softwood cuttings in early summer, or by semiripe cuttings in summer.
• OTHER NAME *A. deltoidea* 'J. S. Baker'.

Z 5–8

HEIGHT
2in (5cm)

SPREAD
20in (50cm)

Cruciferae/ Brassicaceae	

AUBRIETA x *CULTORUM* 'Hartswood Purple'

Habit Vigorous, mat-forming, evergreen, perennial. ***Flowers*** Single, ⅝in (15mm) across, borne in clusters in spring. Violet-purple. ***Leaves*** Oval to oblong, slightly toothed. Soft mid-green.
• NATIVE HABITAT Garden origin.
• CULTIVATION Grow in well-drained, neutral to alkaline soil in sun. Trim lightly after flowering.
• PROPAGATION By softwood cuttings in early summer, or by semiripe cuttings in mid-summer.
• OTHER NAME *A.* 'Carnival'.

Z 5–8

HEIGHT
4in (10cm)

SPREAD
20in (50cm)

Polygalaceae	

POLYGALA CHAMAEBUXUS var. *GRANDIFLORA*

Habit Low-spreading, evergreen, shrub. ***Flowers*** Pea-like, ⅝in (15mm) long, borne in late spring and early summer. Yellow, with purple-pink wings. ***Leaves*** Lance-shaped and leathery. Dark green.
• NATIVE HABITAT Alps, Carpathian mountains.
• CULTIVATION Needs moist, leaf-rich soil.
• PROPAGATION By softwood or semiripe cuttings in summer, or by seed when ripe in an open frame.
• OTHER NAMES *P. c.* var. *purpurea*, *P. c.* var. *rhodoptera*.

Z 5–8

HEIGHT
2–6in (5–15cm)

SPREAD
12in (30cm)

Ranunculaceae	HEPATICA

HEPATICA NOBILIS

Habit Slow-growing, clumping, semi-evergreen, perennial. ***Flowers*** Saucer-shaped, 1in (2.5cm) across, borne in early spring. Purple, white or pink. ***Leaves*** Leathery, rounded or kidney-shaped, divided into 3 lobes. Mid-green, often mottled.
• NATIVE HABITAT Woodland, Europe.
• CULTIVATION Needs fertile, moist, well-drained soil. Mulch with leaf mold in autumn or spring.
• PROPAGATION By seed as soon as ripe in an open frame, or by careful division in spring.
• OTHER NAMES *Anemone hepatica*, *Hepatica triloba*.

Z 4–8

HEIGHT
4in (10cm)

SPREAD
6in (15cm)

Polygalacae	

POLYGALA CALCAREA 'Lillet'

Habit Creeping, prostrate, robust, free-flowering, evergreen, shrub. ***Flowers*** Pea-like, with broad, petal-like wings and a keel with a fringed tip, to 1¼in (3cm) long, borne in terminal clusters over long periods from late spring to early summer. Intense, deep blue with fringed, white lips, ***Leaves*** Oval and leathery. Mid-green.

• NATIVE HABITAT Garden origin.

• CULTIVATION Suitable for growing in a rock garden, trough, raised bed. Ideal as a pot plant in an alpine house. It is more robust and easier to grow than the species, and produces intensely colored flowers. Grow in sharply drained, moderately fertile soil that is enriched with organic matter, in a sunny site

• PROPAGATION By softwood cuttings in early summer, or by semiripe cuttings in mid- to late summer.

Z 5–7

HEIGHT
2in (5cm)

SPREAD
8in (20cm)

Cruciferae/ Brassicaceae	

Aubrieta 'Cobalt Violet'

Habit Vigorous, mat-forming, evergreen, perennial. ***Flowers*** Single, short-stemmed, to ⅝in (15mm) across, borne in spring. ***Leaves*** Small, oval to oblong, entire or toothed, hairy. Mid-green.

- NATIVE HABITAT Garden origin.
- CULTIVATION Grow in neutral to alkaline, well-drained soil in sun, and trim after flowering.
- PROPAGATION Take softwood cuttings in early summer, or semiripe ones in summer.
- OTHER NAMES *A.* x *cultorum* 'Cobalt Violet', *A. deltoidea* 'Cobalt Violet.

Z 5–8

HEIGHT 4in (10cm)

SPREAD to 8in (20cm) or more

Ranunculaceae	JAPANESE HEPATICA

Hepatica nobilis var. *japonica*

Habit Slow-growing, semievergreen, perennial. ***Flowers*** Star-shaped, 1in (2.5cm) across, borne in early spring. Blue. ***Leaves*** Rounded or kidney-shaped, with pointed lobes. Dark green.

- NATIVE HABITAT Woodland, Japan.
- CULTIVATION More compact than the species. Needs moist but well-drained, neutral to alkaline soil that is rich in organic matter. Apply an annual mulch of leaf mold in autumn.
- PROPAGATION By seed as soon as ripe in an open frame, or by careful division in spring.

Z 4–8

HEIGHT 3in (8cm)

SPREAD 6in (15cm)

Berberidaceae	

Jeffersonia dubia

Habit Tufted, perennial. ***Flowers*** Solitary, cup-shaped, 1¼in (3cm) across, borne in late spring or early summer. Lavender-blue, sometimes white. ***Leaves*** Rounded or kidney-shaped and notched at apex. Blue-green, often tinted purple.

- NATIVE HABITAT Damp woods, northeast Asia.
- CULTIVATION Good for a peat bed or shaded rock garden, in moist soil enriched with organic matter.
- PROPAGATION By seed in an open frame as soon as ripe. Divide well-established plants in spring.
- OTHER NAME *Plagiorhegma dubia*.

Z 5–8

HEIGHT 8in (20cm)

SPREAD 12in (30cm)

Boraginaceae	OYSTER PLANT

Mertensia maritima

Habit Prostrate, spreading, semievergreen, perennial. ***Flowers*** Bell-shaped, ⅓in (8mm) across, borne in branched, terminal heads in early summer. Bright blue. ***Leaves*** Fleshy, spoon-shaped, glaucous, tasting of oysters. Blue-green.

- NATIVE HABITAT Eastern N. America, Greenland.
- CULTIVATION Best in a deep bed of coarse sand or grit, with sharply drained, low-fertility soil. Very prone to slug damage.
- PROPAGATION By seed in autumn, or by careful division in spring.

Z 3–7

HEIGHT 4in (10cm)

SPREAD 12in (30cm)

Ranunculaceae	

HEPATICA TRANSSILVANICA

Habit Slow-growing, semievergreen, clump-forming, perennial. ***Flowers*** Cup-shaped, many-petaled, 1½in (4cm) across, with 3 leaflike bracts immediately below, borne in early spring before the leaves have developed fully. Usually bright blue, sometimes white or pale pink. ***Leaves*** Rounded or kidney-shaped, hairy, and divided into 3 oval, scalloped lobes. Pale to mid-green.

- NATIVE HABITAT Woodland, Romania.
- CULTIVATION Excellent for planting in shady areas in a rock or woodland garden, and thrives in sites with heavy soil. Needs moist but well-drained soil that is neutral to alkaline and enriched with organic matter. Apply an annual mulch of leaf mold in autumn or late spring, and protect from birds in spring. Tends to be slow establishing large clumps.
- PROPAGATION By seed as soon as ripe in a cold frame, or by careful division in spring. The stout rootstock resents disturbance and divisions may be slow to reestablish.
- OTHER NAME *H. angulosa.*

Z 5–8

HEIGHT
6in (15cm)

SPREAD
8in (20cm)

Scrophulariaceae	COLUMBIA SYNTHYRIS

SYNTHYRIS STELLATA

Habit Rhizomatous, clump-forming, semi-evergreen, perennial. ***Flowers*** Bell-shaped, ¼in (6mm) long, borne in dense, oblong clusters in spring and early summer. Violet-blue. ***Leaves*** Rounded, heart-shaped, and jagged-toothed. Dark green.

- NATIVE HABITAT Woodlands, northwest USA.
- CULTIVATION Needs moist but well-drained soil rich in organic matter, in partial or deep shade.
- PROPAGATION By seed in autumn in an open frame, or by division in spring.

Z 5–7

HEIGHT 6in (15cm)

SPREAD 10in (25cm)

Boraginaceae	

ANCHUSA CAESPITOSA

Habit Mound-forming, bristly, perennial. ***Flowers*** Forget-me-not-like, ½in (12mm) across, borne in clusters in spring. Intense blue, with white eye. ***Leaves*** Linear, in rosettes. Dark green.

- NATIVE HABITAT Mountain rocks, Crete.
- CULTIVATION Grow as a pot plant in an alpine house. Needs moist but moderately fertile, sharply drained soil in sun. Dislikes excessive moisture.
- PROPAGATION By seed in spring, by root cuttings in winter, or by careful division.
- OTHER NAME *A. cespitosa.*

Z 5–7

HEIGHT 2–4in (5–10cm)

SPREAD 4–8in (10–20cm)

Salicaceae	NET-LEAVED WILLOW

SALIX RETICULATA

Habit Dwarf, prostrate, stem-rooting, deciduous, shrub. ***Flowers*** Male or female, upright, slender, catkins, 1in (2.5cm) long, borne in early spring. Yellow, with pink tips. ***Leaves*** Rounded to oval, glossy. Dark green, with white-haired underside.

- NATIVE HABITAT Rocky mountain habitats, northern Europe, northern Asia, and N. America.
- CULTIVATION Suits a trough with fertile, gritty, sharply drained soil. Dislikes drought conditions.
- PROPAGATION By softwood cuttings in summer, or by hardwood cuttings in winter.

Z 2–5

HEIGHT 3in (8cm)

SPREAD 12in (30cm)

Compositae/Asteraceae	

Leptinella atrata

Habit Tufted, creeping, mat-forming, evergreen, perennial. ***Flowers*** Rounded, fluffy, ⅝in (15mm) across, borne in late spring. Deep purple, with yellow anthers at maturity. ***Leaves*** Fernlike and finely divided. Gray-green, tinted purple.
• NATIVE HABITAT Alpine habitats, New Zealand.
• CULTIVATION Suitable for growing in a scree bed, with gritty, sharply drained soil
• PROPAGATION By seed in an open frame when ripe, or by division in spring.
• OTHER NAME *Cotula atrata.*

Z 7–9

HEIGHT 6in (15cm)

SPREAD 8in (20cm)

Euphorbiaceae	

Euphorbia myrsinites

Habit Semiprostrate, evergreen, with milky juice, perennial. ***Flowers*** Borne in terminal clusters, to 3in (8cm) across, in spring. Bright greenish-yellow, with numerous bracts. ***Leaves*** Oval, pointed, and fleshy, arranged in spirals. Blue-green.
• NATIVE HABITAT Dry, rocky places, from southern and eastern Europe, to Turkey and central Asia.
• CULTIVATION Suits a sheltered raised bed or rock garden in sun. Needs light, well-drained soil.
• PROPAGATION By seed as soon as ripe or in spring in a cold frame. Often self-sows.

Z 5–8

HEIGHT 4in (10cm)

SPREAD 20in (50cm)

Umbelliferae/Apiaceae	

Hacquetia epipactis

Habit Clump-forming, rhizomatous, herbaceous, perennial. ***Flowers*** Tiny, to 1½in (4cm) across. borne in dense clusters in late winter and early spring. Yellow, with apple-green bracts below. ***Leaves*** Lobed, rounded, toothed, glossy. Emerald.
• NATIVE HABITAT Central and eastern Europe.
• CULTIVATION Grow in a rock garden, woodland, or peat bed, in moist, neutral to acid, leaf-rich soil.
• PROPAGATION Sow ripe seed in a cold frame, divide in spring, or take root cuttings in winter.
• OTHER NAME *Dondia epipactis.*

Z 5–7

HEIGHT 2in (5cm), taller after flowering

SPREAD 6–12in (15–30cm)

Cruciferae/ Brassicaceae	

Draba rigida

Habit Cushion-forming, evergreen, perennial. ***Flowers*** Cross-shaped, ⅙–⅕in (4–5mm) across, borne in clusters in late spring. Yellow. ***Leaves*** Small, linear to oval, hairy-margined, forming dense rosettes. Dark green.
• NATIVE HABITAT Mountain screes, Turkey.
• CULTIVATION Grows best in an alpine house, with a mix of equal parts soil, leaf-mold and grit, top-dressed with grit. Water sparingly in winter.
• PROPAGATION By seed in a cold frame in autumn or early spring. Root rosette cuttings in late spring.

Z 4–6

HEIGHT 2in (5cm)

SPREAD 8in (20cm)

Cruciferae/Brassicaceae	YELLOW WHITLOW GRASS

DRABA AIZOIDES

Habit Tufted- or cushion-forming, evergreen, perennial. ***Flowers*** Cross-shaped, ⅓–½in (8–12mm) across, borne in dense clusters in late spring. Bright yellow. ***Leaves*** Linear to lance-shaped, bristle-margined, forming dense rosettes. Dark green.
• NATIVE HABITAT Mountain screes and other rocky habitats, central and southern Europe.
• CULTIVATION Suitable for planting in a rock garden, scree bed, raised bed, or trough, and for growing in tufa. Needs gritty, sharply drained soil in full sun. Protect plants from winter moisture. Alternatively, grow in an alpine house, in a mix of equal parts soil, leaf mold, and grit, top-dressed with grit. Water plant from below.
• PROPAGATION Sow seed in a cold frame in autumn, or root individual rosettes as cuttings in late spring. Often self-sows in gardens under favorable conditions.

☼ ◊

Z 4–6

HEIGHT
4in (10cm)

SPREAD
10in (25cm)

Primulaceae	

DIONYSIA ARETIOIDES

Habit Cushion-forming, evergreen, perennial. ***Flowers*** Scented, solitary, stemless, to 3/8in (1cm) across, with notched petals, borne in early spring. Bright yellow. ***Leaves*** Aromatic, oblong to spoon-shaped, softly hairy, recurved margins. Gray-green.
• NATIVE HABITAT Mountain cliffs, northern Iran.
• CULTIVATION Grow in tufa or in a trough with sharply drained soil, and a top-dressing of grit to keep the plant collar dry. Keep moist in winter.
• PROPAGATION By seed as soon as ripe in a cold frame. Root rosette cuttings in summer.

Z 6–8

HEIGHT
3in (7cm)

SPREAD
to 12in
(30cm)

Cruciferae/ Brassicaceae	

DRABA LONGISILIQUA

Habit Soft cushion-forming, evergreen, perennial. ***Flowers*** Cross-shaped, to 3/8in (1cm) across, borne in dense clusters in spring. Yellow. ***Leaves*** Oval, gray-hairy, in firm, tight rosettes. Silvery-green.
• NATIVE HABITAT Screes, Caucasus.
• CULTIVATION Grow in a scree bed with protection from winter moisture, or in an alpine house, in equal parts soil, leaf mold and grit, top-dressed with grit. Avoid wetting the foliage.
• PROPAGATION Sow seed in containers in a cold frame in autumn. Root rosettes in late spring.

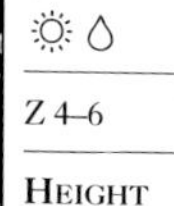

Z 4–6

HEIGHT
3½in (9cm)

SPREAD
to 10in
(25cm)

Cruciferae/ Brassicaceae	

DRABA MOLLISSIMA

Habit Soft cushion-forming, evergreen, perennial. ***Flowers*** Cross-shaped, to 5/16in (8mm) across, borne in tight clusters in late spring. Bright yellow. ***Leaves*** Oblong, hairy, in rosettes. Gray-green.
• NATIVE HABITAT Screes, Caucasus.
• CULTIVATION Grows best as a pot plant in an alpine house, in a mix of equal parts soil, leaf mold, and grit, top-dressed with grit. Avoid wetting the foliage.
• PROPAGATION Sow seed in containers in a cold frame in autumn.

Z 4–6

HEIGHT
3in (8cm)

SPREAD
to 8in
(20cm)

Primulaceae	

DIONYSIA TAPETODES

Habit Dense, cushion-forming, evergreen, perennial. ***Flowers*** Solitary, stemless, long-tubed, to 3/8in (1cm) across, borne in spring and early summer. Yellow. ***Leaves*** Small, oval, oblong, or spoon-shaped, forming rosettes. Mid-green.
• NATIVE HABITAT Northeast Iran and Afghanistan.
• CULTIVATION Excellent as a pot plant in an alpine house, and can also be grown in tufa. Keep the plant collar dry. Protect from winter moisture.
• PROPAGATION By seed when ripe in a cold frame. Root rosettes as cuttings in summer.

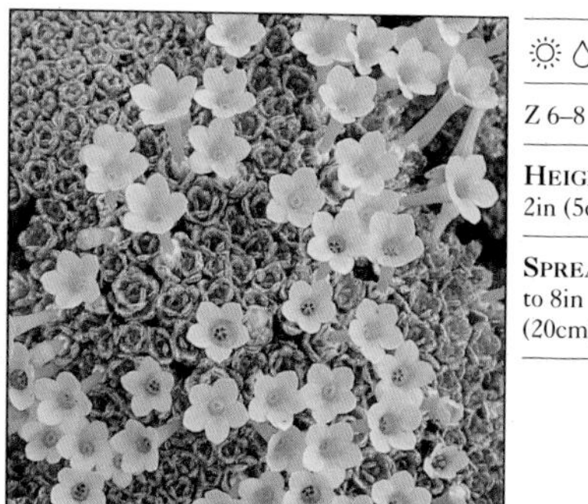

Z 6–8

HEIGHT
2in (5cm)

SPREAD
to 8in
(20cm)

Primulaceae	

VITALIANA PRIMULIFLORA

Habit Tufted, mat- or cushion-forming, evergreen perennial, with creeping stems. ***Flowers*** Solitary, almost stemless, tubular with 5 spreading lobes, giving a star-shaped outline, to ¾in (2cm) across, borne in spring. Bright yellow. ***Leaves*** Narrow, oblong to lance-shaped, pointed, usually hairy. Pale green, with silver margins.

• NATIVE HABITAT Screes, rocks, and alpine and subalpine meadows in the mountains from southwest and central Europe to southeastern Alps and Apennines.

• CULTIVATION Suitable for growing in a trough, scree bed, or rock garden in moist but sharply drained, gritty, moderately fertile soil. Protect from winter moisture. Alternatively, grow in an alpine house in a mix of 1 part soil and leaf mold, with 3 parts grit.

• PROPAGATION By seed as soon as ripe in containers in a cold frame. Separate offsets in spring and early summer.

• OTHER NAMES *Androsace vitaliana, Douglasia vitaliana.*

☼ ◊

Z 4–8

HEIGHT
to 1in (2.5cm)

SPREAD
To 10in (25cm)

Cruciferae/
Brassicaceae

MORISIA MONANTHOS

Habit Tap-rooted, rosette-forming, evergreen, perennial. ***Flowers*** Cross-shaped, short-stemmed, to ⅝in (15mm) across, borne in late spring and early summer. Golden-yellow. ***Leaves*** Lance-shaped, divided into slightly fleshy segments. Dark green.
• NATIVE HABITAT Sandy areas, Corsica, Sardinia.
• CULTIVATION Needs gritty, very sharply drained soil and protection from excessive winter moisture.
• PROPAGATION By seed in containers in a cold frame, in spring. Take root cuttings in winter.
• OTHER NAME *M. hypogaea*.

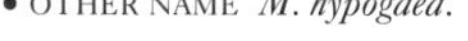

Z 5–7

HEIGHT
18ft (5.5m)

SPREAD
10ft (3m)

Ranunculaceae

TROLLIUS PUMILUS

Habit Tufted, perennial. ***Flowers*** Solitary, cup-shaped, opening flat, ¾–1⅜in (2–3.5cm) across, borne in late spring and early summer. Bright yellow. ***Leaves*** Divided into 5 toothed, oblong to lance-shaped lobes. Mid-green.
• NATIVE HABITAT Damp mountain meadows, Himalaya, eastern Tibet, and western China.
• CULTIVATION Grow in deep, moist, fertile soil, in sun or partial shade.
• PROPAGATION Divide as growth begins in spring. Sow seed when ripe in containers in a cold frame.

Z 4–7

HEIGHT
to 12in (30cm)

SPREAD
to 8in (20cm)

Ranunculaceae

RANUNCULUS FICARIA FLORE-PLENO

Habit Tuberous, herbaceous, perennial. ***Flowers*** Solitary, pompon-like, to 1¼in (3cm) across, borne in early spring. Bright yellow. ***Leaves*** Basal, broadly heart-shaped, glossy, dying back soon after flowering. Dark green.
• NATIVE HABITAT Europe, northwest Africa, and southwest Asia.
• CULTIVATION Spreads rapidly, but is not as invasive as the species. Suits wild gardens or may be naturalized in turf, in sun or deep shade.
• PROPAGATION Divide in spring or autumn.

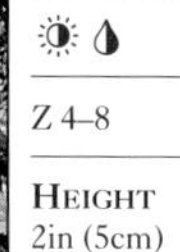

Z 4–8

HEIGHT
2in (5cm)

SPREAD
12in (30cm) or more

Ranunculaceae

RANUNCULUS FICARIA var. *AURANTIACUS*

Habit Tuberous, herbaceous, perennial. ***Flowers*** Solitary, saucer-shaped, to 1¼in (3cm) wide, borne in early spring. Copper-orange. ***Leaves*** Basal, broadly heart-shaped, glossy, dying back soon after flowering. Dark green.
• NATIVE HABITAT Europe and northwest Africa.
• CULTIVATION Suitable for naturalizing in turf. Needs a site in sun or deep shade. Spreads rapidly.
• PROPAGATION Divide in spring or autumn.
• OTHER NAME *R. ficaria* 'Cupreus'.

Z 4–8

HEIGHT
2in (5cm)

SPREAD
12in (30cm) or more

SAXIFRAGA

The genus *Saxifraga* is an important group of alpine plants. Many of them suit rock gardens and alpine-house culture.

Cultivation requirements for the genus are grouped as follows.

Group 1 Moist but well-drained soil, in partial or deep shade.

Group 2 Moist, sharply drained, fertile, neutral to alkaline soil, in light shade.

Group 3 Moist but sharply drained, moderately fertile, neutral to alkaline soil, protected from the hottest summer sun.

Group 4 Sharply drained, alkaline soil, in full sun. In an alpine house, use shallow pans and a mix of 2 parts soil, and 1 part limestone chips.

Sow seed when fresh or in autumn, or root rosette cuttings in late spring.

S. *GRANULATA*

Habit Clump-forming, summer-herbaceous, perennial, with stem and root bulbils.
Flowers Saucer-shaped, ⅝in (15mm) across, borne in clusters of 10–20, in late spring. White.
Leaves Kidney-shaped, toothed, in fairly large rosettes. Mid-green.

- CULTIVATION 2.
- HEIGHT 10in (25cm).
- SPREAD 12in (30cm).

S. granulata
Fair maids of France, Meadow saxifrage

Z 4–6

S. *HIRSUTA*

Habit Mound-forming, evergreen, perennial.
Flowers Star-shaped, to ⅜in (8mm) across, borne in loose clusters in spring or early summer. White.
Leaves Kidney-shaped to rounded, toothed. Mid-green, often with purple underside.

- CULTIVATION 1.
- HEIGHT to 8in (20cm).
- SPREAD 8in (20cm).

S. hirsuta
Kidney saxifrage

Z 5–8

S. *CUNEIFOLIA*

Habit Carpet-forming, evergreen, perennial.
Flowers Star-shaped, ¼in (7mm) across, borne in loose clusters in spring and early summer. White.
Leaves Wedge-shaped, sometimes oval or rounded, toothed and leathery. Fresh green.

- CULTIVATION 1.
- HEIGHT 8in (20cm).
- SPREAD 12in (30cm).

S. cuneifolia
Shield-leaved saxifrage

Z 4–6

S. *LONGIFOLIA*

Habit Monocarpic, evergreen, perennial.
Flowers Saucer-shaped, ½in (1cm) across, borne in large, arching, pyramidal spray to 28in (70cm) long, in summer. White.
Leaves Linear, lime-encrusted, in a single, large, tough rosette. Silver-gray.

- CULTIVATION 4.
- HEIGHT 24in (60cm).
- SPREAD 8in (20cm).

S. longifolia
Pyrenean saxifrage

Z 5–8

S. 'Tumbling Waters'
Habit Tufted, evergreen, perennial.
Flowers Open saucer-shaped, ⅜in (1cm) across, borne in spring. White.
Leaves Linear, in large rosettes. Silver-green.
- CULTIVATION 4.
- OTHER NAME *S. longifolia* 'Tumbling Waters'.
- HEIGHT 18in (45cm).
- SPREAD 8in (20cm).

S. 'Tumbling Waters'

Z 5–7

S. SCARDICA
Habit Cushion-forming, evergreen, perennial.
Flowers Cupped, upturned, ⅝in (15mm) across, borne in clusters on red-tinted stems, in spring. White.
Leaves Oblong and fleshy, forming rosettes. Blue-green.
- CULTIVATION 3.
- HEIGHT 3in (8cm).
- SPREAD 6in (15cm).

S. scardica

Z 6–8

S. BURSERIANA
Habit Cushion-forming, evergreen, perennial.
Flowers Solitary, cup-shaped, ⅜in (1cm) across, borne on red stems in early spring. White.
Leaves Pointed, firm, and narrowly lance-shaped, in small, compact rosettes. Gray-green.
- CULTIVATION 3.
- HEIGHT 2in (5cm).
- SPREAD 6in (15cm).

S. burseriana

Z 5–8

S. x *GEUM*
Habit Mat-forming, evergreen, perennial.
Flowers Star-shaped, ⅓in (8mm) across, borne in loose sprays during summer. White.
Leaves Spoon-shaped, long-stalked, and sparsely haired, with scalloped margins, in large rosettes. Mid-green.
- CULTIVATION 1.
- HEIGHT 8in (20cm).
- SPREAD 8in (20cm).

S. x *geum*

Z 3–7

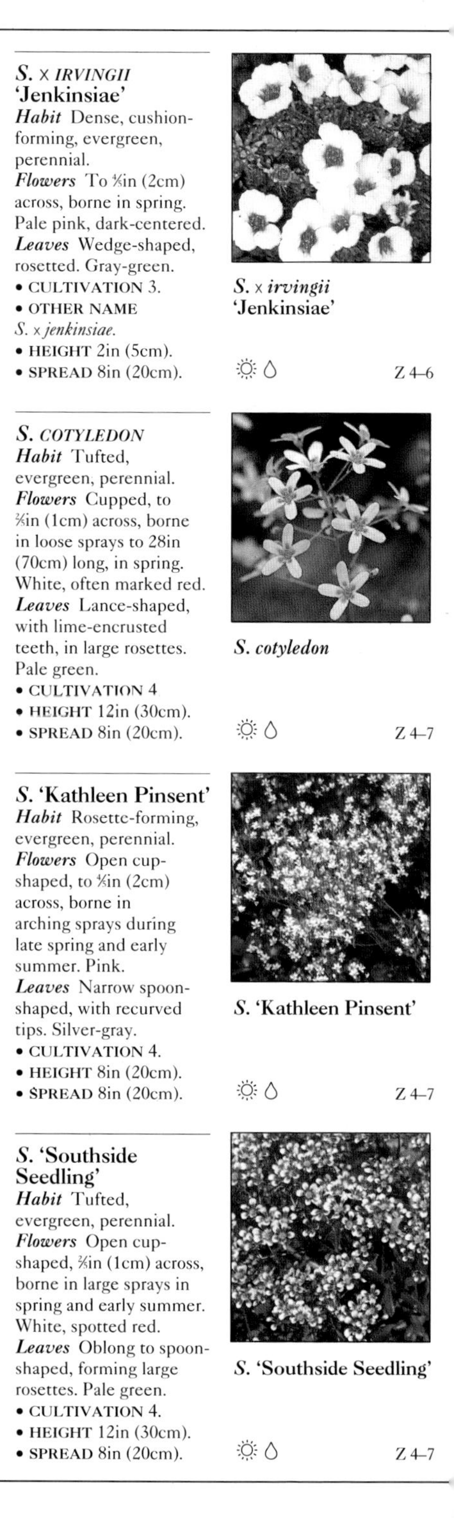

S. x *IRVINGII* 'Jenkinsiae'
Habit Dense, cushion-forming, evergreen, perennial.
Flowers To ¾in (2cm) across, borne in spring. Pale pink, dark-centered.
Leaves Wedge-shaped, rosetted. Gray-green.
- CULTIVATION 3.
- OTHER NAME *S.* x *jenkinsiae.*
- HEIGHT 2in (5cm).
- SPREAD 8in (20cm).

S. x *irvingii* 'Jenkinsiae'

Z 4–6

S. COTYLEDON
Habit Tufted, evergreen, perennial.
Flowers Cupped, to ⅜in (1cm) across, borne in loose sprays to 28in (70cm) long, in spring. White, often marked red.
Leaves Lance-shaped, with lime-encrusted teeth, in large rosettes. Pale green.
- CULTIVATION 4
- HEIGHT 12in (30cm).
- SPREAD 8in (20cm).

S. cotyledon

Z 4–7

S. 'Kathleen Pinsent'
Habit Rosette-forming, evergreen, perennial.
Flowers Open cup-shaped, to ¾in (2cm) across, borne in arching sprays during late spring and early summer. Pink.
Leaves Narrow spoon-shaped, with recurved tips. Silver-gray.
- CULTIVATION 4.
- HEIGHT 8in (20cm).
- SPREAD 8in (20cm).

S. 'Kathleen Pinsent'

Z 4–7

S. 'Southside Seedling'
Habit Tufted, evergreen, perennial.
Flowers Open cup-shaped, ⅜in (1cm) across, borne in large sprays in spring and early summer. White, spotted red.
Leaves Oblong to spoon-shaped, forming large rosettes. Pale green.
- CULTIVATION 4.
- HEIGHT 12in (30cm).
- SPREAD 8in (20cm).

S. 'Southside Seedling'

Z 4–7

S. *FEDERICI-AUGUSTI*
subsp. *GRISEBACHII*
'Wisley Variety'
Habit Cushion-forming, evergreen, perennial.
Flowers To ¼in (6mm) across, borne on leafy, hairy stems in late spring. Red-purple, with green tips.
Leaves Spoon-shaped, in flat rosettes. Silver.
• CULTIVATION 4.
• HEIGHT 4in (10cm).
• SPREAD 4in (10cm).

***S. federici-augusti* subsp. *grisebachii* 'Wisley Variety'**

Z 6–8

S. *OPPOSITIFOLIA*
Habit Flat, mat-forming, evergreen, perennial.
Flowers Solitary, almost stemless, cup-shaped, to ¾in (2cm) across, borne in spring or sometimes late winter. Red-purple to pink, or white.
Leaves Tiny, stiff, oval or oblong. Dark green.
• CULTIVATION 2.
• HEIGHT 1in (2.5cm).
• SPREAD 8in (20cm).

S. oppositifolia
Purple saxifrage

Z 2–6

S. *STRIBRNYI*
Habit Cushion-forming, evergreen, perennial.
Flowers Cupped, ⅜in (1cm) across, borne in spikes on crooklike stems, in late spring and early summer. Deep violet-purple.
Leaves Pointed, lance-shaped, lime-encrusted, in rosettes. Blue-green.
• CULTIVATION 4.
• HEIGHT 4in (10cm).
• SPREAD 8in (20cm).

S. stribrnyi

Z 5–8

S. *SEMPERVIVUM*
Habit Cushion-forming, evergreen, perennial.
Flowers Open cup-shaped, ¼in (6mm) across, borne in spikes on silver-haired, crosier-like stems, in spring. Deep red-purple.
Leaves Linear and lime-encrusted. Silver-green.
• CULTIVATION 4.
• OTHER NAME
S. porophylla var. *thessalica.*
• HEIGHT 4in (10cm).
• SPREAD 8in (20cm).

S. sempervivum

Z 6–8

S. x *ANGLICA*
'Cranbourne'
Habit Cushion-forming. evergreen, perennial.
Flowers Solitary, cup-shaped, almost stemless, to ¾in (2cm) across, borne in early summer. Lilac-purple.
Leaves Linear, forming dense rosettes. Gray-green.
• CULTIVATION 3.
• HEIGHT 1in (2.5cm).
• SPREAD 8in (20cm).

***S.* x *anglica* 'Cranbourne'**

Z 5–8

S. x *BOYDII*
'Hindhead Seedling'
Habit Tight cushion-forming, evergreen, perennial.
Flowers Solitary, cupped, erect, to 1¼in (3cm) across, borne in spring. Pale yellow.
Leaves Linear to lance-shaped, and pointed. Blue-green.
• CULTIVATION 3.
• OTHER NAME
S. 'Hindhead Seedling'.
• HEIGHT 2in (5cm).
• SPREAD 2in (5cm).

S. x ***boydii***
'Hindhead Seedling'

Z 5–8

S. *SANCTA*
Habit Spreading, hummock-forming, evergreen, perennial.
Flowers Open cup-shaped, ⅓in (8mm) across, borne in compact clusters in spring. Deep yellow.
Leaves Narrowly lance-shaped, forming tight rosettes. Dark green.
• CULTIVATION 3.
• OTHER NAME
S. juniperifolia subsp. *sancta*.
• HEIGHT 2in (5cm).
• SPREAD 8in (20cm).

S. *sancta*

S. x *APICULATA*
Habit Cushion-forming, evergreen, perennial.
Flowers Cup-shaped, ⅓in (8mm) across, borne in clusters in early spring. Yellow.
Leaves Linear to lance-shaped, forming tight rosettes. Dark green.
• CULTIVATION 3.
• HEIGHT 4in (10cm).
• SPREAD 12in (30cm).

S. x ***apiculata***

Z 5–8

S. 'Carmen'
Habit Cushion-forming, evergreen, perennial.
Flowers Upright, cupped, ⅓in (8mm) across, borne in spring. Bright yellow.
Leaves Linear, pointed, in rosettes. Dark green.
• CULTIVATION 3.
• OTHER NAME
S. x *elizabethae*.
• HEIGHT 1in (2.5cm).
• SPREAD 4–6in (10–15cm).

S. 'Carmen'

Z 4–6

S. *EXARATA*
subsp. *MOSCHATA*
'Cloth of Gold'
Habit Tufted, evergreen, perennial.
Flowers Star-like, ⅓in (8mm) across, sparsely borne in flat-topped clusters in late spring and early summer. White.
Leaves Entire or lobed, in soft rosettes. Yellow.
• CULTIVATION 1.
• HEIGHT 4in (10cm).
• SPREAD 12in (30cm).

S. *exarata*
subsp. *moschata*
'Cloth of Gold'

Z 5–8

Caryophyllaceae

SILENE ALPESTRIS

Habit Branching, loosely tufted, evergreen, perennial. ***Flowers*** Saucer-shaped, 3/8in (1cm) across, with fringed petals, borne in open sprays in early summer. White, sometimes pink-flushed. ***Leaves*** Linear to lance-shaped. Mid-green.

- NATIVE HABITAT Eastern Alps, Europe.
- CULTIVATION Grow in gritty, sharply drained, neutral to slightly alkaline soil.
- PROPAGATION By seed in autumn, in containers in a cold frame. Take basal cuttings in spring.
- OTHER NAME *Heliosperma alpestris.*

Z 4–7

HEIGHT
6in (15cm)

SPREAD
8in (20cm)

Rosaceae

POTENTILLA ALBA

Habit Spreading, clumping, evergreen, perennial. ***Flowers*** Saucer-shaped, 1in (2.5cm) across, borne in loose clusters in late spring and early summer. White, with golden anthers. ***Leaves*** Palmate, with oblong to oval leaflets. Light green, hairy below.

- NATIVE HABITAT Central and southern Europe.
- CULTIVATION Suitable for growing in scree beds, rock gardens, and border fronts. Needs poor to moderately fertile, well-drained soil.
- PROPAGATION Divided in autumn or spring. Sow seed when ripe, in containers in a cold frame.

Z 4–7

HEIGHT
3in (8cm)

SPREAD
to 12in (30cm)

Gesneriaceae

HABERLEA RHODOPENSIS 'Virginalis'

Habit Rosette-forming, evergreen, perennial. ***Flowers*** Trumpet-shaped, two-lipped, to 1in (2.5cm) across, borne in lax clusters in spring and early summer. Pure white. ***Leaves*** Coarsely scalloped, oval, and softly hairy. Dark green.

- NATIVE HABITAT Shady, rocky places and mountains of Bulgaria and northeastern Greece.
- CULTIVATION Needs moist but well-drained, gritty, fertile soil that is neutral to acid.
- PROPAGATION By leaf cuttings or division, both in spring. Sow seed at 55°F (13°C) in spring.

Z 5–7

HEIGHT
to 6in (15cm)

SPREAD
to 10in (25cm)

Portulacaceae | BITTERROOT

LEWISIA REDIVIVA (White form)

Habit Tufted, rosette-forming, herbaceous, perennial. ***Flowers*** Broadly funnel-shaped, 2in (5cm) across, with narrow petals, borne in early spring to summer. White. ***Leaves*** Linear to club-shaped, dying back after flowering. Dark green.

- NATIVE HABITAT Open, stony mountain grassland, Canada and USA.
- CULTIVATION Needs sharp drainage. Protect from excess winter moisture.
- PROPAGATION By seed in containers in a cold frame, in autumn.

Z 5–7

HEIGHT
2in (5cm)

SPREAD
4in (10cm)

Campanulaceae

CYANANTHUS LOBATUS 'Albus'

Habit Tufted, spreading, tap-rooted, herbaceous, perennial. ***Flowers*** Single, funnel-shaped, with 5 lobes ¾–1½in (2–4cm) across, borne in late summer. White. ***Leaves*** Oval, deeply lobed. Dull green.
• NATIVE HABITAT Cool moist habitats in China and Himalaya.
• CULTIVATION Grow in moderately fertile, moist but well-drained soil that is neutral to slightly acid.
• PROPAGATION By softwood cuttings in late spring or early summer. Sow seed as soon as ripe, or in early spring, in containers in a cold frame.

Z 6–7

HEIGHT 2in (5cm)

SPREAD to 12in (30cm)

Caryophyllaceae

ARENARIA MONTANA

Habit Vigorous, spreading, prostrate, evergreen, perennial. ***Flowers*** Saucer-shaped, to ¾in (2cm) across, borne in early summer. White. ***Leaves*** Paired, narrowly lance-shaped. Grayish-green.
• NATIVE HABITAT Mountains, southwest Europe.
• CULTIVATION Good for growing in a rock garden, or in rock or paving crevices. Easily grown in poor, sandy, moist but sharply drained soil.
• PROPAGATION Divide after flowering, take basal cuttings in early summer, or sow seed in autumn, in containers in a cold frame.

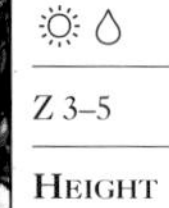

Z 3–5

HEIGHT to 2in (5cm)

SPREAD to 12in (30cm)

Geraniaceae

GERANIUM FARRERI

Habit Tap-rooted, rosette-forming, herbaceous, perennial. ***Flowers*** Saucer-shaped, to 1½in (3.5cm) across, with wavy margins, borne in early summer. Pale pink, with black anthers. ***Leaves*** Kidney-shaped, divided. Mid-green, with red margins.
• NATIVE HABITAT Mountains, western China.
• CULTIVATION Outdoors, grow in a scree bed and protect from winter moisture. In an alpine house, use equal parts soil, leaf mold, and grit.
• PROPAGATION By seed when ripe in containers in a cold frame, or take basal cuttings in spring.

Z 5–8

HEIGHT to 5in (12cm)

SPREAD to 6in (15cm)

Onagraceae

EPILOBIUM CHLORIFOLIUM var. *KAIKOURENSE*

Habit Woody-based, clump-forming, evergreen, perennial. ***Flowers*** Funnel-shaped, with spreading lobes ⅝in (15mm) across, borne in summer. White or pale pink. ***Leaves*** Oval, toothed. Bronze-green.
• NATIVE HABITAT Stony slopes, New Zealand.
• CULTIVATION Grow in fertile, moist but well-drained soil, with shade from the hottest sun.
• PROPAGATION By seed when ripe or in spring, in containers in a cold frame. By division in autumn or spring.

Z 6–8

HEIGHT to 12in (30cm)

SPREAD to 6in (15cm)

Cruciferae/ Brassicaceae	

IBERIS SAXATILIS

Habit Evergreen, subshrub. ***Flowers*** Cross-shaped, borne in flattened clusters 1¼–1½in (3–4cm) across, in late spring and summer. White, sometimes tinted purple. ***Leaves*** Linear, fleshy, almost cylindrical. Dark green.
• NATIVE HABITAT Southern Europe.
• CULTIVATION Needs well-drained, moderately fertile soil that is neutral to alkaline.
• PROPAGATION Take softwood cuttings in early summer or semiripe cuttings in mid-summer. Sow seed when ripe in containers in a cold frame.

Z 4–8

HEIGHT to 6in (15cm)

SPREAD to 12in (30cm)

Geraniaceae	

GERANIUM SESSILIFLORUM subsp. *NOVAE-ZELANDIAE* 'Nigricans'

Habit Rosette-forming, evergreen, perennial. ***Flowers*** Upright, funnel-shaped, ¼in (7mm) across, borne in loose clusters in summer. Gray-white. ***Leaves*** Divided. Olive-bronze.
• NATIVE HABITAT Garden origin.
• CULTIVATION Good for scree or rock gardens, in moist but well-drained, poor to moderately fertile soil. Self-sows freely; seedlings come true.
• PROPAGATION Sow seed when ripe in containers in a cold frame.

Z 4–8

HEIGHT to 3in (8cm)

SPREAD 6in (15cm)

Cornaceae	CREEPING DOGWOOD, DWARF CORNEL

CORNUS CANADENSIS

Habit Creeping, rhizomatous, evergreen, perennial. ***Flowers*** Tiny, borne in dense clusters, with 4–6 bracts to ¾in (2cm) long, in late spring and early summer. Green, with white bracts. ***Fruit*** Rounded berry. Bright red. ***Leaves*** Oval to lance-shaped, in terminal whorls. Bright green.
• NATIVE HABITAT Woods, USA and Greenland.
• CULTIVATION Prefers a site in partial shade, with moist, leaf-rich acid soil.
• PROPAGATION By division in spring or autumn.
• OTHER NAME *Chamaepericlymenum canadense.*

Z 2–6

HEIGHT to 6in (15cm)

SPREAD indefinite

Compositae/Asteraceae	NEW ZEALAND DAISY

CELMISIA RAMULOSA

Habit Branching, evergreen, subshrub. ***Flowers*** Daisy, 1in (2.5cm) across, borne on sticky white stems in late spring and early summer. White, with yellow disc. ***Leaves*** Linear to oblong, overlapping, stiff. Dark green, with white-woolly underside.
- NATIVE HABITAT Moorland and scree, high altitudes, mountains of New Zealand.
- CULTIVATION Grow in moist but well-drained, acid soil that is rich in organic matter, in sun or light shade. Grows best in cool, moist climates.
- PROPAGATION Root rosettes as cuttings in spring.

Z 6–9

HEIGHT to 10in (25cm)

SPREAD to 10in (25cm)

Scrophulariaceae	

OURISIA CAESPITOSA

Habit Mat-forming, evergreen, perennial. ***Flowers*** Tubular, 2-lipped, ⅝in (15mm) across, borne in whorls on leafless stems, in summer. White, with yellow throat. ***Leaves*** Broadly oval to spoon-shaped, entire or notched. Gray-green.
- NATIVE HABITAT Alpine areas, New Zealand.
- CULTIVATION Grow in reliably moist but well-drained soil, preferably in cool, damp climates. Good for a rock garden, peat bed, or wall crevice.
- PROPAGATION By seed as soon as ripe or in spring, in a cold frame. Divide in spring.

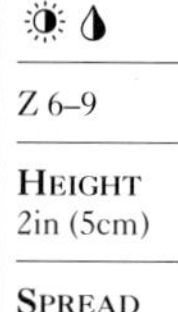

Z 6–9

HEIGHT 2in (5cm)

SPREAD to 8in (20cm)

Solanaceae	WHITE CUP

NIEREMBERGIA REPENS

Habit Mat-forming, stem-rooting, perennial. ***Flowers*** Upright, open bell, 1–2in (2.5–5cm) across, borne in summer. White, with yellow eye. ***Leaves*** Rounded, spoon-shaped. Light green.
- NATIVE HABITAT Andes.
- CULTIVATION Suitable for planting in paving crevices. Grow in dry, sandy soils in a warm, sunny site. Tends to be invasive, so site away from small, more precious alpines.
- PROPAGATION By seed or division in spring.
- OTHER NAME *N. rivularis.*

Z 6–9

HEIGHT 2in (5cm)

SPREAD 24in (60cm) or more

Compositae/Asteraceae	

ANACYCLUS PYRETHRUM var. *DEPRESSUS*

Habit Mat-forming, evergreen, perennial. ***Flowers*** Daisy, to 2in (5cm) across, borne in summer. White with red reverse and yellow disc. ***Leaves*** Finely divided, forming rosettes. Gray-green.
- NATIVE HABITAT Stony slopes, Atlas Mountains.
- CULTIVATION Needs gritty, sharply drained, fertile soil. Protect from winter moisture.
- PROPAGATION Take softwood cuttings in spring. Sow seed in autumn in containers in a cold frame.
- OTHER NAME *A. depressus.*

Z 6–8

HEIGHT 1–2in (2.5–5cm) or more

SPREAD 4in (10cm)

Rosaceae	MOUNTAIN AVENS

DRYAS OCTOPETALA

Habit Mat-forming, evergreen, subshrub. ***Flowers*** Upright, cup-shaped, to 1½in (4cm) across, borne in late spring and early summer. White. ***Leaves*** Oblong, scalloped and glossy. Dark green. ***Fruits*** Fluffy,.silky-haired seedheads.
• NATIVE HABITAT Moorland, northern Europe.
• CULTIVATION Suitable for growing on a rock garden. Prefers gritty, well-drained, fertile soil.
• PROPAGATION By seed when ripe in a cold frame, by softwood cuttings in early summer, or by separation of rooted stems in spring.

Z 3–6

HEIGHT 4in (10cm)

SPREAD 36in (90cm) or more

Ranunculaceae	

THALICTRUM KIUSIANUM

Habit Mat-forming, rhizomatous, herbaceous, perennial. ***Flowers*** Many-petaled, to ⅜in (1cm) across, borne in few-flowered, fluffy clusters in early summer. Pale pink-mauve. ***Leaves*** Finely divided, fern-like, with oval lobes. Blue-green.
• NATIVE HABITAT Damp shady habitats, Japan.
• CULTIVATION Ideal for a rock garden, peat bed, or trough. Grow in moist, sandy, leaf-rich soil.
• PROPAGATION Sow seed when ripe or in early spring, in containers in a cold frame. Divide carefully, in spring, as new growth begins.

Z 7–9

HEIGHT to 4in (10cm)

SPREAD to 12in (30cm) or more

Compositae/Asteraceae	STEMLESS CARLINE THISTLE

CARLINA ACAULIS

Habit Rosette-forming, prickly, herbaceous, perennial. ***Flowers*** Measuring 4in (10cm) across, borne at the center of the rosettes in mid- and late summer. Silvery-white, with brown disc. ***Leaves*** Deeply cut, oval, with spiny margins. Green.
• NATIVE HABITAT Southern and eastern Europe.
• CULTIVATION Grow in poor, sharply drained soil.
• PROPAGATION Sow seed in autumn in containers in a cold frame.

Z 5–7

HEIGHT to 4in (10cm)

SPREAD to 10in (25cm)

Caprifoliaceae	TWIN FLOWER

LINNAEA BOREALIS

Habit Mat-forming, stem-rooting, evergreen, sub-shrub. ***Flowers*** Paired, nodding bell-shaped, to ⅜in (1cm) long, borne in summer. Palest pink. ***Leaves*** Paired, oval to rounded, scalloped, glossy. Dark green, with pale green or buff underside.
• NATIVE HABITAT Woods, tundra, and heath Eurasia and N. America.
• CULTIVATION Needs moist, fertile, acid soil.
• PROPAGATION Separate rooted stems between autumn and spring, root softwood cuttings in early summer. Sow seed in autumn in a cold frame.

pH

Z 2–6

HEIGHT to 3in (8cm)

SPREAD 36in (90cm) or more

Corydalis

The genus *Corydalis* consists of about 300 species of annuals, biennials, and perennials, often from scree, woods, and mountain meadows. For ease of reference, cultivation needs are grouped as follows:
Group 1 Full sun or partial shade, in fertile, well-drained soil.
Group 2 Full sun, in moderately fertile, sharply drained soil.
Group 3 Partial shade and moist but well-drained, leaf-rich, fertile soil.
Group 4 In an alpine house, in a mix of equal parts soil, leaf mold and grit.

Propagate by dividing spring-flowering species in late summer before growth resumes, or summer-flowering species in spring. Sow seed as soon as ripe in a cold frame. Germination may be erratic.

C. OCHROLEUCA
Habit Clump-forming, fibrous-rooted, evergreen, perennial.
Flowers Two-lipped, ⅝in (15mm) long, borne in oblong clusters in late spring and summer. Creamy-white, with yellow tip.
Leaves Finely divided and oval. Pale green.
- CULTIVATION 1.
- HEIGHT 12in (30cm).
- SPREAD 12in (30cm).

C. ochroleuca

Z 4–7

C. MALKENSIS
Habit Compact, tuberous, herbaceous, perennial.
Flowers Two-lipped, 1in (2.5cm) long, borne in spikes in spring. Cream.
Leaves Finely divided and oval. Pale green.
- CULTIVATION 2 or 3.
- OTHER NAME *C. caucasica* var. *alba* of gardens.
- HEIGHT 3–6in (8–15cm).
- SPREAD to 4in (10cm).

C. malkensis

Z 5–8

C. POPOVII
Habit Tuberous, herbaceous, perennial.
Flowers Two-lipped, to 1¾in (4.5cm) long, borne in loose spikes in late spring. White or pale violet, with maroon lips.
Leaves Finely divided and oval. Blue-green.
- CULTIVATION 4.
- HEIGHT 6in (15cm).
- SPREAD 5in (12cm).

C. popovii

Z 7–9

C. DIPHYLLA
Habit Tuberous, herbaceous, perennial.
Flowers Two-lipped, to 1¼in (3cm) long, borne in loose spikes in spring. Pale violet, with white spurs and red-violet lips.
Leaves Narrowly lance-shaped and finely divided. Glaucous, mid-green.
- CULTIVATION 2.
- HEIGHT 6in (15cm).
- SPREAD 4in (10cm).

C. diphylla

Z 4–7

C. SOLIDA
'George Baker'
Habit Clump-forming, tuberous, herbaceous, perennial.
Flowers Two-lipped, 4/5in (2cm) long, borne in erect spikes in spring. Deep salmon-rose.
Leaves Finely dissected. Grayish-green.
• CULTIVATION 1 or 2.
• OTHER NAME *C. solida* 'G. P. Baker'.
• HEIGHT 6in (15cm).
• SPREAD 8in (20cm).

C. solida
'George Baker'

Z 5–8

C. CASHMERIANA
Habit Tufted, tuberous, perennial.
Flowers Two-lipped, 1/2in 1cm) long, with curved spurs, borne in sprays in summer. Bright blue.
Leaves Finely divided, with oval to elliptic lobes. Bright green.
• CULTIVATION 3.
• HEIGHT 4–10in (10–25cm).
• SPREAD 3–6in (8–15cm).

C. cashmeriana

Z 6–8

C. FLEXUOSA
'China Blue'
Habit Scaly-rooted, summer-dormant, rhizomatous, perennial.
Flowers Two-lipped, 1in (2.5cm) long, borne in oblong clusters in late spring and summer. Bright blue.
Leaves Finely divided, and oval. Bluish-green.
• CULTIVATION 3.
• HEIGHT 12in (30cm).
• SPREAD 16in (40cm) or more.

C. flexuosa
'China Blue'

Z 6–8

C. CHEILANTHIFOLIA

Habit Rosette-forming, fibrous-rooted, evergreen, perennial.
Flowers Two-lipped, ⅝in (15mm) long, borne in dense spikes in spring and summer. Deep yellow.
Leaves Fernlike and finely divided. Pale to mid-green.

- CULTIVATION 1.
- HEIGHT 12in (30cm).
- SPREAD 10in (25cm).

C. cheilanthifolia

Z 5–8

C. WILSONII

Habit Tap-rooted, rosetted, evergreen, perennial.
Flowers Two-lipped, ¾in (2cm) long, borne in lax spikes in spring and summer. Canary-yellow, with green tips.
Leaves Fleshy, divided, and smooth. Blue-green.

- CULTIVATION 4.
- HEIGHT 4–8in (10–20cm).
- SPREAD 8–12in (20–30cm).

C. wilsonii

Z 6–8

C. LUTEA

Habit Rhizomatous, mound- or tuft-forming, evergreen, perennial.
Flowers Two-lipped, to ¾in (2cm) long, borne in spikes from spring to autumn. Golden-yellow.
Leaves Fernlike and arching. Pale green.

- CULTIVATION 1, 2, or 3.
- OTHER NAME *Pseudofumaria lutea.*
- HEIGHT 16in (40cm).
- SPREAD 12in (30cm).

C. lutea

Z 5–8

PHLOX

The genus *Phlox* consists of 67 species of evergreen, semievergreen, and herbaceous perennials, with a few annuals and subshrubs. They bear heads or clusters of usually salver- but occasionally funnel-shaped flowers, with 5 spreading petal lobes. Many phloxes, mostly those found in dry, rocky mountain habitats or woodlands in North America, are suitable in scale for growing in a rock garden and are easily cultivated. Many are also suitable for planting in or trailing over walls, and used as border edging. Phloxes are valued for their foliage, and the profusion of small, usually brilliantly colored flowers, borne during spring and summer. The flowers, which are often so abundant that they almost obscure the foliage, are also attractive to butterflies. For ease of reference, their cultivation requirements may be grouped as follows:

Group 1 Fertile, moist but well-drained soil that is enriched with organic matter, in partial shade.
Group 2 Well-drained, fertile soil in sun, or in light, dappled shade in areas with low rainfall.
Group 3 Poor to moderately fertile, gritty, sharply drained soil, in full sun. Best suited to rock gardens, raised beds, and troughs. Grow as a pot plant in an alpine house, in a mix of equal parts soil, leaf mold, and sharp sand.

Propagate by taking softwood cuttings of leafy, non-flowering shoots in spring. Separate self-rooted stem sections of trailing species and cultivars in spring or early autumn. Sow seed in containers in a cold frame, as soon as ripe or in early spring. In areas with cold, wet winters, overwinter young plants in a cold frame, and set them out in their permament positions in spring.

P. STOLONIFERA 'Ariane'
Habit Spreading, stoloniferous, semi-evergreen, perennial.
Flowers Salver-shaped, 1¼in (3cm) across, borne in early summer. White, with yellow eye.
Leaves Oval. Dark green.
• CULTIVATION 1.
• HEIGHT 4–6in (10–15cm).
• SPREAD 12in (30cm).

P. stolonifera 'Ariane'

Z 2–8

P. 'Kelly's Eye'
Habit Vigorous, mound-forming, evergreen, perennial.
Flowers Salver-shaped, ⅝in (15mm) across, borne during late spring and early summer. Pale pink, with red-purple eye.
Leaves Narrowly lance-shaped. Dark green.
• CULTIVATION 2.
• HEIGHT 4in (10cm).
• SPREAD 12in (30cm).

P. 'Kelly's Eye'

Z 5–8

P. ADSURGENS 'Wagon Wheel'
Habit Stem-rooting, mat-forming, evergreen, perennial.
Flowers To 1in (25mm) across, borne in late spring and early summer. Salmon-pink.
Leaves Rounded to narrowly oval. Mid-green.
• CULTIVATION 1.
• HEIGHT 12in (30cm).
• SPREAD 12in (30cm) or more.

P. adsurgens 'Wagon Wheel'

Z 7–9

P. NIVALIS 'Camla'
Habit Trailing or mat-forming, evergreen, subshrub.
Flowers Salver-shaped, ⅝in (15mm) across, borne in lax clusters in summer. Warm pink.
Leaves Lance-shaped and hairy. Mid-green.
• CULTIVATION 2.
• HEIGHT 8in (20cm).
• SPREAD 12in (30cm).

P. nivalis 'Camla'

Z 5–8

P. SUBULATA 'Marjorie'

Habit Mound-forming, evergreen, perennial. ***Flowers*** Star-shaped, 1¼in (30mm) wide, borne in clusters in late spring and early summer. Deep pink, with yellow eye edged dark pink. ***Leaves*** Linear to elliptic, hairy. Bright green.
- CULTIVATION 2.
- HEIGHT 4in (10cm).
- SPREAD 8in (20cm).

P. subulata 'Marjorie'

Z 2–9

P. DOUGLASII 'Crackerjack'

Habit Compact, mound-forming, evergreen, perennial. ***Flowers*** Salver-shaped, ⅝in (15mm) across, borne in late spring and early summer. Magenta. ***Leaves*** Stiff and narrowly lance-shaped. Dark green.
- CULTIVATION 2.
- HEIGHT 5in (12cm).
- SPREAD 8in (20cm).

P. douglasii 'Crackerjack'

Z 5–8

P. NANA 'Arroya'

Habit Spreading, semievergreen or deciduous, perennial. ***Flowers*** Solitary, salver-shaped, 1in (25mm) across, borne throughout summer. Bright magenta, with white eye. ***Leaves*** Narrowly lance-shaped. Gray-green.
- CULTIVATION 3.
- HEIGHT 8in (20cm).
- SPREAD 12in (30cm).

P. nana 'Arroya'

Z 6–8

P. DOUGLASII 'Red Admiral'

Habit Mound-forming, evergreen, perennial. ***Flowers*** Salver-shaped, ⅝in (15mm) across, borne in clusters during late spring and early summer. Deep crimson. ***Leaves*** Narrowly lance-shaped. Dark green.
- CULTIVATION 2.
- HEIGHT 8in (20cm).
- SPREAD 12in (30cm).

P. douglasii 'Red Admiral'

Z 5–8

P. NANA 'Mary Maslin'

Habit Spreading, semievergreen or deciduous, perennial. ***Flowers*** Solitary, salver-shaped, 1in (25mm) across, borne in lax clusters in summer. Scarlet, with yellow eye. ***Leaves*** Linear to narrow lance-shaped and downy. Gray-green.
- CULTIVATION 3.
- HEIGHT 8in (20cm).
- SPREAD 12in (30cm).

P. nana 'Mary Maslin'

Z 6–8

P. DOUGLASII 'Boothman's Variety'

Habit Mound-forming, evergreen, perennial. ***Flowers*** Salver-shaped, ⅝in (15mm) across, borne in late spring and early summer. Violet-pink, with dark eye. ***Leaves*** Narrowly lance-shaped. Dark green.

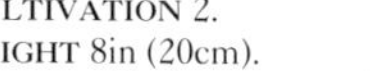

- CULTIVATION 2.
- HEIGHT 8in (20cm).
- SPREAD 12in (30cm).

P. douglasii 'Boothman's Variety'

Z 5–8

P. DIVARICATA 'Dirigo Ice'

Habit Stem-rooting, spreading, perennial, semievergreen. ***Flowers*** Salver-shaped, to 1¼in (30mm) across, borne in lax clusters in early summer. Clear pale blue. ***Leaves*** Oval and hairy. Mid-green.
- CULTIVATION 1.
- HEIGHT 14in (35cm).
- SPREAD 20in (50cm).

P. divaricata 'Dirigo Ice'

Z 3–9

P. BIFIDA
Habit Mound-forming, evergreen, perennial.
Flowers Scented, star-shaped, ¾in (20mm) across, deeply cleft, borne in lax clusters in spring. Deep lavender-blue to white.
Leaves Linear, spiny and hairy. Mid-green.
- CULTIVATION 2 or 3.
- HEIGHT 8in (20cm).
- SPREAD 6in (15cm).

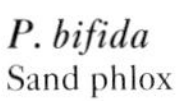

P. bifida
Sand phlox

Z 5–8

P. 'Chatahoochee'
Habit Tufted, short-lived, semievergreen, perennial.
Flowers Salver-shaped, to 1in (25mm) across, borne in summer and early autumn. Lavender-blue, with maroon eye.
Leaves Lance-shaped. Mid-green, flushed purple when young.
- CULTIVATION 1 or 2.
- HEIGHT 6in (15cm).
- SPREAD 12in (30cm).

P. 'Chatahoochee'

Z 4–7

P. 'Emerald Cushion'
Habit Mound-forming, evergreen, perennial.
Flowers Salver-shaped, to 1in (25mm) wide, with notched petals, borne in lax clusters in late spring and early summer. Pale violet.
Leaves Linear to elliptic. Light green.
- CULTIVATION 2.
- HEIGHT 3in (8cm).
- SPREAD 8in (20cm).

P. 'Emerald Cushion'

Z 4–7

P. DIVARICATA subsp. LAPHAMII
Habit Stem-rooting, spreading, perennial, semievergreen.
Flowers Salver-shaped, to 1¼in (30mm) across, borne in heads in early summer. Pale to deep lilac-blue.
Leaves Oval and hairy. Mid-green.
- CULTIVATION 1.
- HEIGHT 14in (35cm).
- SPREAD 20in (50cm).

P. divaricata **subsp.** ***laphamii***

Z 3–9

P. SUBULATA 'G.F. Wilson'
Habit Vigorous, cushion-forming, evergreen, perennial.
Flowers Star-shaped, 1¼in (30mm) wide, borne in lax clusters in late spring and early summer. Deep lavender-blue.
Leaves Linear to elliptic and hairy. Bright green.
- CULTIVATION 2.
- HEIGHT 4in (10cm).
- SPREAD 8in (20cm).

P. subulata
'G.F. Wilson'

Z 2–9

Caryophyllaceae	

GYPSOPHILA REPENS 'Dorothy Teacher'

Habit Mat-forming, semievergreen, perennial. ***Flowers*** Saucer-shaped, ⅝in (15mm) across, borne in sprays in summer. Pale to dark pink. ***Leaves*** Paired, linear or sickle-shaped. Blue-green.

- NATIVE HABITAT Garden origin.
- CULTIVATION Best grown in a rock garden, raised bed, or sunny bank, in light, gritty, sharply drained, and slightly alkaline soil.
- PROPAGATION By division in spring, or take basal cuttings.

Z 3–8

HEIGHT 2in (5cm)

SPREAD to 16in (40cm)

Campanulaceae	

HYPSELA RENIFORMIS

Habit Vigorous, stem-rooting, creeping, perennial. ***Flowers*** Solitary, tubular, with pointed lobes, ⅜in (8mm) across, borne in late spring and summer. White to pale pink, with crimson veins. ***Leaves*** Rounded to kidney-shaped. Bright green.

- NATIVE HABITAT Moist sites, S. America.
- CULTIVATION Tolerates sun or shade, in gritty, fertile soil. Best planted away from small alpines.
- PROPAGATION Divide or sow seed at 43–54°F (6–12°C), both in spring.
- OTHER NAME *H. longiflora.*

Z 7–9

HEIGHT ¾in (2cm)

SPREAD indefinite

Caryophyllaceae	TUNIC FLOWER

PETRORHAGIA SAXIFRAGA

Habit Tufted to mat-forming, semievergreen, perennial. ***Flowers*** Saucer-shaped, ⅜in (1cm) across, borne in delicate clusters during summer. White or pink, with dark pink veins. ***Leaves*** Paired, linear, pointed, grasslike. Deep green.

- NATIVE HABITAT Sandy and rocky sites, southern and central Europe.
- CULTIVATION Prefers gritty, low-fertility soil.
- PROPAGATION Sow seed in autumn, in containers in a cold frame; will self-seed freely.
- OTHER NAME *Tunica saxifraga.*

Z 4–7

HEIGHT 4in (10cm)

SPREAD 8in (20cm)

Geraniaceae	

GERANIUM SANGUINEUM var. *STRIATUM*

Habit Spreading, rhizomatous, part-evergreen, hummock-forming, perennial. ***Flowers*** Saucer-shaped, to 1½in (4cm) across, borne in summer. Pale pink, with deep veins. ***Leaves*** Deeply cut, sparsely toothed. Dark green.

- NATIVE HABITAT Cumbria, United Kingdom.
- CULTIVATION Ideal for borders and rock gardens, in any well-drained, moderately fertile soil.
- PROPAGATION By division in spring.
- OTHER NAME *G. sanguineum* var. *lancastriense.*

☼ ◊

Z 4–8

HEIGHT
4in (10cm)

SPREAD
12in (30cm) or more

Rubiaceae	

ASPERULA SUBEROSA

Habit Soft, clump-forming, spreading, evergreen, perennial. ***Flowers*** Tubular, with spreading lobes, ¼in (6mm) long, borne in clusters in early summer. Pink. ***Leaves*** Small, lance-shaped, hairy, whorled. Gray-green.

- NATIVE HABITAT Mountains, Greece, Bulgaria.
- CULTIVATION Needs sharply drained, moderately fertile soil. Dislikes excessive winter moisture.
- PROPAGATION Divide in spring or autumn, or sow seed in containers in a cold frame, in autumn.
- OTHER NAME *A. athoa* of gardens.

☼ ◊

Z 6–8

HEIGHT
to 3in (8cm)

SPREAD
to 8in (20cm)

Scrophulariaceae	

OURISIA MICROPHYLLA

Habit Cushion-forming, semievergreen, perennial. ***Flowers*** Solitary, salver-shaped, ⅜in (1cm) across, borne in profusion in late spring and early summer. Pale pink, with white eye. ***Leaves*** Heath-like, close to the stems. Pale green.

- NATIVE HABITAT Alpine areas, Chile, Argentina.
- CULTIVATION Grows best in an alpine house. Prefers cool, damp climates, and needs reliably moist but well-drained soil.
- PROPAGATION By seed as soon as ripe or in spring, in a cold frame. Divide in spring.

◑ ♦

Z 7–8

HEIGHT
2in (5cm)

SPREAD
6in (15cm)

Geraniaceae	

ERODIUM CORSICUM

Habit Mat- or cushion-forming perennial. ***Flowers*** Saucer-shaped; ¾in (2cm) across, borne in clusters of 1–3, from late spring to summer. Rose-pink, with darker veins. ***Leaves*** Oval, silver-downy, and crumpled. Gray-green.

- NATIVE HABITAT Sea cliffs, Corsica, Sardinia.
- CULTIVATION Suitable for a trough or raised bed. Needs gritty, sharply drained, neutral to slightly alkaline soil. Protect from winter moisture.
- PROPAGATION Divide in spring, or sow seed in containers in a cold frame as soon as ripe.

☼ ◊

Z 7–9

HEIGHT
3in (8cm)

SPREAD
8in (20cm)

Caryophyllaceae

SAPONARIA x *OLIVANA*

Habit Firm, cushion-forming, evergreen, perennial. ***Flowers*** Solitary, flat, 5-petaled, ⅝in (15mm) across, borne on short stems all over the cushions in summer. Pale pink. ***Leaves*** Narrowly lance-shaped. Mid-green.

- NATIVE HABITAT Garden origin.
- CULTIVATION Suitable for a rock garden, trough, or raised and scree beds. Prefers gritty, sharply drained soil that is neutral to alkaline.
- PROPAGATION Root stem tip cuttings in early summer.

Z 4–7

HEIGHT 2in (5cm)

SPREAD 6in (15cm)

Cruciferae/ Brassicaceae

AETHIONEMA 'Warley Rose'

Habit Compact, tufted, semi- or evergreen, subshrub. ***Flowers*** Cross-shaped, ¼in (7mm) across, borne in clusters in late spring and early summer. Rich pink. ***Leaves*** Linear. Blue-green.

- NATIVE HABITAT Garden origin.
- CULTIVATION Suitable for growing in a rock garden, raised bed, or wall crevice. Needs a site with fertile, well-drained, alkaline soil.
- PROPAGATION Take softwood cuttings in late spring or early summer. Tends to be short-lived, so propagate regularly to maintain stock.

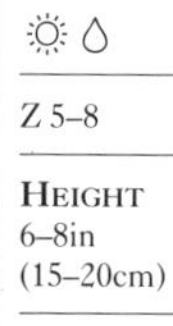

Z 5–8

HEIGHT 6–8in (15–20cm)

SPREAD 6–8in (15–20cm)

Polygonaceae

PERSICARIA AFFINIS 'Donald Lowndes'

Habit Mat-forming, evergreen, perennial. ***Flowers*** Small, cup-shaped, borne in spikes to 3in (8cm) long, in mid- to late summer. Pale pink, deep rose at maturity. ***Leaves*** Lance-shaped. Bright green.

- NATIVE HABITAT Garden origin.
- CULTIVATION Ideal at the base of rockwork. Will thrive in reliably moist soil, in sun or partial shade.
- PROPAGATION By division in spring or autumn.
- OTHER NAME *Polygonum affine* 'Donald Lowndes'.

Z 3–7

HEIGHT to 8in (20cm)

SPREAD 12in (30cm)

Geraniaceae

GERANIUM DALMATICUM

Habit Creeping, rhizomatous, tough-stemmed, semievergreen, perennial. ***Flowers*** Almost flat, to 1⅜in (3.5cm) across, borne in clusters in summer. Pale to bright pink. ***Leaves*** Deeply divided. Glossy, light green.

- NATIVE HABITAT Montenegro and Albania.
- CULTIVATION Suitable for a rock garden, scree bed or at the front of a flower border. Needs sharply drained soil that is rich in organic matter.
- PROPAGATION Divide in spring, or sow seed as soon as ripe, in containers in a cold frame.

Z 4–8

HEIGHT to 6in (15cm)

SPREAD to 20in (50cm) or more

Caryophyllaceae	ALPINE CAMPION, ALPINE CATCHFLY

LYCHNIS ALPINA

Habit Tufted, herbaceous, perennial. ***Flowers*** Saucer-shaped, ¾in (2cm) across, with notched petals, borne in dense, terminal clusters in summer. Bright purplish-pink. ***Leaves*** Oblong to lance-shaped, forming rosettes. Dark green.

• NATIVE HABITAT Montane and subarctic habitats, northern hemisphere.

• CULTIVATION Suitable for a rock garden or raised bed in well-drained, moderately fertile soil.

• PROPAGATION Divide in early spring, or sow seed when ripe in containers in a cold frame.

Z 4–7

HEIGHT
6in (15cm)

SPREAD
6in (15cm)

Labiatae/Lamiaceae	CORSICAN MINT

MENTHA REQUIENII

Habit Creeping, mat-forming, stem-rooting, evergreen, perennial. ***Flowers*** Tiny, two-lipped, 1/12in (2mm) long, borne in whorls in summer. Lilac. ***Leaves*** Strongly peppermint-scented, oval to rounded. Bright green.

• NATIVE HABITAT Sandy areas, Corsica, Sardinia.

• CULTIVATION Ideal for planting in paving crevices. Prefers low-fertility, gritty or sandy soil that is moist but well-drained.

• PROPAGATION Divide in spring or autumn

• OTHER NAME *M. corsica.*

Z 7–9

HEIGHT
to ⅜in (1cm)

SPREAD
indefinite

Asteraceae/Compositae	WALL DAISY

ERIGERON KARVINSKIANUS

Habit Vigorous, rhizomatous, tufted, mounded, evergreen, perennial. ***Flowers*** Daisy, ¾in (2cm) across, borne in summer. White with yellow disc, maturing to pink and purple. ***Leaves*** Oval to lance-shaped, hairy. Gray-green.

• NATIVE HABITAT Mexico and Panama.

• CULTIVATION Ideal for wall crevices and pockets in a rock garden. Needs fertile, well-drained soil.

• PROPAGATION Divide or take basal cuttings in spring. Sow seed in spring in pots in a cold frame.

• OTHER NAME *E. mucronatus.*

Z 6–9

HEIGHT
6–12in (15–30cm)

SPREAD
36in (90cm) or more

Plumbaginaceae	

ACANTHOLIMON GLUMACEUM

Habit Cushion-forming, evergreen, perennial. ***Flowers*** Funnel-shaped, borne in short, dense clusters in summer. Deep pink. ***Leaves*** Spiny, stiff, narrowly lance-shaped, rosetted. Dark green.
• NATIVE HABITAT Caucasus, Turkey, Armenia.
• CULTIVATION Suitable for growing in a rock garden or scree bed. Needs a warm site with very well-drained, moderately fertile soil in full sun.
• PROPAGATION Sow seed as soon as ripe in containers in a cold frame. Layer stem tips into sandy soil mix in spring.

Z 7–9

HEIGHT to 3in (8cm)

SPREAD 8–12in (20–30cm)

Cruciferae/ Brassicaceae	STONE CRESS

AETHIONEMA ARMENUM

Habit Compact, evergreen or semievergreen, subshrub. ***Flowers*** Cross-shaped, ¼in (5mm) across, borne in dense clusters in late spring. Pale pink. ***Leaves*** Linear to oblong. Blue-green.
• NATIVE HABITAT Open sites, mountains of Turkey and the Caucasus.
• CULTIVATION Suitable for a rock garden or wall crevice. Grow in fertile, well-drained, alkaline soil.
• PROPAGATION By softwood cuttings in late spring or early summer, or by seed in spring. Propagate regularly. Will self-sow in favored gardens.

Z 6–9

HEIGHT 6–8in (15–20cm)

SPREAD 6–8in (15–20cm)

Caryophyllaceae	

SAPONARIA CAESPITOSA

Habit Tufted, mat-forming, evergreen, perennial. ***Flowers*** Salver-shaped, ⅜in (1cm) across, borne in few-flowered heads in summer. Pink to purple. ***Leaves*** Narrowly lance-shaped. Mid-green.
• NATIVE HABITAT Pyrenees.
• CULTIVATION Suitable for a rock garden, trough, or raised and scree beds. Needs gritty, sharply drained soil that is neutral to alkaline.
• PROPAGATION Root stem tip cuttings in early summer. Sow seed in containers in a cold frame, in autumn or spring.

Z 4–7

HEIGHT 6in (15cm)

SPREAD 6in (15cm)

Geraniaceae

ERODIUM x *VARIABILE* 'Ken Aslet'

Habit Spreading, mat-or cushion-forming, perennial, with prostrate stems. ***Flowers*** Solitary, single, ⅜in (1cm) across, 5-petaled, borne throughout summer. Deep pink, with darker veins and paler center. ***Leaves*** Oval, scalloped or lobed, heart-shaped at the base. Mid-green.

• NATIVE HABITAT Garden origin. A selection of the hybrid between *E. corsicum* and *E. reichardii*.

• CULTIVATION Suitable for growing in a rock garden, raised bed, or trough, and ideal for planting in the crevices of well-drained paving. Needs a site in full sun with gritty, sharply drained, neutral to alkaline soil that is enriched with organic matter. Protect from excessive winter moisture, with an overhead cloche or glass. Where grown in an alpine house, use a mix of equal parts soil, leaf mold, and grit.

• PROPAGATION By division in spring.

Z 6–9

HEIGHT
4in (10cm)

SPREAD
12in (30cm)

Caryophyllaceae	TUMBLING TED, ROCK SOAPWORT

SAPONARIA OCYMOIDES

Habit Spreading, mat-forming, perennial. ***Flowers*** Flat, 3/8in (1cm) across, borne in loose clusters in summer. Pink. ***Leaves*** Oval to lance-shaped, hairy. Bright green.

- NATIVE HABITAT Mountains, Spain to Yugoslavia.
- CULTIVATION Suitable for a larger rock garden or sunny bank. Needs gritty, sharply drained, neutral to alkaline soil. Trim plant lightly after flowering.
- PROPAGATION Root stem tip cuttings in early summer. Sow seed in containers in a cold frame, in autumn or early spring.

Z 2–7

HEIGHT 3in (8cm)

SPREAD 18in (45cm) or more

Geraniaceae	

GERANIUM CINEREUM 'Ballerina'

Habit Compact, tufted, semievergreen, perennial. ***Flowers*** Upright, saucer-shaped, to 1in (2.5cm) across, borne from late spring to early autumn. Purplish-pink, with darker eye and veins. ***Leaves*** Rounded, deeply lobed. Gray-green.

- NATIVE HABITAT Garden origin.
- CULTIVATION Ideal for rock gardens, raised beds, or on top of dry retaining walls. Needs sharply drained soil that is rich in organic matter.
- PROPAGATION By division or take basal cuttings, both in spring.

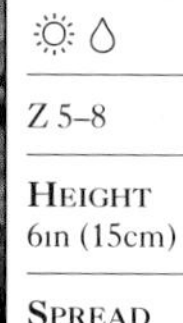

Z 5–8

HEIGHT 6in (15cm)

SPREAD to 12in (30cm)

Rosaceae	PINK CINQUEFOIL

POTENTILLA NITIDA

Habit Tufted, semi-evergreen, perennial. ***Flowers*** Solitary or paired, saucer-shaped, 1in (2.5cm) across, borne in summer. Pale to deep pink, rarely white. ***Leaves*** Three-lobed, with lance-shaped segments. Silver-haired.

- NATIVE HABITAT Alps and Apennines.
- CULTIVATION Suitable for a trough or scree bed. Grows best in low-fertility, sharply drained, gritty soil, but is not always free-flowering.
- PROPAGATION By division in autumn or spring, or sow seed when ripe, in containers in a cold frame.

Z 5–8

HEIGHT to 4in (10cm)

SPREAD 6in (15cm)

Labiatae/Lamiaceae	

TEUCRIUM POLIUM

Habit Semideciduous, mound-forming, subshrub. ***Flowers*** Two-lipped, to 3/8in (1cm) long, borne in flat-topped clusters in summer. Pink-purple, or pale yellow. ***Leaves*** Oblong to lance-shaped, wrinkled and woolly. Gray-green.

- NATIVE HABITAT Mediterranean, western Asia.
- CULTIVATION Prefers a site with poor, gritty soil.
- PROPAGATION By seed as soon as ripe, in containers in a cold frame. Root softwood or semiripe cuttings in early or mid-summer with bottom heat.

Z 6–9

HEIGHT 12in (30cm)

SPREAD 12in (30cm)

Portulacaceae	BITTERROOT

LEWISIA REDIVIVA [Pink form]

Habit Herbaceous, rosette-forming, perennial. ***Flowers*** Broadly funnel-shaped, 2in (5cm) across, with narrow, overlapping petals, borne in early spring and summer. Pink. ***Leaves*** Linear to club-shaped, succulent, dying back after flowering. Dark green.
• NATIVE HABITAT Western Canada, western USA.
• CULTIVATION Grow in pots in an alpine house or in a cold frame, and keep dry after flowering.
• PROPAGATION Sow seed as soon as ripe in containers in a cold frame, in autumn.

Z 3–7

HEIGHT
2in (5cm)

SPREAD
4in (10cm)

Caryophyllaceae	

SILENE SCHAFTA

Habit Clump-forming, semievergreen, perennial. ***Flowers*** Flat, long-tubed, ¾in (2cm) across, with notched petals, borne in open clusters in late summer and autumn. Deep magenta. ***Leaves*** Lance-shaped. Bright green.
• NATIVE HABITAT Subalpine rocks. western Asia.
• CULTIVATION Suitable for growing on a raised bed or at the front of a border. Needs well-drained soil that is neutral to slightly alkaline soil.
• PROPAGATION By seed in containers in a cold frame, in autumn. Take basal cuttings in spring.

Z 4–8

HEIGHT
10in (25cm)

SPREAD
12in (30cm)

Geraniaceae	

GERANIUM CINEREUM var. *SUBCAULESCENS*

Habit Vigorous, tufted, semievergreen, perennial. ***Flowers*** Saucer-shaped, 1in (2.5cm) across, borne in late spring. Brilliant magenta, with black eye. ***Leaves*** Deeply lobed. Dark gray-green.
• NATIVE HABITAT Balkans, northeast Turkey.
• CULTIVATION Suitable for growing in a rock garden or raised bed, in sharply drained soil.
• PROPAGATION Divide or take basal cuttings, in spring. Sow seed in a cold frame in spring.
• OTHER NAME *G. subcaulescens.*

Z 5–8

HEIGHT
6in (15cm)

SPREAD
12in (30cm)

THYMUS

The genus *Thymus*, commonly known as thyme, consists of about 350 species of aromatic evergreen perennials, subshrubs, and shrubs. Many of them suit a rock garden or raised bed, while the prostrate species and cultivars also suit paving crevices, releasing scent when crushed.

Need well-drained, neutral to alkaline, gritty soil in full sun. Trim lightly after flowering to keep compact. Some species, such as *T. cilicicus*, dislike winter moisture and are best grown in an alpine house, in equal parts of soil, leaf mold, and grit.

Take semiripe cuttings in mid- to late summer. Separate self rooted stems and grow on in pots until well-established. Sow seed of species in early spring or autumn, in a cold frame.

T. VULGARIS 'Silver Posie'

Habit Bushy, mound-forming, evergreen, subshrub.
Flowers Two-lipped, borne in rounded clusters in late spring and early summer. Pale mauve.
Leaves Aromatic and oval. Gray-green, with white margins.
• HEIGHT 6–12in (15–30cm).
• SPREAD 12in (30cm).

***T. vulgaris* 'Silver Posie'**

Z 4–8

T. LONGIFLORUS

Habit Densely branched, evergreen, sub-shrub.
Flowers Two-lipped, ⅓in (8mm) long, borne in egg-shaped clusters during summer. Pink, with distinctive greenish-purple bracts.
Leaves Narrow, elliptical to linear, hairy. Grayish-green.
• HEIGHT 12in (30cm).
• SPREAD 10in (25cm).

T. longiflorus
Long-flowered thyme

Z 4–8

T. 'Doone Valley'

Habit Mat-forming, spreading, evergreen, subshrub.
Flowers Two-lipped, borne in rounded clusters during summer. Lavender-pink, opening from red buds.
Leaves Lance-shaped, irregular. Deep olive-green, with yellow spots.
• HEIGHT 5in (12cm).
• SPREAD 14in (35cm).

***T.* 'Doone Valley'**

Z 4–8

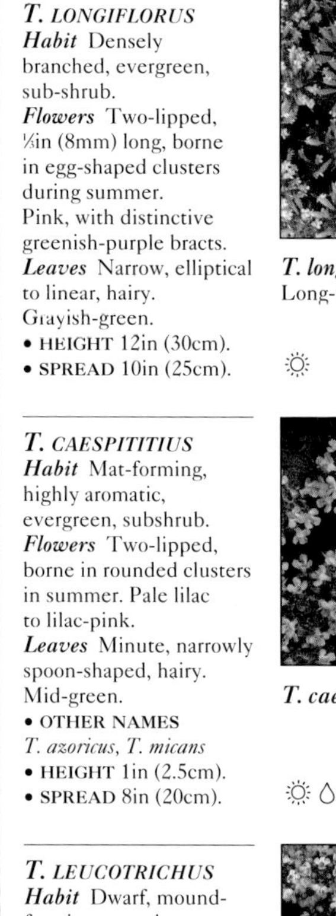

T. CAESPITITIUS

Habit Mat-forming, highly aromatic, evergreen, subshrub.
Flowers Two-lipped, borne in rounded clusters in summer. Pale lilac to lilac-pink.
Leaves Minute, narrowly spoon-shaped, hairy. Mid-green.
• OTHER NAMES *T. azoricus*, *T. micans*
• HEIGHT 1in (2.5cm).
• SPREAD 8in (20cm).

T. caespititius

Z 4–8

T. PULEGIOIDES

Habit Spreading, strongly aromatic, evergreen, subshrub.
Flowers Two-lipped, borne in short, interrupted spikes in late spring and early summer. Pink to purple.
Leaves Oblong to lance-shaped. Mid-green.
• HEIGHT 2–10in (5–25cm).
• SPREAD 12in (30cm).

T. pulegioides
Large thyme

Z 4–8

T. LEUCOTRICHUS

Habit Dwarf, mound-forming, creeping, evergreen, subshrub.
Flowers Two-lipped, borne in large, rounded clusters, in early summer. Pale purplish-pink.
Leaves Narrowly lance-shaped, hairy. Gray-green.
• HEIGHT 6in (15cm).
• SPREAD 8in (20cm).

T. leucotrichus

Z 4–8

T. CILICICUS
Habit Compact, upright, evergreen, subshrub.
Flowers Two-lipped, borne in dense, rounded clusters in early summer. Lilac to mauve.
Leaves Linear, with finely hairy underside and margins. Dark green.

• HEIGHT 6in (15cm).
• SPREAD 8in (20cm).

T. cilicicus

Z 5–8

T. RICHARDII subsp. *NITIDUS* 'Peter Davis'
Habit Dwarf, bushy, free-flowering, evergreen, subshrub.
Flowers Two-lipped, borne in rounded clusters in late spring. Pink.
Leaves Oval and aromatic. Gray-green.
• HEIGHT 6in (15cm).
• SPREAD 6in (15cm).

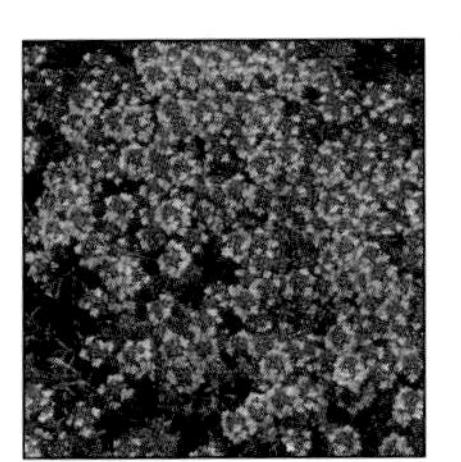

T. richardii subsp. *nitidus* 'Peter Davis'

Z 5–8

T. DOERFLERI 'Bressingham'
Habit Prostrate, mat-forming, evergreen subshrub.
Flowers Two-lipped, borne in lax clusters in summer. Clear pink.
Leaves Linear and very fragrant. Gray-green.
• HEIGHT 4in (10cm).
• SPREAD 14in (35cm).

T. doerfleri 'Bressingham'

Z 4–8

T. SERPYLLUM COCCINEUS
Habit Mat- or mound forming, evergreen, subshrub.
Flowers Two-lipped, borne in rounded clusters in summer. Crimson-pink.
Leaves Elliptical to oval. Mid-green.
• HEIGHT 10in (25cm).
• SPREAD 18in (45cm).

T. serpyllum coccineus

Z 4–8

T. SERPYLLUM 'Annie Hall'
Habit Mat-forming, spreading, evergreen, subshrub.
Flowers Two-lipped, borne in rounded clusters in summer. Purple-pink.
Leaves Elliptical to oval. Pale green.
• HEIGHT 3–4in (8–10cm).
• SPREAD 10in (25cm).

T. serpyllum 'Annie Hall'

Z 4–8

T. HERBA-BARONA
Habit Dwarf, mat-forming, evergreen, perennial.
Flowers Two-lipped, borne in loose, interrupted, oblong or rounded clusters during summer. Pale pink.
Leaves Oval to lance-shaped, caraway-scented. Dark green.
• HEIGHT 4in (10cm).
• SPREAD 8in (20cm).

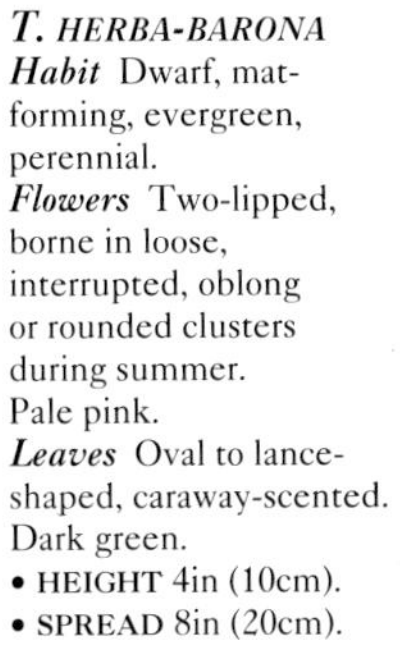

T. herba-barona
Caraway thyme

Z 4–7

T. x *CITRIODORUS*
Habit Rounded, bushy evergreen, shrub.
Flowers Two-lipped, with leaflike bracts, borne in interrupted, oblong clusters during summer. Pale lavender-pink.
Leaves Oval to lance-shaped, lemon-scented. Mid-green.
• HEIGHT 12in (30cm).
• SPREAD 10in (25cm).

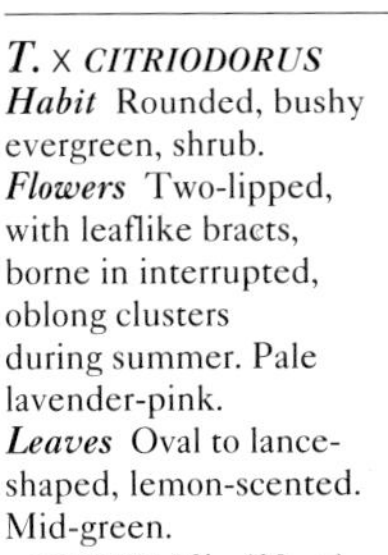

T. x *citriodorus*
Lemon-scented thyme

Z 4–8

OXALIS

The genus *Oxalis*, commonly known as shamrock or sorrel, consists of about 500 species of tuberous, bulbous, fibrous-rooted, or rhizomatous annuals and perennials, some of which are pernicious weeds. Oxalis are widely distributed in the wild, being found in a range of habitats from open sites to woodland. Many of the most ornamental species come from South America and South Africa.

The plants described here are suitable for rock gardens, raised beds, troughs, or pots in an alpine house. The native *Oxalis acetosella* and its cultivars are best grown in a woodland garden, shady border, or naturalized beneath shrubs, as they are generally too invasive for the rock garden. Many of the hardy species, as well as various cultivars are suitable for growing in a rock garden, a raised bed, or a trough. In colder areas, the less-hardy species should be grown in a warm greenhouse.

The cultivated species of *Oxalis* are valued for their silky, widely funnel- or cup-shaped flowers that open from furled umbrella-like buds. In many species, both the flowers and the foliage fold or close up at night and during wet or cloudy weather. The flowers frequently open fully only in sunlight or bright light.

Oxalis should be grown in full sun, with well-drained, moderately fertile soil. In an alpine house, use a mix of equal parts soil, leaf mold, and grit. Keep pot-grown plants just moist when dormant. (Note that *O. lobata* is dormant in summer). *O. acetosella* needs leaf-rich, fertile, moist but well-drained soil that is rich in organic matter, in deep or partial shade.

Propagate by division in spring. Small sections of the rhizomatous species will root readily with bottom heat. Sow seed of species in late winter or early spring, in pots in a cold frame.

O. ENNEAPHYLLA
Habit Tufted, clump-forming, perennial, with short, scaly rhizomes.
Flowers Solitary, scented, funnel-shaped, to 1in (2.5cm) across, borne in spring and early summer. White to red-pink, with deeper veins.
Leaves Pleated, with heart-shaped lobes, fleshy. Blue-gray.
• **HEIGHT** 3in (8cm).
• **SPREAD** 6in (15cm).

O. enneaphylla

Z 7–9

O. ACETOSELLA
Habit Mat-forming, creeping, rhizomatous, perennial.
Flowers Solitary, cup-shaped, to ¾in (2cm) across, borne during spring. White or deep pink, with pale purple veins.
Leaves Cloverlike, with heart-shaped lobes. Pale green.
• **HEIGHT** 2in (5cm).
• **SPREAD** indefinite.

O. acetosella
Wood sorrel

Z 3–7

O. OBTUSA
Habit Mat-forming, rhizomatous, herbaceous, perennial, spreading by runners and bulbils.
Flowers Solitary, funnel-shaped, to ¾in (2cm) wide, borne in spring. Rose-pink, or brick-red, with yellow throat.
Leaves Rounded, with heart-shaped lobes. Gray-green.
• **HEIGHT** 2in (5cm).
• **SPREAD** 8in (20cm).

O. obtusa

Z 7–9

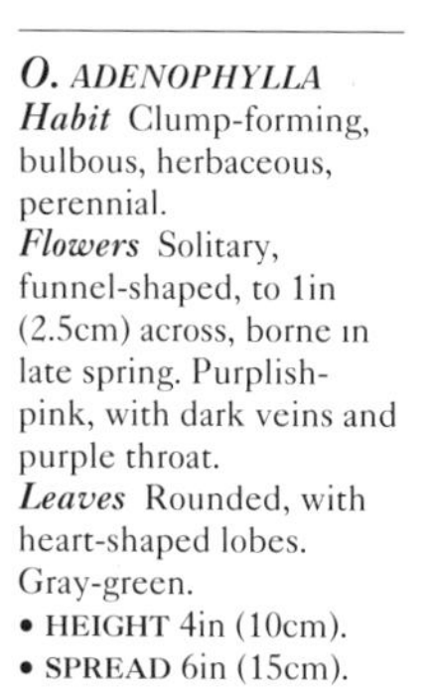

O. ADENOPHYLLA
Habit Clump-forming, bulbous, herbaceous, perennial.
Flowers Solitary, funnel-shaped, to 1in (2.5cm) across, borne in late spring. Purplish-pink, with dark veins and purple throat.
Leaves Rounded, with heart-shaped lobes. Gray-green.
• **HEIGHT** 4in (10cm).
• **SPREAD** 6in (15cm).

O. adenophylla

Z 7–10

O. *ENNEAPHYLLA*
'Rosea'
Habit Tufted, clumping, herbaceous, perennial, with scaly rhizomes.
Flowers Solitary, funnel-shaped, to 1in (2.5cm) across, borne in spring and early summer. Pale purple-pink, with deeper pink veins.
Leaves Umbrella-like, fleshy, with narrowly-oblong and pleated lobes. Blue-gray.
• HEIGHT 3in (8cm).
• SPREAD 6in (15cm).

O. enneaphylla **'Rosea'**

Z 7–9

O. *DEPRESSA*
Habit Clump-forming, bulbous, herbaceous, perennial.
Flowers Solitary, funnel-shaped, to ⅘in (2cm) across, borne during summer. Deep rose-pink.
Leaves Divided, with oval to triangular lobes. Gray-green.
• OTHER NAME *O. inops*.
• HEIGHT 2in (5cm).
• SPREAD 8in (20cm).

O. depressa

Z 4–7

O. *TETRAPHYLLA*
Habit Clump-forming, bulbous, perennial.
Flowers Funnel-shaped, ⅘–1⅕in (2–3cm) across, borne in clustered heads during summer. Deep pink, with yellow-green throat.
Leaves Divided, with heart-shaped lobes. Mid-green with a brown-purple basal band.
• HEIGHT 6in (15cm).
• SPREAD 6in (15cm).

O. tetraphylla
Good luck plant,
Lucky clover

Z 7–9

O. *TETRAPHYLLA*
'Iron Cross'
Habit Clump-forming, bulbous, perennial.
Flowers Funnel-shaped, ⅘–1⅕in (2–3cm) across, borne in clustered heads in summer. Pink, with yellow-green throat.
Leaves Divided, with heart-shaped lobes. Green, with V-shaped, deep-purple basal mark.
• HEIGHT 6in (15cm).
• SPREAD 6in (15cm).

O. tetraphylla
'Iron Cross'

Z 7–9

O. *LOBATA*
Habit Clump-forming, bulbous, herbaceous, perennial.
Flowers Funnel-shaped, to ⅘in (2cm) across, borne during autumn. Bright yellow.
Leaves Divided, with heart-shaped lobes. Bright green.
• OTHER NAME
O. perdicaria.
• HEIGHT 4in (10cm).
• SPREAD 4in (10cm).

O. lobata

Z 7–9

DIANTHUS

The genus *Dianthus* consists of more than 300 species of evergreen subshrubs, perennials, and annuals, including a group of compact, fully hardy, perennial alpine species together with the hybrids and cultivars derived from them. The alpine pinks occur naturally in a range of mountain habitats, from dry, rocky, grassy habitats at low altitude, to scree, moraine, and rock crevices at high altitude. Most are found on limestone rocks and prefer slightly alkaline soils, but will tolerate neutral to slightly acid conditions. The smaller pinks are ideal for rock gardens and scree beds, and especially for the tops of dry-stone, retaining walls, raised beds, and troughs, where those with a strong fragrance can be appreciated at close range. The more vigorous varieties can also be used for edging along borders and paths, or in scree plantings. Most alpine pinks have a neat, cushion- or mat-forming habit, with paired, linear to narrowly lance-shaped leaves, which are often gray- or silvery-green and sometimes stiff and prickly. Alpine pinks are particularly valued for their flowers, which are borne in summer and range from ⅖–1⅗in (1–4cm) across. The flowers are either solitary or borne in few-flowered clusters, and may be single, semidouble, or double.

Grow in a gritty, well-drained, moderately fertile, neutral to alkaline soil, in full sun. *D. pavonius* and *D. microlepis* prefer acid soils that are rich in organic matter. Deadhead to keep the plant vigorous and neat, unless seed is needed for propagation.

Sow seed of alpine species from autumn to early spring, in pots in a cold frame. Cultivars will not always come true. Take cuttings of nonflowering shoots, or Irishman's cuttings (see p.172) of self-layering, mat-forming types in summer.

D. 'Pike's Pink'
Habit Compact, cushion-forming, evergreen, perennial.
Flowers Solitary, double, about 1in (2.5cm) across, clove-scented, borne in summer. Pale pink, with darker base.
Leaves Narrowly lance-shaped, sharply pointed. Gray-green.
- **HEIGHT** 6in (15cm).
- **SPREAD** 6in (15cm).

D. 'Pike's Pink'

☼ ◊ Z 4–8

D. ERINACEUS
Habit Dense cushion-forming, evergreen, perennial.
Flowers Solitary or paired, often sparse, ½in (15mm) across, with toothed and bearded petals, borne on short stems in summer. Pink.
Leaves Stiff and linear to narrowly lance-shaped, sharply pointed. Mid-green.
- **HEIGHT** 2in (5cm).
- **SPREAD** 20in (50cm) or more.

D. erinaceus

☼ ◊ Z 5–8

D. MICROLEPIS
Habit Compact, cushion-forming, evergreen, perennial.
Flowers Solitary, ⅝in (15mm) across, with slightly toothed petals, borne during early summer. Pink or purple.
Leaves Linear, soft. Silver-gray to green.
- HEIGHT 2in (5cm).
- SPREAD 6in (15cm).

D. microlepis

Z 3–7

D. 'Little Jock'
Habit Cushion-forming, evergreen, perennial.
Flowers Solitary, semidouble, strongly scented, about 1in (2.5cm) across, with fringed petals, borne in summer. Pale pink, with maroon eye.
Leaves Pointed and narrowly lance-shaped. Gray-green.
- HEIGHT 4in (10cm).
- SPREAD 4in (10cm).

D. **'Little Jock'**

Z 3–7

D. MYRTINERVIS
Habit Dense, evergreen, mat-forming, perennial.
Flowers Solitary, ⅜in (1cm) across, borne just above the leaves in summer. Deep pink, with paler eye.
Leaves Tiny and elliptical to oblong. Bright green.
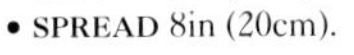
- TIPS Best grown in a scree bed or trough.
- HEIGHT 2in (5cm).
- SPREAD 8in (20cm).

D. myrtinervis

Z 5–8

D. 'La Bourboule'
Habit Compact, tuft-forming or matted, evergreen, perennial.
Flowers Strongly scented, ⅝–¾in (1.5–2cm) across, borne in clusters in summer. Clear pink.
Leaves Narrowly lance-shaped and pointed, but soft. Grayish-green.
- OTHER NAME *D.* 'La Bourbille'.
- HEIGHT 2in (5cm).
- SPREAD 3in (8cm).

D. **'La Bourboule'**

Z 3–7

D. CARTHUSIANORUM
Habit Tufted, evergreen, perennial,
Flowers Solitary, to ¾in (2cm) across, with toothed, bearded petals, borne in clusters during summer. Dark red-pink, or white.
Leaves Linear, soft. Pale green.
- HEIGHT to 16in (40cm).
- SPREAD 8–12in (20–30cm).

D. carthusianorum
Carthusian pink

Z 3–7

D. GRATIANOPOLITANUS
Habit Mat-forming, evergreen, perennial.
Flowers Solitary, strong-scented, to 1¼in (3cm) across, with bearded, toothed petals, borne in summer. Deep pink.
Leaves Linear, soft. Gray-green.
- OTHER NAME *D. caesius*.
- HEIGHT 6in (15cm).
- SPREAD 16in (40cm).

D. gratianopolitanus
Cheddar pink

Z 5–8

D. ALPINUS

Habit Cushion- or mat-forming, evergreen, perennial.
Flowers Solitary, to 1½in (4cm) wide, with bearded, toothed petals, borne in summer. Deep pink to crimson, with paler spots.
Leaves Narrow-oblong, blunt, soft, and glossy. Dark green.
• TIPS Needs gritty soil that is rich in organic matter.
• HEIGHT 3in (8cm).
• SPREAD 10in (25cm).

D. alpinus
Alpine pink

Z 3–7

D. PAVONIUS

Habit Mat-forming, evergreen, perennial.
Flowers Solitary, to 1¼in (3cm) across, with toothed, bearded petals, borne in summer. Pale to deep pink, with buff reverse.
Leaves Pointed and linear. Gray-green.
• OTHER NAME *D. neglectus*.
• HEIGHT 3in (8cm).
• SPREAD to 8in (20cm).

D. pavonius

Z 3–7

D. DELTOIDES 'Leuchtfunk'

Habit Mat-forming, evergreen, perennial.
Flowers Solitary, ¾in (2cm) across, with toothed, bearded petals, borne in summer. Cerise.
Leaves Narrowly lance-shaped, soft. Dark green.
• OTHER NAME *D.* 'Flashing Light'.
• HEIGHT 8in (20cm).
• SPREAD 12in (30cm) or more.

***D. deltoides* 'Leuchtfunk'**

Z 3–7

D. 'Annabelle'

Habit Compact, clump-forming, free-flowering, evergreen, perennial.
Flowers Solitary, double, strongly scented, about ¾in (2cm) across, borne in summer. Cerise-pink.
Leaves Linear, pointed, soft. Gray-green.
• HEIGHT 4in (10cm).
• SPREAD 4in (10cm).

***D.* 'Annabelle'**

Z 3–7

D. ALPINUS 'Joan's Blood'

Habit Cushion- or mat-forming, evergreen, perennial.
Flowers Solitary, 1½in (4cm) wide, with bearded, toothed petals, borne during summer. Deep magenta.
Leaves Linear to lance-shaped. Dark green.
• HEIGHT 3in (8cm).
• SPREAD 4in (10cm).

***D. alpinus* 'Joan's Blood'**

Z 3–7

Plumbaginaceae	

ARMERIA MARITIMA 'Vindictive'

Habit Cushion-forming, evergreen, perennial. ***Flowers*** Small, cup-shaped, borne on stiff stems in dense, rounded heads to ¾in (2cm) across, in late spring and summer. Deep rose-pink. ***Leaves*** Linear. Dark green.

• NATIVE HABITAT Garden origin.

• CULTIVATION Good for growing in a rock garden or as path edging. Needs well-drained, poor or moderately fertile soil in an open site.

• PROPAGATION Divide in early spring, or root basal cuttings in summer.

Z 3–7

HEIGHT 8in (20cm)

SPREAD 12in (30cm)

Globulariaceae	GLOBE DAISY

GLOBULARIA MERIDIONALIS

Habit Mat-forming, evergreen, subshrub. ***Flowers*** Tiny, 2-lipped, borne in dense heads to ¾in (2cm) across, in summer. Lavender. ***Leaves*** Lance-shaped, leathery, glossy. Dark green.

• NATIVE HABITAT Southeast Alps, central and southern Apennines, and Greece.

• CULTIVATION Grows best in troughs or on raised beds, with sharply drained, neutral to alkaline soil.

• PROPAGATION By seed in autumn in containers under a cold frame, or root rosettes in spring.

• OTHER NAMES *G. bellidifolia*, *G. pygmaea*.

Z 5–7

HEIGHT to 4in (10cm)

SPREAD to 12in (30cm)

Dipsacaceae	

PTEROCEPHALUS PERENNIS

Habit Mat-forming, evergreen, perennial. ***Flowers*** Tubular, borne in dense, flattened, scabiouslike heads to 1½in (4cm) across, in summer. Pale pink-purple. ***Leaves*** Oval, scalloped, hairy. Gray-green.

• NATIVE HABITAT Dry, rocky slopes, Greece.

• CULTIVATION Suitable for growing in a rock garden or raised bed. Tolerates well-drained soil in full sun, but dislikes very acid soils.

• PROPAGATION By seed in pots in a cold frame in autumn, or by stem-tip cuttings in summer.

• OTHER NAME *P. parnassia*.

Z 5–8

HEIGHT 3in (8cm)

SPREAD 8in (20cm)

Campanulaceae	

PHYSOPLEXIS COMOSA

Habit Tufted, herbaceous, perennial. ***Flowers*** Bottle-shaped, borne in rounded, terminal clusters, to ¾in (2cm) across, in summer. Pale violet with dark violet tips. ***Leaves*** Oval to heart-shaped and deeply toothed. Dark green.

• NATIVE HABITAT Rocks, southeastern Alps.

• CULTIVATION Grows best in pots in an alpine house, or in troughs or on tufa outdoors. Very susceptible to slug damage.

• PROPAGATION By seed in a cold frame in autumn.

• OTHER NAME *Phyteuma comosum*.

Z 5–7

HEIGHT 3in (8cm)

SPREAD 4in (10cm)

Labiatae/Lamiaceae	LARGE SELF-HEAL

PRUNELLA GRANDIFLORA

Habit Vigorous, semievergreen, perennial. ***Flowers*** Two-lipped, to 1¼in (3cm) long, borne in dense whorls on upright stems; during summer. Purple. ***Leaves*** Paired, oval to lance-shaped and toothed. Dark green.
- NATIVE HABITAT Woods and meadows, Europe.
- CULTIVATION Tolerates any soil in sun or part shade. Good as groundcover but invasive so avoid siting near smaller plants. Self-seeds freely.
- PROPAGATION Divide in spring or autumn, or sow seed at 43–54°F (6–12°C) in spring.

Z 5–8

HEIGHT 6in (15cm)

SPREAD 3ft (90cm) or more

Compositae/Asteraceae	ALPINE ASTER

ASTER ALPINUS

Habit Clump-forming, spreading, semi-evergreen, perennial. ***Flowers*** Solitary, daisylike, to 2in (5cm) across, borne on upright stems in early to mid-summer. Violet, with a yellow disc. ***Leaves*** Spoon- to narrowly lance-shaped. Mid-green.
- NATIVE HABITAT Meadows, stony places, Alps.
- CULTIVATION Suitable for planting in a large rock garden or at the front of a flower border. Prefers a site with well-drained soil.
- PROPAGATION Sow seed in pots in a cold frame or divide, both in early spring or autumn.

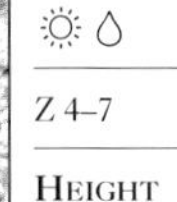

Z 4–7

HEIGHT to 10in (25cm)

SPREAD 18in (45cm)

Campanulaceae	GRASSY BELLS

EDRAIANTHUS SERPYLLIFOLIUS

Habit Tufted, mat-forming, evergreen, perennial. ***Flowers*** Solitary, erect, bell-shaped, to ¾in (2cm) long, borne in early summer. Deep violet. ***Leaves*** Linear to spoon-shaped. Dark green.
- NATIVE HABITAT Mountains of Croatia, Bosnia and Albania.
- CULTIVATION Grow in light, sharply drained alkaline soil. Protect from excess winter moisture.
- PROPAGATION Sow seed in an open frame in autumn, or take stem-tip cuttings in early summer.
- OTHER NAME *Wahlenbergia serpyllifolia.*

Z 4–7

HEIGHT 2in (5cm)

SPREAD 6in (15cm)

Leguminosae/ Papilionaceae	

PAROCHETUS COMMUNIS

Habit Tuberous-rooted, carpeting, perennial. ***Flowers*** Pea, solitary or paired, 1in (2.5cm) across, borne in succession from late summer to autumn. Bright blue. ***Leaves*** Clover-like, with heart-shaped leaflets. Mid-green, with bronze markings.
- NATIVE HABITAT Himalaya and southwest China.
- CULTIVATION Needs moist but well-drained soil, and protection from excessive winter moisture.
- PROPAGATION By division or separation of rooted runners in spring. Needs to be propagated regularly as it tends to be short-lived.

Z 8–10

HEIGHT 4in (10cm)

SPREAD 12in (30cm) or more

Campanulaceae

CYANANTHUS MICROPHYLLUS

Habit Mat-forming, stout-rooted, herbaceous, perennial. ***Flowers*** Solitary, broad funnel-shaped, 1in (2.5cm) across, borne in late summer. Violet-blue. ***Leaves*** Oval to oblong. Dark green.
• NATIVE HABITAT Nepal to southeast Tibet.
• CULTIVATION Grows best in a peat bed or rock garden with moderately fertile, moist but well-drained soil that is neutral to slightly acid.
• PROPAGATION By softwood cuttings in late spring or early summer. Sow seed as soon as ripe or in early spring, in containers in a cold frame.

Z 5–7

HEIGHT
1in (2.5cm)

SPREAD
to 10in (25cm)

Campanulaceae

EDRAIANTHUS PUMILIO

Habit Cushion-forming, evergreen, perennial. ***Flowers*** Solitary, erect, bell-shaped, ⅜in (1cm) long, borne in early summer. Pale to deep violet. ***Leaves*** Linear and finely haired. Silver-green.
• NATIVE HABITAT Mountains of southern Croatia.
• CULTIVATION Grow in light, sharply drained alkaline soil. Protect the overwintering buds from excessive moisture.
• PROPAGATION Sow seed in pots in a cold frame in autumn, or take stem-tip cuttings in early summer.
• OTHER NAME *Wahlenbergia pumilio.*

Z 4–7

HEIGHT
1in (2.5cm)

SPREAD
to 6in (15cm)

Gesneriaceae

RAMONDA MYCONI

Habit Rosette-forming, evergreen, perennial. ***Flowers*** Flat, 5-petaled, 1in (2.5cm) across, borne in late spring and early summer. Violet-blue or pink, with yellow anthers. ***Leaves*** Leathery, oval, crinkled. Dark green, with rusty hairs underneath.
• NATIVE HABITAT Pyrenees, northeast Spain.
• CULTIVATION Plant between peat blocks, or sideways in crevices. Dislikes winter moisture.
• PROPAGATION By leaf cuttings in early autumn, or by ripe seed in a shaded, cold frame.
• OTHER NAME *R. pyrenaica.*

Z 5–7

HEIGHT
4in (10cm)

SPREAD
8in (20cm)

Iridaceae

SISYRINCHIUM IDAHOENSE

Habit Semievergreen, tufted, perennial. ***Flowers*** Star-shaped, to 1in (2.5cm) across, borne on erect stems during summer. Deep violet-blue, with yellow throat. ***Leaves*** Sword-shaped. Mid-green.
• NATIVE HABITAT Mountains, across the USA.
• CULTIVATION Prefers a site with gritty, poor or moderately fertile soil that is neutral to alkaline.
• PROPAGATION Sow seed in containers in a cold frame in autumn or early spring. Self-seeds freely.
• OTHER NAMES *S. bellum* of gardens, *S. macounii.*

Z 7–8

HEIGHT
5in (12cm)

SPREAD
6in (15cm)

Globulariaceae	GLOBE DAISY

GLOBULARIA CORDIFOLIA

Habit Mat-forming, evergreen, perennial. ***Flowers*** Tiny, two-lipped, borne in stemless, rounded heads, to ¾in (2cm) across, in summer. Lavender-blue. ***Leaves*** Spoon-shaped, glossy, notched at the tip. Dark green.

• NATIVE HABITAT Rocky, mountain habitats, central and southern Europe, and western Turkey.

• CULTIVATION Grow in sharply drained, neutral to alkaline soil, in a rock garden or retaining wall.

• PROPAGATION By seed in autumn in containers in a cold frame, or root rosettes in spring.

Z 5–7

HEIGHT to 2in (5cm)

SPREAD to 8in (20cm)

Compositae/Asteraceae	

TOWNSENDIA GRANDIFLORA

Habit Short-lived, evergreen, perennial or biennial. ***Flowers*** Daisy-head, 1¼in (3cm) across, borne in summer. Violet-blue, with a greenish-yellow disc. ***Leaves*** Elliptical and leathery. Dark green, bronze-tinted.

• NATIVE HABITAT Central USA.

• CULTIVATION Suitable for growing in pots in an alpine house. Needs gritty, sharply drained soil and protection from excessive winter moisture.

• PROPAGATION Sow seed as soon as ripe or in early spring, in containers under a cold frame.

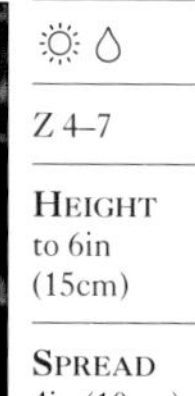

Z 4–7

HEIGHT to 6in (15cm)

SPREAD 4in (10cm)

Boraginaceae	

OMPHALODES LUCILIAE

Habit Semievergreen, perennial. ***Flowers*** Forget-me-not-like, to ⅓in (8mm) across, borne in terminal sprays in summer. Clear pale blue, opening from pink buds. ***Leaves*** Oval or oblong. Pale gray-blue.

• NATIVE HABITAT Greece, Turkey, western Iran.

• CULTIVATION Grows best in tufa or very gritty, sharply drained, alkaline soil in troughs and raised beds. Very susceptible to slug damage.

• PROPAGATION Divide in early spring, or sow seed in spring, in containers in a cold frame.

Z 6–7

HEIGHT 4in (10cm)

SPREAD to 6in (15cm)

Campanulaceae	

PRATIA PEDUNCULATA

Habit Prostrate, stem-rooting, invasive, evergreen, perennial. ***Flowers*** Star-shaped, ¼in (6mm) across, borne in summer. Pale blue. ***Leaves*** Oval to rounded. Bright green.

- NATIVE HABITAT Damp, shady places, Australia.
- CULTIVATION Good for paving crevices and as low groundcover in a rock garden. Prefers fertile, loamy, moist but well-drained soil.
- PROPAGATION Divide during the growing season or take self-rooted cuttings in spring and summer.
- OTHER NAME *Lobelia pedunculata.*

Z 5–7

HEIGHT
1/2in
(15mm)

SPREAD
indefinite

Campanulaceae	

TRACHELIUM ASPERULOIDES

Habit Cushion-forming, evergreen, perennial. ***Flowers*** Star-shaped, ¼in (6mm) across, borne in late summer. Lavender-blue or white. ***Leaves*** Small, rounded, overlapping. Glossy mid-green.

- NATIVE HABITAT Southern Greece.
- CULTIVATION Grows best in a pot in an alpine house. Outdoors, grow in a trough with sharply drained, alkaline soil. Avoid winter moisture.
- PROPAGATION Sow seed as soon as ripe in containers in a cold frame.
- OTHER NAME *Diosphaera asperuloides.*

Z 5–7

HEIGHT
to 2in
(5cm)

SPREAD
to 6in
(15cm)

Rubiaceae	CREEPING BLUETS

HEDYOTIS MICHAUXII

Habit Mat-forming, stem-rooting, evergreen, perennial. ***Flowers*** Salver-shaped, 4–10 lobed, to ⅜in (1cm) across, borne in late spring and early summer. Pale blue, with white eye. ***Leaves*** Rounded to oval. Glossy-green.

- NATIVE HABITAT Damp woods and rocks, USA.
- CULTIVATION Grow in moist but well-drained, preferably acid soil that is rich in organic matter.
- PROPAGATION Divide in spring or autumn, or sow seed in spring in containers under a cold frame.
- OTHER NAME *H. serpyllifolia.*

pH

Z 5–8

HEIGHT
3in (7cm)

SPREAD
to 12in
(30cm)
or more

Polygalaceae	

POLYGALA CALCAREA 'Bulley's Form'

Habit Creeping, prostrate, evergreen, subshrub. ***Flowers*** Pea-like, ¼in (6mm) long, borne in terminal clusters, to 1¼in (3cm) long, in late spring to early summer. Intense, deep blue, with white fringed lip. ***Leaves*** Oval and leathery. Mid-green.
• NATIVE HABITAT Garden origin.
• CULTIVATION Good for a rock garden or trough, in sharply drained, moderately fertile soil.
• PROPAGATION By softwood cuttings in early summer, or by semiripe ones in mid- to late summer.

Z 5–7

HEIGHT
2in (5cm)

SPREAD
to 8in (20cm)

Polygalaceae	CHALK MILKWORT

POLYGALA CALCAREA

Habit Creeping, prostrate, evergreen, subshrub. ***Flowers*** Pea-like, ¼in (6mm) long, borne in terminal clusters, to 1¼in (3cm) long, in late spring and early summer. Deep blue, with a white, fringed lip. ***Leaves*** Oval and leathery. Mid-green.
• NATIVE HABITAT Grassland, western Europe.
• CULTIVATION Good for a rock garden or trough, in sharply drained, moderately fertile soil.
• PROPAGATION By softwood cuttings in early summer, or by semiripe ones in mid- to late summer. By seed in autumn in a cold frame.

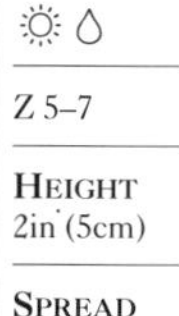

Z 5–7

HEIGHT
2in (5cm)

SPREAD
to 8in (20cm)

Gunneraceae	

GUNNERA MAGELLANICA

Habit Carpeting, perennial. ***Flowers*** Tiny, borne in oblong clusters, ⅝–5in (1.5–12cm) long, in summer. Green. ***Fruits*** Very small, egg-shaped to rounded. Red. ***Leaves*** Kidney-shaped, cupped, and scalloped. Shiny, dark green.
• NATIVE HABITAT Damp habitats, S. America and Falkland Islands.
• CULTIVATION Grow in moist, fertile soil in part shade. Prefers a site in areas with cool summers.
• PROPAGATION Divide in spring, or sow seed as soon as ripe. Keep cool but frost-free in winter.

Z 5–7

HEIGHT
6in (15cm)

SPREAD
12in (30cm) or more

Saxifragaceae	

MITELLA BREWERI

Habit Clump-forming, rhizomatous, evergreen, perennial. ***Flowers*** Tiny, bell-shaped, with fringed petals, borne in spikes ¾–1½in (2–4cm) long in late spring and early summer. Yellow-green. ***Leaves*** Broadly oval, hairy, lobed. Mid-green.
• NATIVE HABITAT Western to central N. America.
• CULTIVATION Suitable for growing in a peat bed, woodland garden, or shady corner of a rock garden. Needs moist but well-drained, leaf-rich, acid soil.
• PROPAGATION Divide in spring, or sow seed in autumn, in containers in a cold frame.

pH

Z 5–7

HEIGHT
6in (15cm)

SPREAD
8in (20cm)

Scrophulariaceae	CREEPING SNAPDRAGON

ASARINA PROCUMBENS

Habit Trailing, evergreen, perennial. ***Flowers*** Snapdragon-like, 2-lipped, to 1½in (3.5cm) long, borne in summer. Pale yellow, with darker throat and purple veins. ***Leaves*** Paired, shallowly lobed, kidney-shaped, sticky-haired. Gray-green.
• NATIVE HABITAT Shady rocks, Pyrenees.
• CULTIVATION Suitable over rocks and walls, or beneath conifers. Needs well-drained, sandy soil.
• PROPAGATION By seed at 61°F (16°C) in early spring, or by tip-cuttings in summer.
• OTHER NAME *Antirrhinum asarina.*

Z 6–8

HEIGHT 2in (5cm)

SPREAD to 24in (60cm)

Polygalaceae	SHRUBBY MILKWORT

POLYGALA CHAMAEBUXUS

Habit Dwarf, spreading, evergreen, shrub. ***Flowers*** Pea-like, ⅝in (15mm) long, borne in late spring and early summer. Yellow, maturing to brown-crimson, with white or yellow wings. ***Leaves*** Lance-shaped and leathery. Dark green.
• NATIVE HABITAT Western central Europe.
• CULTIVATION Good for growing in a rock garden, in sharply drained, moderately fertile soil.
• PROPAGATION By softwood cuttings in early summer, by semiripe ones in mid- to late summer, or by seed in autumn or early spring.

Z 5–7

HEIGHT 2–6in (5–15cm)

SPREAD to 12in (30cm)

Papaveraceae	

PAPAVER FAURIEI

Habit Short-lived, tufted, semievergreen, annual or perennial. ***Flowers*** Solitary, bowl-shaped, ⅘–1¼in (2–3cm) across, borne in summer. Pale yellow to greenish-yellow. ***Leaves*** Lance-shaped and deeply lobed, bristly. Gray-green.
• NATIVE HABITAT N. Kurile Islands and Japan.
• CULTIVATION Grow in a site with moderately fertile, sharply drained soil, and protect from excessive winter moisture.
• PROPAGATION By seed in spring in a cold frame.
• OTHER NAME *P. miyabeanum* of gardens.

Z 6–9

HEIGHT to 4in (10cm)

SPREAD to 4in (10cm)

Labiatae/Lamiaceae	

SCUTELLARIA ORIENTALIS

Habit Rhizomatous, woody-based, evergreen, mat-forming, perennial. ***Flowers*** Two-lipped, ⅝–1⅛in (1.5–3cm) long, borne in 4-angled clusters on hairy stems, in summer. Bright yellow, often with red lips. ***Leaves*** Oblong to broadly oval, toothed. Dark gray-green.
- NATIVE HABITAT Mountains, southeast Europe.
- CULTIVATION Suits a rock garden or border in light, gritty, well-drained, neutral to alkaline soil.
- PROPAGATION Sow seed in autumn in containers in a cold frame, or divide in spring.

Z 5–8

HEIGHT 10in (25cm)

SPREAD 12in (30cm)

Onagraceae	OZARK SUNDROPS

OENOTHERA MACROCARPA

Habit Vigorous, evergreen, perennial, with trailing, red-tinted stems. ***Flowers*** Solitary, cup-shaped, to 5in (12.5cm) across, borne in succession from late spring to early autumn. Bright yellow. ***Leaves*** Lance-shaped, toothed. Pale to mid-green.
- NATIVE HABITAT Rocky areas, USA.
- CULTIVATION Suitable for a sunny bank or scree bed. Prefers poor, gritty, sandy, or stony soils.
- PROPAGATION By seed in spring, in pots in a cold frame, or by stem tip cuttings in summer.
- OTHER NAME *O. missouriensis.*

Z 4–7

HEIGHT 6in (15cm)

SPREAD to 20in (50cm)

Compositae/Asteraceae	

ERIGERON AUREUS 'Canary Bird'

Habit Mound-forming, evergreen, perennial. ***Flowers*** Solitary, daisy, ¾in (2cm) across, borne in summer. Bright canary-yellow. ***Leaves*** Broadly oval to spoon-shaped, leathery, hairy. Gray-green.
- NATIVE HABITAT Garden origin.
- CULTIVATION Ideal in pots in an alpine house. Outdoors, suits scree or raised beds and troughs. Needs moist but sharply drained soil and protection from excessive winter moisture.
- PROPAGATION By division or basal cuttings, both in spring.

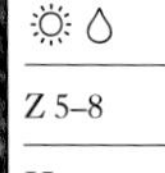

Z 5–8

HEIGHT 4in (10cm)

SPREAD 6in (15cm)

Rosaceae	

POTENTILLA ERIOCARPA

Habit Carpet-forming, rhizomatous, semi-evergreen, perennial. ***Flowers*** Saucer-shaped, to 1½in (4cm) across, borne singly or in small clusters in early summer. Deep yellow. ***Leaves*** Divided, toothed, wedge-shaped. Bright green.
- NATIVE HABITAT Himalaya, western China.
- CULTIVATION Suitable for growing in a rock garden, at the foot of rock work or at the front of a border. Needs gritty, well-drained soil.
- PROPAGATION By division or seed in containers in a cold frame, both in autumn and spring.

Z 5–7

HEIGHT 3in (8cm)

SPREAD 12in (30cm)

Linaceae	

LINUM FLAVUM 'Compactum'

Habit Compact, upright, woody-based, evergreen, perennial. ***Flowers*** Upward-facing, funnel-shaped, to 1in (2.5cm) across, borne in dense branched, terminal clusters, opening in full sunshine, during summer. Flowers are individually short-lived, but are produced in succession over long periods. Bright yellow. ***Leaves*** Spoon- to lance-shaped. Dark green.

• NATIVE HABITAT Garden origin. The species is found in scrub and on dry grassy slopes, in the hills and mountains of central and southern Europe.

• CULTIVATION Grow in light, moderately fertile, well-drained soil that is rich in organic matter, in a warm, sunny, sheltered site. Protect from excessive winter moisture.

• PROPAGATION Sow seed in autumn or spring, in containers under a cold frame. Take stem-tip cuttings in early summer. Propagate regularly since they are often short-lived.

☼ ◊

Z 4–8

HEIGHT
6in (15cm)

SPREAD
6in (20cm)

ANEMONE

The genus *Anemone* consists of about 120 species of perennials, most of which suit growing in flower borders. For ease of reference, their cultivation requirements may be grouped as follows:

Group 1 Moist but well-drained soil, enriched with organic matter, in partial shade. Tolerate drier conditions when dormant in summer.

Group 2 Well-drained soil that is enriched with organic matter, in sun or partial shade.

Group 3 Light, sandy soil in full sun.

Sow seed of species when fresh in containers in a cold frame. Divide rhizomatous species in spring or after the leaves have faded. Separate tubers when dormant in summer.

A. NEMOROSA 'Bracteata Pleniflora'

Habit Rhizomatous, patch-forming, herbaceous, perennial.
Flowers Star-shaped, semidouble, borne in late spring. White, often with a green ruff.
Leaves Deeply divided. Mid-green.
• **CULTIVATION** 1 or 2.
• **HEIGHT** 5in (12cm).
• **SPREAD** 12in (30cm).

A. nemorosa **'Bracteata Pleniflora'**

Z 4–8

A. BLANDA 'White Splendour'

Habit Tuberous, herbaceous, perennial.
Flowers Solitary, star-shaped, 2in (5cm) across, borne during spring. White, with a pink tint on the outside.
Leaves Deeply divided. Dark green.
• **CULTIVATION** 1 or 2.
• **HEIGHT** 6in (15cm).
• **SPREAD** 6in (15cm).

A. blanda **'White Splendour'**

Z 4–8

A. MULTIFIDA

Habit Vigorous, clump-forming, semievergreen, perennial.
Flowers Cupped, 1in (2.5cm) wide, borne in sprays of 2–3 in summer. Creamy-yellow.
Leaves Rounded, lobed, Shiny, deep green.
• **CULTIVATION** 2.
• **OTHER NAMES** *A. globosa, A. magellanica.*
• **HEIGHT** 12in (30cm).
• **SPREAD** 6in (15cm).

A. multifida

Z 2–6

A. x *LIPSIENSIS*

Habit Rhizomatous, herbaceous, perennial.
Flowers Solitary, flat, to ¾in (2cm) across, borne in spring. Creamy-yellow.
Leaves Rounded and deeply lobed. Mid-green.
• **CULTIVATION** 1 or 2.
• **OTHER NAMES** *A.* x *intermedia, A.* x *seemannii.*
• **HEIGHT** 2–6in (5–15cm).
• **SPREAD** to 18in (45cm).

A.* x *lipsiensis

Z 3–7

A. BLANDA 'Radar'

Habit Tuberous, herbaceous, perennial.
Flowers Solitary, flattened star-shaped, 1½in (4cm) across, borne in spring. Rich magenta, with white center.
Leaves Deeply divided. Dark green.
• **CULTIVATION** 1 or 2.
• **HEIGHT** 6in (15cm).
• **SPREAD** 6in (15cm).

A. blanda **'Radar'**

Z 4–8

A. HORTENSIS

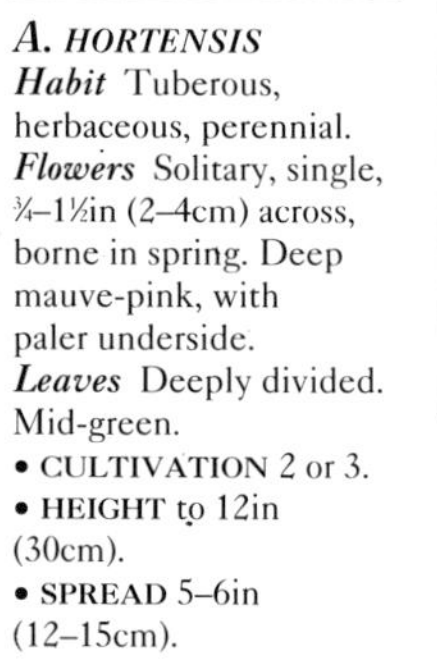

Habit Tuberous, herbaceous, perennial.
Flowers Solitary, single, ¾–1½in (2–4cm) across, borne in spring. Deep mauve-pink, with paler underside.
Leaves Deeply divided. Mid-green.
• **CULTIVATION** 2 or 3.
• **HEIGHT** to 12in (30cm).
• **SPREAD** 5–6in (12–15cm).

A. hortensis

Z 6–9

A. *PAVONINA*
Habit Tuberous, herbaceous, perennial.
Flowers Solitary, saucer-shaped, 1¼–4in (2–10cm) across, borne in early to mid-spring. Pink, red, or purple, often white-eyed.
Leaves Deeply divided. Mid- to dark green.
- CULTIVATION 2 OR 3.
- HEIGHT 10in (25cm).
- SPREAD 6in (15cm).

A. pavonina
Peacock anemone

Z 6–9

A. *NEMOROSA* 'Robinsoniana'
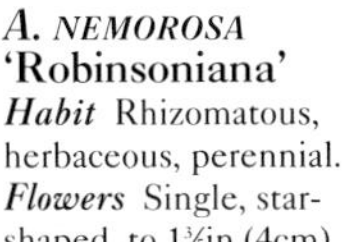
Habit Rhizomatous, herbaceous, perennial.
Flowers Single, star-shaped, to 1½in (4cm) across, borne in spring. Soft mid-blue, with blue-gray reverse.
Leaves Deeply divided. Mid-green.
- CULTIVATION 1 or 2.
- HEIGHT 5–7in (12 18cm).
- SPREAD 12in (30cm).

A. nemorosa 'Robinsoniana'

Z 4–8

A. *OBTUSILOBA*
Habit Compact, tufted, fibrous-rooted, perennial, semievergreen.
Flowers Solitary, ¾in (2cm) across, borne during late spring and early summer. White, blue, or occasionally, yellow.
Leaves Rounded and lobed. Mid-green.
- CULTIVATION 2.
- HEIGHT 6in (15cm).
- SPREAD 8in (20cm).

A. obtusiloba

Z 4–8

A. *APENNINA*
Habit Rhizomatous, patch-forming, herbaceous, perennial.
Flowers Solitary, to 1½in (4cm) across, borne during spring. Bright blue or pink-flushed white.
Leaves Rounded, lobed, and toothed. Mid-green.
- CULTIVATION 1 or 2.
- HEIGHT 8in (20cm).
- SPREAD 8in (20cm).

A. apennina

Z 4–8

A. *BLANDA* [Blue form]
Habit Tuberous, herbaceous, perennial.
Flowers Solitary, star-shaped, 1–1½in (2.5–4cm) across, borne in spring. Mid- to deep blue.
Leaves Deeply divided. Dark green.
- CULTIVATION 1 or 2.
- HEIGHT 6in (15cm).
- SPREAD 6in (15cm).

A. blanda [Blue form]

Z 4–8

A. *BLANDA* 'Ingramii'
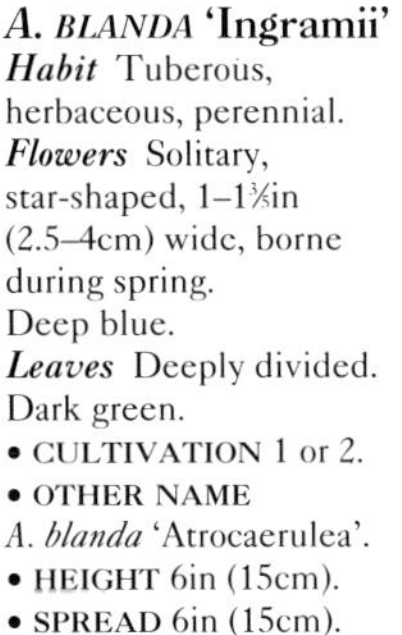
Habit Tuberous, herbaceous, perennial.
Flowers Solitary, star-shaped, 1–1½in (2.5–4cm) wide, borne during spring. Deep blue.
Leaves Deeply divided. Dark green.
- CULTIVATION 1 or 2.
- OTHER NAME *A. blanda* 'Atrocaerulea'.
- HEIGHT 6in (15cm).
- SPREAD 6in (15cm).

A. blanda 'Ingramii'

Z 4–8

A. *RANUNCULOIDES* 'Pleniflora'
Habit Rhizomatous, herbaceous, perennial.
Flowers Solitary, double, ¾–1¼in (2–3cm) across, borne in spring. Yellow.
Leaves Deeply lobed and toothed. Mid-green.
- CULTIVATION 1 or 2.
- OTHER NAME *A. r.* 'Flore Pleno'.
- HEIGHT 2–4in (5–10cm).
- SPREAD 18in (45cm).

A. ranunculoides 'Pleniflora'

Z 3–7

A. *RANUNCULOIDES*
Habit Patch-forming, rhizomatous, herbaceous, perennial.
Flowers Solitary, ¾–1¼in (2–3cm) across, borne in spring. Deep yellow.
Leaves Deeply lobed and toothed. Mid-green.
- CULTIVATION 1 or 2.
- HEIGHT 2–4in (5–10cm).
- SPREAD 18in (45cm).

A. ranunculoides

Z 3–7

CAMPANULA

The genus *Campanula* consists of about 300 species of annuals, biennials, and perennials, some of which are evergreen. Campanulas are valued for their tubular, bell-, funnel-, or star-shaped flowers, which are often borne over long periods. The genus includes many small species and cultivars that are perfect for rock gardens, raised beds, and scree plantings. Most of those described here are robust and easily grown. The smallest, for example *Campanula zoysii* or *C. raineri*, are excellent for troughs, but are very susceptible to slug damage. *C. cochlearifolia* is particularly effective if allowed to colonize areas of gravel paving crevices or the tops of dry-stone, retaining walls by self-sowing. *C. poscharskyana* and *C. portenschlagiana* will thrive on a sunny bank or in a wall crevice. Both species are vigorous, so site them away from smaller less-robust alpines. They also suit growing in containers such

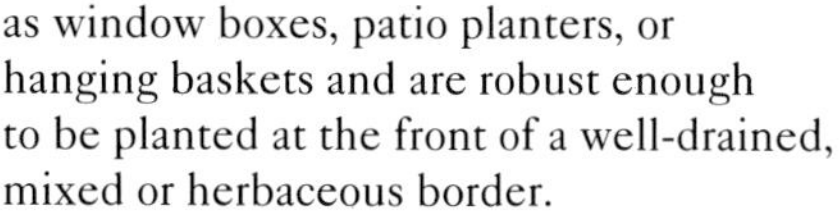

as window boxes, patio planters, or hanging baskets and are robust enough to be planted at the front of a well-drained, mixed or herbaceous border.

Grow in moist but well-drained soil in full sun or light, dappled or partial shade. *C. zoysii* and *C. raineri* need sharper drainage than the other species described, and must have protection from excessive winter moisture, either with a propped pane of glass outdoors, or in an alpine house. Grow in very gritty, sharply drained soil, in a scree bed, in tufa, or in a trough. In an alpine house, use a soil-based potting mix, with up to one-third by volume of added grit.

Divide rhizomatous species and cultivars in autumn or early spring. Take cuttings of new growth or root individual rosettes cuttings, both in early summer. Sow seed of species in pots in a cold frame, as soon as ripe or in autumn.

C. CARPATICA 'Bressingham White'

Habit Clump-forming, herbaceous, perennial.
Flowers Solitary, upright, open bell-shaped, 1¼in (3cm) or more across, borne during summer. White.
Leaves Rounded and heart-shaped. Bright green.

- HEIGHT 6in (15cm).
- SPREAD 12in (30cm).

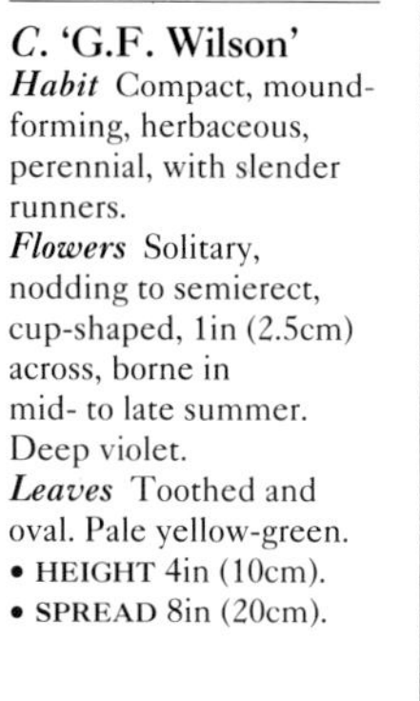

C. carpatica **'Bressingham White'**

Z 4–7

C. POSCHARSKYANA

Habit Vigorous, spreading, evergreen, perennial.
Flowers Star-shaped, to 1in (2.5cm) across, borne in clusters from summer to autumn. Pale lavender.
Leaves Rounded to oval and toothed. Mid-green.

- HEIGHT 6in (15cm).
- SPREAD to 24in (60cm).

C. poscharskyana

Z 4–7

C. 'G.F. Wilson'

Habit Compact, mound-forming, herbaceous, perennial, with slender runners.
Flowers Solitary, nodding to semierect, cup-shaped, 1in (2.5cm) across, borne in mid- to late summer. Deep violet.
Leaves Toothed and oval. Pale yellow-green.

- HEIGHT 4in (10cm).
- SPREAD 8in (20cm).

C. **'G.F. Wilson'**

Z 4–7

C. 'Birch Hybrid'

Habit Vigorous, prostrate, evergreen, perennial, with runners.
Flowers Open bell-shaped, ¾in (2cm) across, prolific, borne in clusters in summer. Mauve-blue.
Leaves Oval to heart-shaped and toothed. Bright green.
• HEIGHT 4in (10cm).
• SPREAD 20in (50cm) or more.

C. 'Birch Hybrid'

Z 4–7

C. COCHLEARIIFOLIA

Habit Tufted, patch-forming, rhizomatous, herbaceous, perennial.
Flowers Drooping, bell-shaped, ½in (15mm) long, borne in summer. White, lavender, or slate-blue.
Leaves Rounded to heart-shaped, toothed, in rosettes. Bright green
• OTHER NAMES *C. bellardii, C. pusilla.*
• HEIGHT 3in (8cm)
• SPREAD 12in (30cm).

C. cohleariifolia
Fairies' thimbles

Z 6–7

C. PORTENSCHLAGIANA

Habit Mound-forming, evergreen, perennial.
Flowers Long bell-shaped, ¾in (2cm) across, borne in spreading sprays from mid- through to late summer. Deep purple.
Leaves Kidney- to heart-shaped. Mid-green.
• OTHER NAME *C. muralis.*
• HEIGHT 6in (15cm).
• SPREAD 20in (50cm).

C. portenschlagiana,
Dalmatian bellflower

Z 4–8

C. RAINERI

Habit Spreading perennial.
Flowers Solitary, upright, open bell-shaped, to 1½in (4cm) across, borne in summer. Pale lavender.
Leaves Oval, toothed. and hairy. Gray-green.
• CULTIVATION Protect from winter moisture and provide sharp drainage.
• HEIGHT 3in (8cm)
• SPREAD 8in (20cm).

C. raineri

Z 4–7

C. BARBATA

Habit Short-lived, rosette-forming, perennial or biennial.
Flowers Drooping, bearded, bell-shaped, to 1¼in (3cm) long, borne in one-sided spikes on upright stems, in early summer. Lavender-blue.
Leaves Narrowly lance-shaped. Pale to mid-green.
• HEIGHT 12in (30cm)
• SPREAD 8in (20cm).

C. barbata
Bearded bellflower

Z 6–8

C. CARPATICA var. *TURBINATA* 'Jewel'

Habit Compact, clump-forming, herbaceous, perennial.
Flowers Solitary, upright, open bell-shaped, 1¼in (3cm) or more across, during summer. Bright blue-purple.
Leaves Rounded and heart-shaped. Emerald.
• HEIGHT 4in (10cm).
• SPREAD 12in (30cm).

C. carpatica var. ***turbinata*** 'Jewel'

Z 4–7

C. ZOYSII

Habit Tufted, semi-evergreen, perennial.
Flowers Horizontal to ascending, tubular, to ¾in (2cm) long, borne in mid-summer. Clear to pale lavender-blue.
Leaves Small, toothed, oval, glossy. Mid-green.
- TIPS Needs sharply drained, alkaline soil. Dislikes winter moisture.
- HEIGHT 2in (5cm).
- SPREAD 4in (10cm).

C. zoysii
Crimped bellflower

Z 4–7

C. ARVATICA

Habit Carpet-forming, perennial, with runners.
Flowers Solitary, upright, shallowly funnel-shaped, ¾–1½in (2–4cm) long, borne in summer. Pale blue or white.
Leaves Oval to heart-shaped and toothed. Mid-green.
- OTHER NAME *C. acutangula*.
- HEIGHT 4in (10cm).
- SPREAD 8in (20cm).

C. arvatica

Z 4–7

C. GARGANICA 'Blue Diamond'

Habit Spreading, evergreen, perennial.
Flowers Star-shaped, upright, to 3in (2cm) across, borne profusely in sprays in summer. Gray-blue, with dark blue center.
Leaves Kidney- or heart-shaped to oval and toothed. Gray-green.
- HEIGHT 2in (5cm).
- SPREAD 12in (30cm).

C. garganica
'Blue Diamond'

Z 6–8

Scrophulariaceae	POUCH FLOWER, SLIPPER FLOWER

CALCEOLARIA TENELLA

Habit Vigorous, creeping, evergreen, mat-forming, perennial. ***Flowers*** Slipperlike, pouched, ⅓–⅜in (7–9mm) across, usually borne singly, in summer. Bright yellow, marked red. ***Leaves*** Broadly oval, finely-toothed. Pale yellow-green.
• NATIVE HABITAT Alpine regions, Chile.
• CULTIVATION Needs peat-rich, gritty, moist but well-drained, neutral to acid soil. Shade from hot midday sun, and protect from winter moisture.
• PROPAGATION By seed in autumn or early spring, in containers in a cold frame. Divide in spring.

Z 7–8

HEIGHT
2in (5cm)

SPREAD
to 12in (30cm)

Rosaceae	MOUNTAIN AVENS

GEUM MONTANUM

Habit Clumping, rhizomatous, semievergreen, perennial. ***Flowers*** Solitary, cup-shaped, to 1½in (4cm) across, borne in spring and early summer. Deep yellow. ***Leaves*** Divided, with a large, kidney-shaped or rounded lobe. Dark green.
• NATIVE HABITAT Mountain pastures, central and southern Europe.
• CULTIVATION Grow in a site with fertile, well-drained, preferably gritty soil.
• PROPAGATION By division or by seed in pots ina cold frame, both in autumn and spring.

Z 4–8

HEIGHT
6in (15cm)

SPREAD
16in (40cm)

Cruciferae/ Brassicaceae	

ALYSSUM WULFENIANUM

Habit Tufted, upright or prostrate, evergreen, perennial. ***Flowers*** Cross-shaped, to ¼in (6mm) across, borne in loose, rounded clusters in early summer. Yellow. ***Leaves*** Small, oblong to oval, hairy, forming rosettes. Gray-green.
• NATIVE HABITAT Southeast Alps.
• CULTIVATION Needs well-drained, moderately fertile, gritty soil. Trim lightly after flowering.
• PROPAGATION By softwood cuttings in late spring, or by seed in autumn or early spring, in containers in a cold frame.

Z 5–8

HEIGHT
4–6in (10–15cm)

SPREAD
to 20in (50cm)

Guttiferae/Clusiaceae	

HYPERICUM REPTANS

Habit Mat-forming, stem-rooting, deciduous, sub-shrub. ***Flowers*** Solitary, cup-shaped, to 1¼in (3cm) across, borne in summer. Golden-yellow, opening from crimson buds. ***Leaves*** Oval and leathery, Mid-green, turning red and yellow in autumn.
• NATIVE HABITAT Himalaya, southwest China.
• CULTIVATION Suitable for growing in a rock garden or on a sunny, retaining wall. Needs moist but sharply drained soil.
• PROPAGATION Separate rooted stems in spring. Sow seed in autumn in containers in a cold frame.

Z 6–8

HEIGHT
2in (5cm)

SPREAD
8in (20cm)

Leguminosae/Papilionaceae	WINGED BROOM

GENISTA SAGITTALIS

Habit Prostrate, mat-forming, deciduous, shrub. ***Flowers*** Pea, ⅜in (1cm) long, borne in dense, terminal spikes, to 1⅝in (4cm) long. Bright yellow. ***Leaves*** Few, small, lance-shaped, borne on upright, broadly winged green stems, giving the shrub an evergreen appearance. Mid-green.

• NATIVE HABITAT Meadows, rocky areas, open woodlands, and by roadsides, in the hills and mountains of central and southern Europe.

• CULTIVATION Suitable for growing in a rock garden or on top of a retaining wall, or for clothing a sunny bank. Grow in poor or moderately fertile, light, well-drained soil. Resents being transplanted, so set young plants out directly from their containers into their permanent flowering site as soon as possible.

• PROPAGATION By seed in autumn or spring, in containers in a cold frame, or by semiripe cuttings in summer.

• OTHER NAME *Chamaespartium sagittale.*

Z 3–7

HEIGHT 6in (15cm)

SPREAD to 3ft (1m) or more

Leguminosae/ Papilionaceae	

CYTISUS ARDOINOI

Habit Deciduous, semiprostrate, hummock-forming, shrub. ***Flowers*** Pea, ⅜in (1cm) long, borne in lateral clusters on arching stems, in late spring and summer. Bright yellow. ***Leaves*** Tiny, 3-lobed, divided, and hairy. Grayish-green.

• NATIVE HABITAT Maritime Alps.

• CULTIVATION Suitable for a rock garden or raised bed. Grow in poor, or moderately fertile, light, well-drained, acid or slightly alkaline soil.

• PROPAGATION By seed in autumn or spring, in a cold frame, or by semiripe cuttings in summer.

Z 5–8

HEIGHT 8–24in (20–60cm)

SPREAD 8–24in (20–60cm)

Primulaceae	GOLDEN CREEPING JENNY

LYSIMACHIA NUMMULARIA 'Aurea'

Habit Very vigorous, stem-rooting, prostrate, evergreen, perennial. ***Flowers*** Cup-shaped, to ¾in (2cm) across, borne in summer. Golden-yellow. ***Leaves*** Paired, broadly oval to rounded, with a heart-shaped base. Golden-yellow.

• NATIVE HABITAT Garden selection.

• CULTIVATION Grow in moist but well-drained soil in partial shade. Needs full sun for best leaf color. Rampant, so site away from choice alpines.

• PROPAGATION Separate rooted stems in spring or autumn.

Z 3–8

HEIGHT to 2in (5cm)

SPREAD indefinite

Rosaceae	

POTENTILLA AUREA

Habit Mat-forming, semi-evergreen, perennial. ***Flowers*** Saucer-shaped, ¾in (2cm) across, borne in clusters from late spring to summer. Deep yellow. ***Leaves*** Rounded, with finger-like segments, sharply toothed, glossy, with silver-haired margins. Deep green.

• NATIVE HABITAT Pyrenees and Alps.

• CULTIVATION Suitable for growing in a rock garden in gritty, well-drained soil.

• PROPAGATION By division, or by seed in containers in a cold frame, in autumn or spring.

Z 4–8

HEIGHT 4in (10cm)

SPREAD 8in (20cm)

Leguminosae/ Papilionaceae	HORSESHOE VETCH

HIPPOCREPIS COMOSA

Habit Creeping, woody-based, semi-evergreen, perennial. ***Flowers*** Pea, ⅜in (1cm) across, borne in clusters in spring and late summer. Lemon-yellow. ***Leaves*** Divided, oval. Mid-green.

• NATIVE HABITAT Central and southern Europe.

• CULTIVATION Suitable for growing in rock crevices, retaining walls, or paving. Grow in poor, alkaline, well-drained soil in full sun.

• PROPAGATION Sow scarified seed in autumn or spring, in containers in a cold frame. Will self-sow freely. Take stem-tip cuttings in summer.

Z 6–9

HEIGHT to 16in (40cm)

SPREAD to 16in (40cm)

Guttiferae/Clusiaceae	

HYPERICUM EMPETRIFOLIUM subsp. *OLIGANTHUM*

Habit Prostrate, evergreen, shrub. ***Flowers*** Star-shaped, to ¾in (2cm) across, borne in clusters of 4–7 in summer. Deep yellow. ***Leaves*** Whorled, linear, with inrolled margins. Dark green.
• NATIVE HABITAT Maquis, Greece.
• CULTIVATION Suitable for growing on a sharp-drained rock garden. Dislikes winter moisture.
• PROPAGATION Separate rooted stems in spring, or sow seed in autumn in containers in a cold frame.
• OTHER NAME *H. empetrifolium* var. *prostratum*.

Z 7–9

HEIGHT 2in (5cm)

SPREAD to 12in (30cm) or more

Scrophulariaceae	

CALCEOLARIA 'Walter Shrimpton'

Habit Clumping, evergreen, perennial. ***Flowers*** Slipperlike, 1in (2.5cm) long, borne in clusters of 2–5 in summer. Bronze-yellow, with brown spots and a white band. ***Leaves*** Spoon- to diamond-shaped. glossy, hairy, in rosettes. Dark green.
• NATIVE HABITAT Garden origin.
• CULTIVATION Needs fertile, gritty, neutral to acid soil. Shade from hot midday sun and protect from winter moisture. In an alpine house, grow in equal parts soil, leaf mold, and sharp sand.
• PROPAGATION Root rosettes in early summer.

Z 7–9

HEIGHT 4in (10cm)

SPREAD 9in (23cm)

Compositae/Asteraceae	GOLDEN YARROW, WOOLLY SUNFLOWER

ERIOPHYLLUM LANATUM

Habit Vigorous, clump-forming, semievergreen, perennial. ***Flowers*** Daisy, ¾–1½in (2–4cm) across, borne in succession from late spring to summer. Bright mid-yellow. ***Leaves*** Spoon- to lance-shaped, lobed at stem. Woolly-white to silver-gray.
• NATIVE HABITAT Western N. America.
• CULTIVATION Suits the front of a flower border, dry retaining wall, or paving crevices. Tolerates poor, sharply drained, even dry soil.
• PROPAGATION Divide in spring or after flowering. Sow seed in autumn, in containers in a cold frame.

Z 6–8

HEIGHT 8–20in (20–50cm)

SPREAD 8–24in (20–60cm)

Papaveraceae	WELSH POPPY

MECONOPSIS CAMBRICA

Habit Tap-rooted, semievergreen, tufted, perennial. ***Flowers*** Solitary, shallowly cup-shaped, 2–2½in (5–6cm) across, borne on wiry stems from spring to autumn. Lemon-yellow to orange. ***Leaves*** Finely divided or irregularly lobed, in basal tufts. Pale to blue-green.
• NATIVE HABITAT Woods, western Europe.
• CULTIVATION Grow in any moist but well-drained soil, in sun or part-shade. Self-sows freely.
• PROPAGATION Sow seed when ripe or in early spring, either *in situ* or in pots in a cold frame.

Z 6–8

HEIGHT 18in (45cm)

SPREAD to 10in (25cm)

Polygonaceae	

PERSICARIA VACCINIIFOLIA

Habit Mat-forming, trailing, semievergreen, perennial. ***Flowers*** Tiny, bell-shaped, borne in upright spikes to 3in (8cm) long, in late summer and autumn. Deep pink. ***Leaves*** Oval and glossy. Mid-green, turning red in autumn.
- NATIVE HABITAT Himalaya.
- CULTIVATION Grows best when allowed to tumble over large rocks. Needs moist soil.
- PROPAGATION Divide in early spring or autumn, or sow seed in spring, in containers in a cold frame.
- OTHER NAME *Polygonum vacciniifolium.*

Z 4–8

HEIGHT
8in (20cm)

SPREAD
20in (50cm) or more

Ericaceae	CHECKERBERRY, WINTERGREEN

GAULTHERIA PROCUMBENS

Habit Creeping, rhizomatous, evergreen, shrub. ***Flowers*** Urn-shaped, borne in clusters ⅜–1in (1–2.5cm) long, in summer. White or pale pink. ***Fruits*** Rounded. Red. ***Leaves*** Oval, pointed, leathery. Aromatic when crushed. Dark green.
- NATIVE HABITAT Woods, eastern N. America.
- CULTIVATION Suits a woodland or peat garden. Prefers a site in partial or dappled shade with moist, leaf-rich soil that is acid to neutral.
- PROPAGATION Separate rooted stems in spring, or sow seed in pots in a cold frame in autumn.

Z 3–7

HEIGHT
6in (15cm)

SPREAD
3ft (1m) or more

Papaveraceae	

PAPAVER ATLANTICUM

Habit Short-lived, clump-forming, evergreen, perennial. ***Flowers*** Solitary, saucer-shaped, to 2in (5cm) across, borne in summer. Soft orange. ***Leaves*** Oblong to lance-shaped, coarsely toothed, and very hairy. Mid-green.
- NATIVE HABITAT Morocco.
- CULTIVATION Suitable for growing in a rock or scree garden. Needs sharply drained, moderately fertile soil in partial shade.
- PROPAGATION By seed in spring, in pots in a cold frame. Self-seeds freely.

Z 5–8

HEIGHT
12in (30cm)

SPREAD
6in (15cm)

VIOLA

The genus *Viola* consists of about 500 species of popular annuals, biennials, and perennials, some of which are evergreen or semievergreen. Violets and pansies have a long flowering season and are valued for their often sweetly scented or showy blooms. Several compact species are suitable for the rock garden. Some, like *Viola pedata*, dislike excessive winter moisture and so are best grown in pots in an alpine house. Shade-loving species, like *V. odorata* and *V. riviniana* 'Purpurea', which self-seed freely, are ideal for naturalizing in a woodland garden or shady border but will spread and often become a nuisance in a rock garden. Drifts of self-sown seedlings can look very attractive in scree plantings.

Grow in poor to moderately fertile, moist but well-drained soil in sun or partial shade. Generally, violets need dappled shade, while pansies prefer sun. Deadhead frequently to prolong flowering, and trim back vigorous species and cultivars after flowering to maintain compactness. The smaller alpine species need sharp drainage in gritty, moderately fertile soil, except for *V. calcarata*, which grows best in more fertile soils. In an alpine house, use a mix of soil, leaf mold and grit or tufa chippings. Pot-grown specimens are best re-potted annually in late summer or early autumn.

Propagate species by sowing seed as soon as ripe or in spring, in containers in a cold frame. Divide *V. biflora*, *V. cornuta*, and *V. odorata* in spring or autumn. *V.* 'Huntercombe Purple' and other cultivars should be divided about every three years to maintain vigor. Take softwood cuttings of cultivars, such as *V.* 'Jackanapes', in spring or late summer. Many *Viola* species and cultivars tend to be short-lived, so propagate regularly to maintain stocks.

V. 'Nellie Britton'
Habit Clump-forming, evergreen, perennial.
Flowers Solitary, pansy, 1in (2.5cm) wide, borne in profusion in summer. Pinkish-mauve.
Leaves Oval, toothed, and glossy. Mid-green.
• **TIPS** Needs well-drained but not dry soil.
• **OTHER NAME** *V.* 'Haslemere'.
• **HEIGHT** 6in (15cm).
• **SPREAD** 12in (30cm).

V. 'Nellie Britton'

Z 5–7

V. 'Huntercombe Purple'
Habit Spreading, clumping, evergreen, perennial.
Flowers Solitary, pansy, 1in (2.5cm) wide, borne in summer. Deep violet-purple.
Leaves Oval, toothed, and glossy. Mid-green.
• **TIPS** Best divided every 3 years.
• **HEIGHT** 6in (15cm).
• **SPREAD** 12in (30cm).

V. 'Huntercombe Purple'

Z 5–8

V. PEDATA
Habit Stemless, clump-forming, herbaceous, perennial.
Flowers Violet, short-spurred, 1¼in (3cm) across, borne in late spring and summer. Pale violet with yellow center.
Leaves Finely divided. Mid-green.
• **TIPS** Best grown in an alpine house.
• **HEIGHT** 2in (5cm).
• **SPREAD** 4in (10cm).

V. pedata
Birdsfoot violet, Crowfoot violet

Z 3–8

V. CALCARATA
Habit Clump-forming, perennial.
Flowers Pansy, slender-spurred, to 1½in (4cm) across, borne in late spring and summer. White-lavender.
Leaves Oval or lance-shaped. Mid-green.
• **TIPS** Prefers a site with deep, rich soil.
• **HEIGHT** 4–6in (10–15cm).
• **SPREAD** 8in (20cm).

V. calcarata
Long-spurred pansy

Z 4–7

V. ODORATA

Habit Stoloniferous, mat-forming, perennial, semievergreen.
Flowers Solitary, violet, sweet-scented, ¾in (2cm) across, with short spurs, borne in late winter and spring. Violet or white.
Leaves Heart-shaped. Bright green.
• TIPS Self-seeds freely. Good for naturalizing.
• HEIGHT 8in (20cm).
• SPREAD 12in (30cm).

V. odorata
English violet,
Sweet violet

Z 6–9

V. RIVINIANA 'Purpurea'

Habit Tufted, evergreen, perennial.
Flowers Solitary, violet, to ¾in (2cm) across, borne in late spring and early summer. Violet, with white or pale purple spur.
Leaves Oval, toothed. Dark purplish-green.
• TIPS Suitable for naturalizing.
• HEIGHT 4in (10cm).
• SPREAD 8in (20cm).

V. riviniana 'Purpurea'
Common dog violet,
Wood violet

Z 4–7

V. CORNUTA

Habit Rhizomatous, evergreen, clump-forming, perennial.
Flowers Solitary, pansy, slender-spurred, to 1⅜in (3.5cm) wide, borne from spring to summer. Pale to deep lilac-blue, or white.
Leaves Oval and toothed. Mid-green.
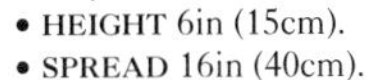
• TIPS Thrives in a sunny or shaded site.
• HEIGHT 6in (15cm).
• SPREAD 16in (40cm).

V. cornuta
Horned violet,
Pyrenean pansy

Z 5–8

V. 'Jackanapes'

Habit Clump-forming, short-lived, evergreen, perennial.
Flowers Pansy, spurred, ¾in (2cm) across, borne in spring and summer. Deep brownish-purple, with yellow lower petals.
Leaves Oval and toothed. Bright green.
• TIPS Short-lived, so take cuttings regularly.
• HEIGHT 5in (12cm).
• SPREAD 12in (30cm).

V. 'Jackanapes'

Z 5–8

V. BIFLORA

Habit Compact, rhizomatous, herbaceous, perennial.
Flowers Solitary or paired, violet, ⅝in (15mm) across, borne in late spring and early summer. Lemon-yellow, veined on lower petal.
Leaves Heart-shaped and toothed. Pale green.
• TIPS Suits naturalizing.
• HEIGHT 3in (8cm).
• SPREAD 8in (20cm).

V. biflora
Twin-flowered violet

Z 4–8

V. AETOLICA

Habit Clump-forming, evergreen, perennial.
Flowers Solitary, pansy, scented, ¾in (2cm) across, borne in late spring and summer. Yellow, with darker lower petals.
Leaves Oval to lance-shaped, scalloped. Mid-green.
• TIPS Suits a rock garden or raised bed.
• HEIGHT 3in (8cm).
• SPREAD 6in (15cm).

V. aetolica

Z 5–7

GENTIANA

The genus *Gentiana*, commonly known as gentians, consists of about 400 species of annuals, biennials, and evergreen and herbaceous perennials. The autumn-flowering gentians are classified as semievergreen. Those described here are alpine species suitable for rock gardens, peat beds, or troughs. Most of them prefer cool, damp climates.

Cultivation requirements for the genus are grouped as follows:
Group 1 Need sunny site and neutral to alkaline soil.
Group 2 Need cool, moist, acid to neutral soil and good light. Dislike dry conditions.

Sow seed of species as soon as ripe in containers in a cold frame. Separate offsets or divide in early spring.

G. SAXOSA

Habit Rosette-forming, short-lived, evergreen, perennial.
Flowers Upright, bell-shaped, ⅘in (2cm) long, borne in summer and early autumn. White, with faint green veins.
Leaves Narrow spoon-shaped and leathery. Dark green.
- CULTIVATION 1.
- HEIGHT 3in (7cm).
- SPREAD 4in (10cm).

G. saxosa
New Zealand gentian

Z 6–9

G. TERNIFOLIA

Habit Semievergreen, perennial, trailing.
Flowers Solitary, bell- to trumpet-shaped, 1⅗in (4cm) long, borne in autumn. Sky-blue, with darker blue stripes.
Leaves Narrowly lance-shaped. Grayish-green.
- CULTIVATION 2.
- HEIGHT 3in (8cm).
- SPREAD 12in (30cm).

G. ternifolia

Z 6–9

G. × MACAULEYI 'Well's Variety'

Habit Clump-forming.
Flowers Solitary, trumpet-shaped, borne during mid- and late summer. Deep blue.
Leaves Linear, pointed, and paired. Mid-green.
- CULTIVATION 2.
- OTHER NAME *G.* 'Wellsii'.
- HEIGHT 3in (8cm).
- SPREAD 12in (30cm).

***G. × macauleyi* 'Well's Variety'**

Z 5–7

G. SINO-ORNATA

Habit Semievergreen, perennial, with prostrate shoots.
Flowers Solitary, trumpet-shaped, 2½in (6cm) long, borne in autumn. Bright deep blue, with white stripes.
Leaves Linear to lance-shaped, paired, and pointed. Mid-green.
- CULTIVATION 2.
- HEIGHT 3in (7cm).
- SPREAD 12in (30cm).

G. sino-ornata
Autumn gentian

Z 5–7

G. 'Kingfisher'

Habit Semievergreen, perennial, with prostrate stems.
Flowers Solitary, trumpet-shaped, to 1⅗in (4cm) long, borne in autumn. Vivid blue.
Leaves Linear to lance-shaped and pointed. Dark green.
- CULTIVATION 2.
- HEIGHT 2in (5cm).
- SPREAD to 12in (30cm).

***G.* 'Kingfisher'**

Z 5–7

G. PARADOXA

Habit Tufted, herbaceous, perennial.
Flowers Solitary, broad trumpet-shaped, to 1⅗–2in (4–5cm) long, borne in late summer. Rich blue, white throat.
Leaves Linear, in whorls of 3–4. Yellow-green.
- CULTIVATION 1.
- HEIGHT 4–8in (10–20cm).
- SPREAD 4–8in (10–20cm).

G. paradoxa

Z 5–7

G. x *STEVENAGENSIS*
Habit Semievergreen, perennial, with branching, prostrate stems.
Flowers Terminal, trumpet-shaped, 2¾in (6.5cm) long, borne in autumn. Purple-blue, with yellow-green stripes.
Leaves Paired, linear, thick. Mid- to dark green.
• CULTIVATION 2.
• HEIGHT 2in (5cm).
• SPREAD 12in (30cm).

G. x *stevenagensis*

Z 4–7

G. 'Inverleith'
Habit Vigorous, semievergreen, perennial.
Flowers Solitary, trumpet-shaped, to 2½in (6cm) long, borne during autumn. Pale blue, with darker stripes outside.
Leaves Lance-shaped, recurved. Mid-green.
• CULTIVATION 2.
• HEIGHT 4in (10cm).
• SPREAD 12in (30cm).

G. 'Inverleith'

Z 4–7

G. VERNA subsp. *BALCANICA*
Habit Clump-forming, evergreen, perennial.
Flowers Solitary, salver-shaped, 1in (2.5cm) across, borne in spring. Deep sky-blue, with white center.
Leaves Small, oval to lance-shaped, in basal rosettes, paired at stems. Dark to mid-green.
• CULTIVATION 1.
• OTHER NAME *G. verna* 'Angulosa'.
• HEIGHT 2½in (6cm).
• SPREAD to 6in (15cm).

G. verna subsp. *balcanica*

Z 4–7

G. SEPTEMFIDA
Habit Spreading to upright, clump-forming, herbaceous, perennial.
Flowers Narrowly bell-shaped, 1½in (3.5cm) long, borne in clusters in late summer. Bright blue, dark stripes, white throat.
Leaves Oval, pointed, paired. Mid-green.
• CULTIVATION 1.
• HEIGHT 6–8in (15–20cm).
• SPREAD 12in (30cm).

G. septemfida

Z 4–8

G. VEITCHIORUM
Habit Semievergreen, perennial with trailing, prostrate stems.
Flowers Solitary, narrowly trumpet-shaped, 2in (5cm) long, borne in autumn. Dark blue, with greenish-yellow stripes outside.
Leaves Linear to oblong, paired. Mid-green.
• CULTIVATION 2.
• HEIGHT 2in (5cm).
• SPREAD to 8in (20cm).

G. veitchiorum

Z 5–7

G. VERNA
Habit Mat-forming, evergreen perennial.
Flowers Solitary, salver-shaped, 1in (2.5cm) across, borne in spring. Pure sky-blue, with white center.
Leaves Oval to lance-shaped, in basal rosettes, paired on the stems. Dark to mid-green.
• CULTIVATION 1.
• HEIGHT 1½in (4cm).
• SPREAD to 4in (10cm).

G. verna
Spring gentian, Star gentian

Z 4–7

G. ACAULIS
Habit Mat-forming, evergreen, perennial.
Flowers Solitary trumpet-shaped, 2in (5cm) long, borne in spring. Vivid, deep blue.
Leaves Oval to lance-shaped, pointed, glossy, and rosetted. Dark green.
• CULTIVATION 1.
• OTHER NAMES *G. excisa*, *G. kochiana*.
• HEIGHT 3in (8cm).
• SPREAD 12in (30cm).

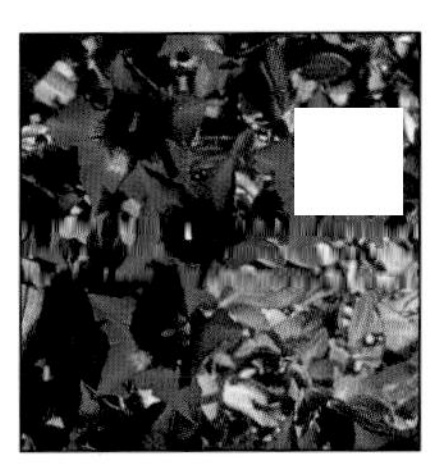

G. acaulis
Trumpet gentian

Z 4–7

Cruciferae/ Brassicaceae	

ARABIS PROCURRENS 'Variegata'

Habit Prostrate, mat-forming, evergreen or semi-evergreen, perennial. ***Flowers*** Cross-shaped, ⅓–⅖in (8–10mm) across, borne in loose clusters in late spring. White. ***Leaves*** Narrowly oblong to lance-shaped, glossy. Mid-green, with cream or pink margins.
• NATIVE HABITAT Garden origin.
• CULTIVATION Tolerates any well-drained soil in sun. Remove all-green shoots to keep variegation.
• PROPAGATION By softwood cuttings in summer.
• OTHER NAME *A. ferdinandi-coburgii* 'Variegata'.

Z 5–8

HEIGHT
2–3in
(5–8cm)

SPREAD
12–16in
(30–40cm)

Ericaceae	COMMON BEARBERRY, KINNIKINNICK

ARCTOSTAPHYLOS UVA-URSI

Habit Low-growing, evergreen, shrub.
Flowers Tiny, urn-shaped, borne in sprays ⅘–1⅕in (2–3cm) long, in summer. White, tinted pink.
Leaves Small, oval, and leathery. Dark green.
Fruits Rounded berries. Scarlet.
• NATIVE HABITAT Moors, heaths, open woodland in northern Eurasia and N. America.
• CULTIVATION Grow in a rock or woodland garden, or peat bed, in moist, acid, leaf-rich soil.
• PROPAGATION By semiripe cuttings in summer, or layer or separate rooted stems in autumn.

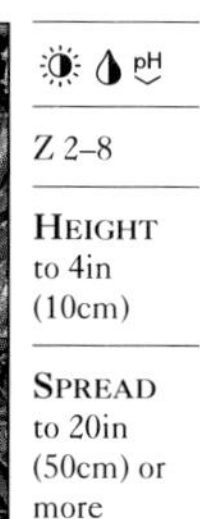

pH

Z 2–8

HEIGHT
to 4in
(10cm)

SPREAD
to 20in
(50cm) or
more

Crassulaceae	COMMON HOUSELEEK

SEMPERVIVUM TECTORUM

Habit Vigorous, clump-forming, fleshy, evergreen, perennial. ***Flowers*** Small, star-shaped, borne in hairy-stemmed dense clusters, 2–4in (5–10cm) across, in summer. Red-purple. ***Leaves*** Thick, oval to narrowly oblong, bristle-tipped, in large rosettes. Blue-green, suffused red-purple.
• NATIVE HABITAT Mountains, southern. Europe.
• CULTIVATION Good for growing on an old roof or in gritty, sharply drained, moderately fertile soil.
• PROPAGATION By seed in spring, or by offsets in spring or early summer.

Z 5–9

HEIGHT
6in (15cm)

SPREAD
to 20in
(50cm)

Crassulaceae	

JOVIBARBA HIRTA

Habit Clumping, stoloniferous, fleshy, evergreen, perennial. ***Flowers*** Bell-shaped, borne in branched clusters, to 3in (8cm) across, in summer. Yellow-brown. ***Leaves*** Lance-shaped, hairy-margined, fleshy, in rosettes. Green, flushed red.
• NATIVE HABITAT Central and southeast Europe.
• CULTIVATION Grow in troughs or on the top of retaining walls, in poor, gritty, sharply drained soil.
• PROPAGATION By offsets in spring or summer.
• OTHER NAMES *J. globifera* subsp. *hirta*, *Sempervivum hirtum*.

Z 5–8

HEIGHT
6in (15cm)

SPREAD
12in (30cm)

Crassulaceae	COBWEB HOUSELEEK

SEMPERVIVUM ARACHNOIDEUM

Habit Clump-forming, evergreen, perennial. ***Flowers*** Small, star-shaped, borne in flat heads, to 1in (2.5cm) across, in summer. Red-pink. ***Leaves*** Oval, fleshy, in tight, crowded rosettes, and cobwebbed with white hairs. Mid-green to red.

- NATIVE HABITAT Mountain rocks, Europe
- CULTIVATION Suitable for growing in a scree bed or trough, with gritty, sharply drained, moderately fertile soil.
- PROPAGATION By seed in spring in pots in a cold frame, or by offsets in spring or early summer.

Z 5–9

HEIGHT 3in (8cm)

SPREAD to 12in (30cm)

Compositae/Asteraceae	

RAOULIA HOOKERI var. *ALBO-SERICEA*

Habit Mat-forming, evergreen, perennial. ***Flowers*** Insignificant, borne in heads to ¼in (7mm) wide, in summer. Pale green or straw-colored. ***Leaves*** Oval to spoon-shaped, intensely silky-haired, closely overlapping along stems. Gray-silver.

- NATIVE HABITAT Gravel and scree, New Zealand.
- CULTIVATION Needs gritty, fertile, moisture-retentive, sharply drained soil. Shade from the hottest sun and protect from winter moisture.
- PROPAGATION Divide in spring.
- OTHER NAME *R. lutescens*.

Z 8–9

HEIGHT 1/2in (1cm)

SPREAD to 8in (20cm) or more

Compositae/Asteraceae	NEW ZEALAND EDELWEISS

LEUCOGENES GRANDICEPS

Habit Mat-forming, evergreen, perennial. ***Flowers*** Small, daisy, flat, ⅜–⅝in (9–15mm) across, with a collar of densely white-woolly bracts, borne in early summer. Yellow. ***Leaves*** Oval to wedge-shaped, downy, closely overlapping on stems. Silver-white.

- NATIVE HABITAT Mountain screes, New Zealand.
- CULTIVATION Needs gritty, fertile, moist but sharply drained soil. Protect from winter moisture.
- PROPAGATION Take stem tip cuttings in late summer, or sow seed as soon as ripe in containers in a cold frame.

Z 6–9

HEIGHT 4–6in (10–15cm)

SPREAD 4–6in (10–15cm)

Compositae/Asteraceae	

ARTEMISIA SCHMIDTIANA 'Nana'

Habit Rhizomatous, tufted, evergreen, perennial. ***Flowers*** Tiny, borne in clusters, to 4in (10cm) long, in summer. Yellow. ***Leaves*** Linear, finely cut, silky-haired, lobed. Silver-white.

- NATIVE HABITAT Garden selection. The species is found in the mountains of Japan.
- CULTIVATION Suitable for growing in rock gardens and raised beds. Needs gritty, well-drained, moderately fertile soil.
- PROPAGATION By heeled, side-shoot cuttings in summer.

Z 3–7

HEIGHT 3in (8cm)

SPREAD 12in (30cm)

Crassulaceae	CILIATE HOUSELEEK

SEMPERVIVUM CILIOSUM

Habit Clump-forming, evergreen, perennial. ***Flowers*** Small, star-shaped, borne in compact, flat clusters 1in (2.5cm) across, in summer. Greenish-yellow. ***Leaves*** Thick, fleshy, lance-shaped, incurved, white-hairy, forming dense rosettes. Gray-green.

• NATIVE HABITAT Rocks and screes, in the mountains of Bulgaria, former Yugoslavia, and northwest Greece.

• CULTIVATION Best in an alpine house in areas prone to damp winters. Even though it is very cold hardy, it dislikes winter moisture. Grow in pans in a mix of equal parts soil-based potting mix and sharp grit. The rosettes die after flowering, but are rapidly replaced by daughter rosettes that emerge from the base of the rosettes on lateral stolons. Sempervivums tolerate poor soils and dry conditions, but will not thrive in warm, humid climates.

• PROPAGATION By seed in spring in containers in a cold frame. Separate offsets in spring or early summer.

☼ ◊

Z 5–9

HEIGHT
3in (8cm)

SPREAD
to 12in
(30cm)

Compositae/Asteraceae	

RAOULIA AUSTRALIS

Habit Mat-forming, evergreen, perennial. ***Flowers*** Insignificant, borne in heads to ⅕in (5mm) wide, in summer. Pale yellow. ***Leaves*** Minute, spoon-shaped, intensely hairy, closely overlapping along the rooting stems. Silver-gray.
• NATIVE HABITAT Gravel and scree, New Zealand.
• CULTIVATION Needs gritty, fertile, moisture-retentive, but sharply drained soil, and some shade from the hottest sun. Protect from winter moisture.
• PROPAGATION Divide carefully in spring.
• OTHER NAME *R. lutescens.*

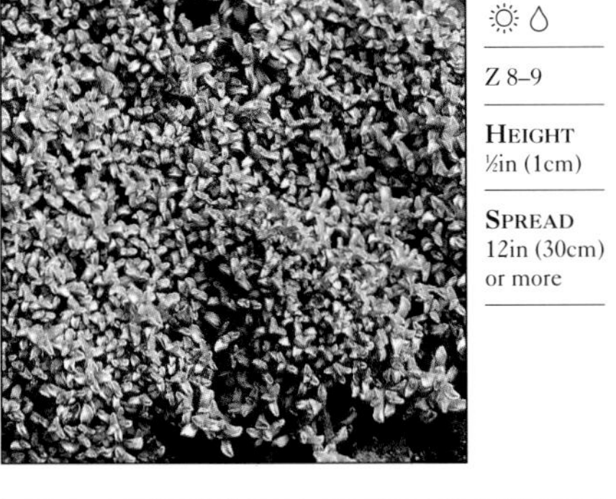

Z 8–9

HEIGHT
½in (1cm)

SPREAD
12in (30cm) or more

Umbelliferae/Apiaceae	

AZORELLA TRIFURCATA

Habit Cushion-forming, evergreen, perennial. ***Flowers*** Tiny, borne in small clusters in summer. Creamy-white. ***Leaves*** Triangular, with sharp-tipped lobes, in dense rosettes. Glossy, dark green.
• NATIVE HABITAT Open, rocky places, Chile and Argentina.
• CULTIVATION Suits a scree or raised bed in poor or moderately fertile, gritty, sharply drained soil.
• PROPAGATION By seed in autumn, in containers in a cold frame. Root rosettes as cuttings in spring.
• OTHER NAME *A. nivalis.*

Z 6–7

HEIGHT
4in (10cm) or more

SPREAD
8in (20cm)

Crassulaceae	

SEMPERVIVUM GIUSEPPII

Habit Vigorous, clump-forming, evergreen, perennial. ***Flowers*** Small, star-shaped, borne in terminal heads, 1⅜in (3.5cm) across, in summer. Dark red. ***Leaves*** Oval, fleshy, hairy when young, in tight rosettes. Pea-green, with dark tips.
• NATIVE HABITAT Mountain rocks, Spain.
• CULTIVATION Good in pots in an alpine house. Outdoors, suits a scree bed or trough, with gritty, sharply drained, moderately fertile soil.
• PROPAGATION By seed in spring, or by offsets in spring or early summer.

Z 5–9

HEIGHT
3in (8cm)

SPREAD
12in (30cm)

Crassulaceae	MOUNTAIN HOUSELEEK

SEMPERVIVUM MONTANUM

Habit Vigorous, mat-forming, evergreen, perennial. ***Flowers*** Small, star-shaped, borne in loose clusters to 2½in (6cm) across, in summer. Red-purple. ***Leaves*** Broadly lance-shaped, sharp-pointed, fleshy, finely haired, rosetted. Dull green.
• NATIVE HABITAT Mountains, central Europe.
• CULTIVATION Suits a scree bed or trough, with gritty, sharply drained, moderately fertile soil.
• PROPAGATION By seed in spring, or by offsets in spring or early summer.
• OTHER NAME *S. helveticum.*

Z 5–9

HEIGHT
4in (10cm)

SPREAD
12in (30cm)

Caryophyllaceae	

SAGINA BOYDII

Habit Very slow-growing, compact, cushion-forming, evergreen, perennial. ***Flowers*** Tiny, usually petalless, borne in summer. Mid-green. ***Leaves*** Rigid, linear to narrowly wedge-shaped, recurved, densely packed in crowded rosettes. Glossy, dark green.

• NATIVE HABITAT Mountains of Scotland.

• CULTIVATION Valued for its neat, symmetrical, compact rosettes of foliage. Best grown in an alpine house in order to maintain its compact form. Grow in a mix of 3 parts grit or sharp sand, with 1 part peat or leaf mold. Provide bright, filtered light, and maintain a cool, moist, buoyant atmosphere as it dislikes hot, dry conditions. Very susceptible to spider mite, under glass. Outdoors, it is ideal for growing in a trough, in very low-fertility, very sharply drained soil, in good light but with shade from hot sun.

• PROPAGATION Root individual rosettes as cuttings in early summer.

Z 4–7

HEIGHT
1in (2.5cm)

SPREAD
3in (8cm)

Umbelliferae/Apiaceae	

BOLAX GUMMIFERA

Habit Slow-growing, cushion-forming, evergreen, perennial. ***Flowers*** Tiny, seldom produced, borne in clusters of 3–20, in summer. Greenish-white. ***Leaves*** Deeply lobed, leathery, forming dense rosettes. Dark blue-green.

- NATIVE HABITAT Southern Chile, southern Argentina, and the Falkland Islands.
- CULTIVATION Needs poor, gritty, sharply drained soil, in a scree or raised bed. May be grown in tufa.
- PROPAGATION Root rosettes as cuttings in spring.
- OTHER NAMES *B. glebaria, Azorella glebaria.*

Z 6–7

HEIGHT
2in (5cm)

SPREAD
6in (15cm)

Plantaginaceae	

PLANTAGO NIVALIS

Habit Rosette-forming, evergreen, perennial. ***Flowers*** Tiny, tubular, borne in spikes to ½in (1cm) across, on long stalks in summer. Green. ***Leaves*** Lance-shaped, silky-haired. Silver-green.

- NATIVE HABITAT Mountains, southern Spain.
- CULTIVATION In an alpine house, use a mix of 4 parts peat or leaf mold to 1 part grit or sharp sand. Outdoors, grow in a trough in low-fertility, sharply drained soil. Protect from winter moisture.
- PROPAGATION Sow seed in autumn, or divide in spring.

Z 5–8

HEIGHT
1in (2.5cm)

SPREAD
3in (8cm)

Caryophyllaceae/ Illecebraceae	

PARONYCHIA KAPELA subsp. *SERPYLLIFOLIA*

Habit Mat-forming, evergreen, perennial. ***Flowers*** Tiny, borne in heads, to ¾in (2cm) across, in summer. Greenish-white, with silvery-white papery bracts. ***Leaves*** Oval to lance-shaped. Silvery blue-green.

- NATIVE HABITAT Hot, dry sites, Mediterranean.
- CULTIVATION Grow in poor, sharply drained soil. Suitable for a trough, a raised bed, or tufa.
- PROPAGATION Sow seed in winter, divide in spring, or take stem-tip cuttings in early summer.

Z 5–7

HEIGHT
2in (5cm)

SPREAD
8in (20cm)

SEDUM

The genus *Sedum*, commonly known as stonecrops, consists of about 400 species of succulent annuals and evergreen, semievergreen, and deciduous perennials. Some of the larger perennials, along with a few shrubs and subshrubs, are sometimes included in the genus *Hylotelephium*. Stonecrops are valued for their neat and attractive, often beautifully colored or bloomed foliage. The star-shaped flowers, although usually individually small, are grouped in showy clusters or sprays. Most of them originate in the mountains of the northern hemisphere, and a few are found in arid areas of South America and Africa.

The stonecrops described here are ideal for growing in rock gardens or for cultivation in an alpine house. They can be used to great effect if planted as a genus collection in a trough or raised bed, and will provide very attractive contrasts of color, texture, and form. The more robust types may also be grown at the front of a sunny, well-drained herbaceous or mixed border.

Stonecrops are best grown in moderately fertile, well-drained, gritty soils in full sun. *Sedum spathulifolium, S. kamschaticum* 'Variegatum', and other vigorous species tolerate light shade. Trim back spreading species after they have flowered to maintain the shape of the plant and prevent encroachment on other, less-vigorous, neighbors.

Propagate species by seed sown in autumn, in pots in a cold frame. Divide during spring and mid-summer. Take stem cuttings of nonflowering shoots or root individual rosette cuttings, in early or mid-summer. Handle stonecrops carefully, since all parts can cause stomach upset if ingested and contact with the sap may irritate the skin.

S. CAUTICOLA

Habit Trailing, stoloniferous, perennial, semievergreen.
Flowers Star-shaped, borne in rounded, terminal clusters, to 4in (10cm) wide, in autumn. Rose-purple aging to carmine-red.
Leaves Rounded to spoon-shaped or oval, borne on purple-tinted stems. Gray-green.
- HEIGHT 3in (8cm).
- SPREAD 12in (30cm).

S. cauticola

Z 4–8

S. LYDIUM

Habit Mat-forming, stem-rooting, evergreen, perennial.
Flowers Star-shaped, borne in flat-topped, terminal clusters 1in (2.5cm) across, during summer. White.
Leaves Cylindrical, fleshy, tightly rosetted. Bright green, with red tips.
- HEIGHT 2in (5cm).
- SPREAD 8in (20cm).

S. lydium

Z 5–7

S. SPATHULIFOLIUM 'Purpureum'

Habit Mat-forming, evergreen, perennial.
Flowers Star-shaped, borne in flat clusters, ⅝in (15mm) across, in summer. Yellow.
Leaves Spoon-shaped and fleshy. Silvery-green, suffused red-purple.
- HEIGHT 4in (10cm).
- SPREAD 24in (60cm).

***S. spathulifolium* 'Purpureum'**

Z 4–7

S. OBTUSATUM
Habit Cushion-forming, evergreen, perennial.
Flowers Star-shaped, to ⅜in (1cm) across, borne in flat, terminal clusters, 4in (10cm) wide, in summer. Bright yellow.
Leaves Spoon-shaped and fleshy. Blue-green, suffused crimson.
• OTHER NAME *S. rubroglaucum*.
• HEIGHT 2in (5cm).
• SPREAD 8in (20cm).

S. obtusatum

Z 5–9

S. KAMSCHATICUM 'Variegatum'
Habit Clump-forming, rhizomatous, perennial, semievergreen.
Flowers Star-shaped, ⅝in (15mm) across, borne in flat-topped clusters, 2in (5cm) wide, in late summer. Golden-yellow.
Leaves Lance- to spoon-shaped. Green, tinted pink, cream-margined.
• HEIGHT 4in (10cm).
• SPREAD 10in (25cm).

***S. kamschaticum* 'Variegatum'**

Z 3–8

S. ACRE
Habit Mat-forming, evergreen, perennial.
Flowers Star-shaped, borne in flat-topped clusters, to 1½in (4cm) across, in summer. Bright yellow.
Leaves Triangular, overlapping, borne on trailing or upright stems. Pale green.
• HEIGHT 2in (5cm).
• SPREAD 24in (60cm).

S. acre
Biting stonecrop, Wallpepper

Z 3–8

S. ACRE 'Aureum'
Habit Mat-forming, evergreen, perennial.
Flowers Star-shaped, borne in flat-topped clusters, to 1½in (4cm) across, in summer. Yellow-green.
Leaves Triangular and overlapping. Bright yellow.
• HEIGHT 2in (5cm).
• SPREAD 24in (60cm).

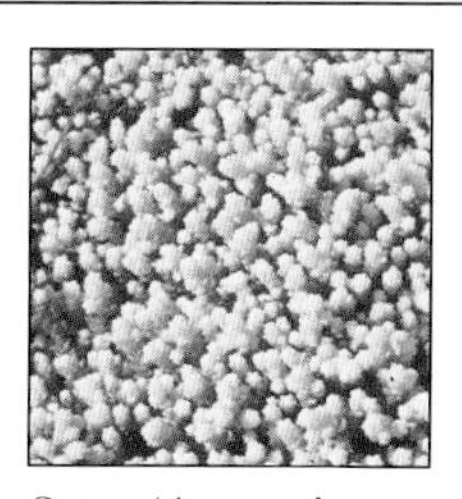

***S. acre* 'Aureum'**

Z 3–8

S. SPATHULIFOLIUM 'Cape Blanco'
Habit Mat-forming, evergreen, perennial.
Flowers Star-shaped, ⅝in (15mm) across, borne in summer. Yellow.
Leaves Spoon-shaped, fleshy, rosetted. Silvery-green, with white bloom.
• OTHER NAME *S. spathulifolium* 'Cappa Blanca'.
• HEIGHT 4in (10cm).
• SPREAD 24in (60cm).

***S. spathulifolium* 'Cape Blanco'**

Z 4–7

S. RUPESTRE
Habit Vigorous, mat-forming, evergreen, perennial.
Flowers Star-shaped, ⅝in (15mm) across, borne in terminal clusters 2½in (6cm) wide, on upright, woody stems, in summer. Yellow.
Leaves Pointed, fleshy, cylindrical. Gray-green.
• OTHER NAME *S. reflexum*.
• HEIGHT 4in (10cm).
• SPREAD 24in (60cm).

S. rupestre
Stone orpine

Z 4–8

Soil Preparation and Planting

The rock garden is perhaps the best-known place for growing rock plants and alpines. However, if space is restricted, raised beds, troughs, sinks, and other containers with free drainage can provide very attractive alternatives. Together with the use of different soil mixes, they also extend the range of plants that can be grown in a garden.

Selecting and buying plants

A well-planned rock garden can provide color throughout the year, more so than other plant groups in the garden. Where early-flowering alpines are grown, it is important to consider their characters, such as form and habit, and the color offered by fruit, foliage, and stems, to ensure year-round interest. Before buying, research the range of plants that are likely to thrive in the soil type, exposure, and climate of the garden, by consulting standard texts and visiting established rock gardens.

Garden centers and other non-specialist outlets generally offer a limited range of rock plants, and these are likely to be the more robust and easily grown. Bear in mind that some may be vigorous species that will overwhelm smaller, more choice alpines, if not sited with due attention to their size, vigor, and propensity for self-seeding.

Specialist nurseries are likely to provide a wider range of unusual plants and can offer guidance on the suitability of plants for a given situation and on their cultural needs. Beware of making expensive purchases of rarities unless confident that their specific needs can be met.

Choose plants that have healthy foliage, with no sign of pests, diseases, root restriction, or water deprivation. Look for a weed-free soil mix surface and, before planting, discard the top layer of soil mix to avoid introducing weed seeds to the rock garden. The

invasion of mat- or cushion-forming alpines by pernicious seeders such as pearlworts and bittercress, will prove tediously difficult to eradicate if they are allowed to establish.

Siting a rock garden

Most alpines need high levels of light and excellent drainage, and so prefer an open, sunny site, away from shade cast by buildings or trees. Although some alpines grow well beneath them, trees can present several problems. For example, dripping water can spoil foliage and set up a site for fungal infection, while fallen leaves can smother small plants in autumn. Moreover, tree roots may compete for water and nutrients, and can even undermine rockwork.

Avoid frost pockets and sites exposed to searing winds. A sloping site is ideal in that drainage is likely to be good and the potential for integrating rocks in a naturalistic manner is far greater than on a flat site. Natural and aesthetically pleasing effects are achieved if the rock garden is set in informally planted surroundings. If the style of the garden is predominantly formal, it may be better to consider rectangular raised beds, which are more easily integrated and unified with a strong geometric layout.

Choosing stone

Using locally available stone is the cheapest option, and will almost certainly harmonize more naturally with the general surroundings. This may not be possible in areas where supplies are limited or where geological formations are unsuitable. For example, shales weather too quickly, and igneous rocks, like granite or basalt, or hard rocks with no clear strata, are difficult to arrange in a natural layout and can take many years to achieve a weathered appearance. Slates can be useful and attractive, but are often difficult to blend in, except in areas where they occur naturally. Avoid buying rock that has been taken from any ecologically sensitive rock formation.

Types of Stone

Sandstone
This is one of the most suitable rocks to use in a rock garden. Its natural strata lines are clearly visible and allow the rock to be split easily.

Tufa
Scarce and expensive, tufa is lightweight and alkaline and its air pockets provide perfect drainage. Niches for cushion plants can easily be drilled or excavated.

Limestone
A good choice, available either second-hand or from quarries. Over time, it releases alkaline compounds and makes growing acid-loving plants difficult.

How to Prepare the Site

1 Place a 6in (15cm) layer of coarse rubble, broken bricks, ballast, or gravel over the base of the site to form a mound and guarantee good drainage at the base.

2 Cover the mound with inverted sod or a punctured plastic sheet to prevent soil mix from percolating through to the rubble, thus impeding drainage.

3 Cover the sod with a 9–12in (23–30cm) layer of soil mix. Using string and pegs, mark the outlines of "keystones" and rock outcrops.

4 Dig out receiving hollows for large rocks, with a spade. Maneuver stones into place with a crowbar. Tip them back slightly and wedge with smaller rocks for stability.

*5 Infill around the rocks with carefully mixed soil (*see *pp.160–1). Check regularly for stability. Firm the soil gently around the stones to eliminate air pockets.*

6 Fill around the stones with soil mix, burying them to one-third of their depth. Top with a final layer of equal parts loam, leaf mold or garden compost, and grit.

Preparation and construction
Perennial weeds can be very difficult to eradicate from established rock gardens, especially if they seed into dense mat- or cushion-forming plants. It is best to begin a program of weed eradication several months before construction starts, using a systemic herbicide to ensure that deep roots are killed completely. Any subsequent seedling regrowth can be readily removed by hand.

Make sure that the site, particularly if level, is well drained and install a French drain or other drainage system, if necessary. This is most important on heavy clay soils. Sloping sites are usually free-draining but may need a drainage ditch or French drain at the lowest point. If the underlying drainage is good, simply dig over the soil and remove any weed regrowth. Consolidate the surface by gentle treading to avoid subsequent soil settlement, then fork over lightly to maintain the soil structure. Never attempt to construct the rock garden when the soil is wet, since the weight of heavy rocks will damage soil structure and cause compaction. This, in turn, will interfere with free drainage, making establishment and healthy root growth difficult.

Wear sturdy gloves and protective footwear throughout construction. Use rollers to move large rocks, and arrange for the consignment to be delivered as close as possible to the construction site. It may be necessary to use a block -and tackle and crowbar to maneuver large rocks into place. Set the rocks tipped backward slightly, so that rainwater runs into the bed rather than onto the plants beneath. Bury about one-third of the rock to ensure stability, checking for any movement as work proceeds.

The largest stones act as "keystones" (the dominant rock of the outcrop), and must be set in place first. Position the remaining rocks with their strata aligned, so that they flow naturally from the keystone to form outcrops in the required direction. Secondary keystones

Planting During Construction

1 *Set plants against a firmed rock with the roots against its face. Place battens on either side so that a second rock can be placed without crushing the plants.*

2 *When the second stone is set firmly in place, remove the battens. Infill around the rocks and at the plant's roots with soil mix (see pp. 160–1). Firm the plant in gently.*

3 *Add a 1in (2.5cm) layer of stone chippings, gravel, or grit as a top-dressing to ensure sharp drainage at the vulnerable neck of the plants, and to create an attractive and natural finish.*

can be used to extend the outcrops. Make regular visual checks and arrange rocks so that they are positioned to provide the widest possible variety of planting niches. Butting rocks face to face will ensure sites for crevice dwellers, while terraces between successive tiers provide suitable conditions for mat-forming alpines. Plants that need a cool, moist root run beneath the rocks can be set in place during construction. Position them between two successive layers of rock, and protect them from crushing with battens or fragments of rocks.

Soils for rock gardens and scree beds
In the wild, many alpines grow in a substrate made up largely of rock fragments, interspersed with detritus that is often rich in organic matter and retains moisture. This substrate is very sharply drained and often low in nutrients. These two factors should be taken into account when creating a mix in which plants will thrive and still retain their natural, compact character. A special soil mix that suits most rock garden plants can be made up of equal parts garden soil, peat or leaf mold, and sharp grit or sharp, salt-free sand. This

Planting a Rock Garden

1 Water plants and allow them to drain. Arrange them on the surface of the soil according to the planting plan.

2 Remove each plant from its pot and loosen the root ball gently. Dispose of the top layer of soil mix, plus weeds and their seeds.

3 With a trowel, make a planting hole large enough to accommodate the root ball. Ease the plant into the hole and label.

4 Infill with soil mix and firm gently. Top-dress with a layer of grit or rock chips, easing a little grit beneath the plant necks.

5 When the entire rock garden is fully planted, fill in any gaps in the top-dressing with grit, and water the plants in well.

should be used to form a top layer of at least ¾in (20mm). Scree plants need a very well-drained, low-fertility soil mix made up of one part of loam and one part of peat or leaf mold, with 3 parts or more of grit or stone chips. In very dry areas, it is wise to use a more moisture-retentive mix of 2 parts each loam and leaf mold, with 1 part coarse sand, and 2 parts stone chips (or less in dry areas). For acid-loving plants use a mix of 4 parts lime-free leaf mold, compost, or ground bark, and one part lime-free grit or coarse sand. On naturally alkaline soils, pocket plantings of this mix are best regarded as short-term, since lime eventually percolates into the mix often causing the plants to perish.

Planting a rock garden

Alpines and rock plants are nearly always pot-grown. Most can be planted at any time of the year if given conscientious aftercare, especially with regard to watering and weeding. Like other plant groups, however, they should not be planted when the soil is wet or frozen, or when the weather is warm and dry. Plants with gray or soft foliage and many cushion-forming alpines are best set out in spring or early summer. Water all plants thoroughly before planting and allow them to drain. Dig a hole that will accommodate the roots without crowding. Slide them gently from their pots and tease out the root ball very carefully. Position the plant in the hole and infill with soil mix, firming gently. Set the plant with its collar slightly above the soil surface, then top-dress with grit or rock chips, easing it in gently around the plant neck with your fingers. Water thoroughly after planting and continue until the plant begins to make new growth. If the weather is dry after planting, water at weekly intervals, if necessary. Check first by feeling the soil beneath the top-dressing, taking care to avoid disturbing the roots. Once they are established, plants seldom need additional watering except in prolonged periods of drought. Netting should be

Planting in a Vertical Crevice

1 Remove soil mix with a spoon or trowel. Wedge a small stone firmly at the base of the crevice, using a hammer if necessary.

2 Add a 1in (2.5cm) layer of soil mix, then gently ease in the small rootball of of a young plant (here, Campanula*).*

3 Cover with soil mix, and wedge in place with a small stone. Add more plants, at least 4in (10cm) apart. Water in carefully.

How to Plant in a Drystone Retaining Wall

1 *Check that there is sufficient soil mix in the planting crevice. Set a small rooted cutting on the flat of the stone. Ease in the roots with a trowel.*

2 *Bed the plant into the soil mix and pack more soil mix into the crevice to hold the plant in place. This is easiest with small plants and slightly moist soil mix. Firm in with your fingers.*

3 *For larger plants, scoop out some soil mix from the crevice. Ease in the rootball and trickle in more soil mix while holding the plant in place. Water in from the wall top or with a mist sprayer.*

used to protect plants, especially woolly-leaved species, since birds may pull out or damage rosette-forming plants, or shred woolly leaves for nest material. Check plants regularly, refirming soil as necessary.

Planting in a scree bed

Key to a successful scree bed are care during planting and conscientious watering until the plants are well established. It can be more difficult to grow plants in a scree bed because the surface layer of sharply drained soil mix dries out before the plants can develop a root system that is able to reach moisture at deeper levels. At the same time, care must be taken not to overwater the site.

When planting, shake off most of the soil mix from the root ball and keep the bare roots moist. Set the plant in a planting hole, spreading the roots out, and then infill carefully with scree mixture. Top-dress with a layer of chips and water each plant immediately and thoroughly. Keep watering regularly until new leaves or shoot growth are evident.

Top-dressing

When planting is complete, it is best to top-dress any bare soil with grit or chips that will blend with the rocks. As well as being aesthetically satisfying, this maintains a perfectly drained layer around the neck of plants, conserves soil moisture, and prevents compaction by heavy rain or watering. It also prevents light from reaching weed seeds at the soil surface. Top-dressing needs to be at least 1in (2.5cm) deep to be effective, preferably twice that, and on scree beds it can be up to 6in (15cm) deep.

Troughs, sinks, and other containers

Almost any perfectly drained, frost-proof container can be used for growing alpines. The advantage of container plantings is that they can be filled with a specific soil mix to suit a given group of plants. Traditional stone troughs are scarce and expensive, but glazed stone sinks make attractive alternatives when coated with hypertufa. This is a mix of 1–2 parts sphagnum peat or sifted peat substitute, 1 part coarse sand or grit, and 1 part cement, mixed with just enough water to form a stiffish paste. Clean glazed sinks thoroughly and score the outer surface with a wire brush or glass cutter. Adhesion will be more secure if the surface is first coated with an epoxy bonding agent. Using gloved hands, apply the fresh hypertufa mix to a thickness of ¾in (2cm), from below the inside rim to just below the expected soil mix level. Roughen the surface to resemble stone. After one week, scrub with a stiff wire brush, then wash with a suspension of manure to encourage rapid colonization by algae, mosses, and lichens to create an attractive weathered appearance. The hypertufa mix can be adjusted, with an increased proportion of sand and grit to 3 parts, to make a stiffer mix that is sufficiently rigid and durable for an entire trough. Use 2 sturdy boxes as a mold, one inside the other, with a cavity of 2–3in (5–7cm) between them.

Place troughs in their final position before filling and planting up, especially if rocks are used. They will be heavy, even when empty, and may prove impossible to move when full. Choose an open site, with at least part-day sun,

How to Make a Hypertufa Trough

1 Coat the surfaces of the inner and outer boxes with oil to prevent sticking. Place a 1in (2.5cm) layer of hypertufa in the outer box.

2 Put wire netting on the hypertufa to reinforce it and push thick pieces of dowel into the bottom to make drainage holes.

3 Reinforce the sides with vertical netting. Place the inner box centrally. Fill the cavity with more hypertufa and tamp down.

4 Cover the top of the hypertufa with plastic sheeting until the mix has set (usually about a week). Keep frost-free.

5 When the hypertufa has set, remove the outer box. If hypertufa has stuck to the box, separate gently with a hammer and chisel.

6 Remove the inner box, again with a hammer and chisel if necessary. Paint with liquid manure to encourage algal growth.

preferably on a hard, level surface with easy access to water. Raise containers off the ground, so as not to hinder drainage, by placing them on sturdy stable pillars of stone or brick. Ensure that there is no danger of them tipping over.

Many rock plants will thrive in a commercial potting mix with about one-third by volume of sharp grit added to improve drainage, and bonemeal. Acid-loving plants need a lime-free soil mix with granitic or acid sandstone chips. Cover drainage holes with crocks or wire gauze and fill the bottom third or quarter of the trough with stone chips. Top with a thin, inverted layer of sod (or peat substitute) and fill to within 2in (5cm) of the rim with soil mix (see pp. 160–1). If rocks or tufa are used, set them in the soil mix to form suitable crevices and niches for the proposed plantings. Water thoroughly to settle in the soil mix and let them drain before planting.

Choose compact, slow-growing plants that will neither dominate the site nor exhaust soil nutrients too quickly. Arrange container-grown plants on the soil mix and, when they are in final position, plant as described for planting in the rock garden (see p. 161). Top-dress with a layer of rock chips and water throughly. In hot weather, provide shade for the plant until it is well established.

How to Plant Up an Alpine Trough

1 If planting in tufa, drill holes about 1in (2.5cm) wide, 3in (7cm) deep, and 4in (10cm) apart. Immerse tufa in water overnight.

2 Lay fine-mesh netting over the trough base, cover the holes with crocks, and add 3–4in (7–10cm) of coarse grit.

3 Partly fill the trough with a gritty, moist soil mix, firming in stages. Set the tufa in place, buried by at least ⅓–½ its depth.

4 Fill the trough with soil mix to within 2in (5cm) of the rim. Trickle a little soil mix into the tufa cavities.

5 Wash the roots of plants to go in the tufa; ease into the planting holes. Dribble in soil mix, firm in, wedge with small stones.

6 Arrange plants in their pots to check the arrangement and spacing. Then plant, firm them in, and water well.

ROUTINE CARE

As with any other group of plants, alpines and rock plants need regular care and maintenance if they are to continue to give their best. In most routine maintenance, perhaps the primary difference is that of scale.

Weeding

Thorough site preparation and the use of sterilized soil mix when planting helps to minimize weed problems, at least for the first few years. It is vital, however, to remove any seedling weeds as soon as they emerge, and to remove all weeds before they seed. Once weeds have rooted into dense mats or compact cushions they are very difficult to extract without resorting to the use of snub-nosed tweezers. It is possible to treat perennial weeds by painting with a systemic weed killer, but bear in mind that these are so effective that they will also kill any alpine plant that they come into contact with. For weeding around alpine plants, use a 3-pronged cultivator, which helps to loosen and aerate the surrounding soil.

Feeding

If the original soil mix has been prepared properly, newly planted areas will not need feeding for several years. Eventually, however, the soil will be depleted of nutrients and growth, and flowering may begin to deteriorate. Although an annual dressing in spring of slow-release fertilizer and bonemeal can be given, slow-release fertilizers tend to cause uneven growth in alpines. A better method, therefore, is to carefully remove the top-dressing and the top ½in (1cm) of soil mix, and replace it with fresh soil mix and a further top-dressing of grit. The top-dressing on the surface of the rock garden is likely to need topping up occasionally,

WEEDING

Before

Use a 3-pronged cultivator to weed around young plants. This also loosens and aerates the soil. Remove top-dressing first, and replace it after weeding.

REMOVING DEAD GROWTH

Before

When danger of frost has passed in spring, remove any dieback by cutting back to healthy growth with sharp scissors or pruners.

Renewing Top-dressing

1 *Remove the old top-dressing as well as the top layer, to about ⅜in (1cm), of soil mix. Fill in around the plants with fresh soil mix.*

2 *Top-dress the bed with a fresh layer of coarse grit or rock chips, lifting cushions gently, if necessary, to renew top-dressing around the plant collar.*

Removing Dead Rosettes

1 *Dead rosettes may cause rot if not removed. Cut out carefully with a sharp knife or scissors without disturbing the rest of the plant.*

2 *Top-dress any exposed soil. This prevents weed from becoming established in the gaps before the plant produces new growth to fill the space.*

especially on slopes. Recover any bare patches of soil, paying particular attention in autumn, to ensure good soil coverage during winter. Top up again, as required, in spring, applying a slow-release fertilizer at the same time, if needed.

Watering

Once rock plants are well established, they root deeply and seldom need more water than is provided by rainfall. In prolonged drought, however, they should be soaked thoroughly in the early morning or evening, but not during the heat of the day. If the soil is dry to a depth of about 2in (5cm), soak until water has penetrated to the full depth of the roots. Containers used for alpines need more attention because they dry out quickly in hot weather, and the plants have a confined volume of soil from which to extract moisture. Overhead irrigation for troughs is best done in the early morning or evening.

Trimming and pruning

The routine pruning of shrubs, subshrubs, and evergreen perennials in a rock garden is limited, for the most part, to the removal of dead, diseased, or damage wood to keep them healthy. They are usually so slow-growing that they seldom need pruning to restrict size, but when this does become necessary it is very important to maintain the natural form and habit of the plant. A few species, notably *Helianthemum*, *Arabis*, *Aubrieta*, and *Aurinia*, benefit from hard annual clipping after flowering to keep them dense and compact.

Where over-vigorous plants threaten to encroach upon their neighbors, they can be cut back in spring. It may be sufficient to pull out excess growth by hand from the margins of vigorous mat-forming species, and refirm any rooted stems that have been lifted by mistake. On other plants, excess growth may need to be lifted with a handfork. Clear sufficient space to allow for regrowth of the pruned plant without further impeding the growth of the surrounding plants. Plants that are hard-pruned will benefit from an application of balanced fertilizer to promote new growth.

It is more important with alpines than with other plants to remove dead leaves and flowers, especially tree leaves, toward autumn. If left in place, these may cause rotting in winter. Carefully cut out dead rosettes from plants such as saxifrages, using sharp scissors, but do not pull them out since this is likely to dislodge healthy rosettes at the same time. Dead material from the smallest alpines should be picked out carefully by hand, or by using tweezers if necessary. Routine deadheading of alpines is also important, especially with plants that are known to self-seed freely, like *Campanula cochlearifolia* or violas.

Renovating an Alpine Bed

1 *Vigorously spreading plants may encroach on smaller neighbors. Dig out, pull up, or trim back in spring, to give nearby plants space to grow.*

2 *Once the bed has been cleared of unwanted growth, add a dressing of balanced fertilizer before replacing a fresh layer of grit or gravel on the surface of the soil mix around the plants.*

Pests and diseases

Good garden hygiene and cultural practices are the primary approach when controlling pests and diseases in the rock garden. Aphids may need to be controlled, but are most likely to be a problem where plants are grown in over-fertile soils. Rich soils produce soft growth that is not only more prone to attack by sap-sucking insects, but also less tolerant of winter cold. A sharp surface of top-dressing goes some way to deterring slugs and snails but, even then, some luscious plants like *Campanula zoysii* are still likely to need additional protection.

Insects such as ants can also cause damage when they build nests beneath cushion-forming plants. It is important to control these nests before extensive colonies become established.

Protection from birds in the form of netting is important for new plantings. Nesting birds in spring are particularly determined to uproot rosettes.

PROPAGATION

Most species of alpine and rock plant can be raised from seed but a few, like the celmisias, may produce infertile seed in cultivation. Some cultivars come true from seed, but most need to be increased vegetatively.

Seed collection

Since many alpines flower early in the year, seed is often ripe by mid-summer and may be sown at once. Germination is usually rapid, producing strong seedlings before winter. Any autumn-sown seed that germinates quickly should be overwintered in a cold frame. Collect the ripe seed, taking off the seedhead and its stem. Place in a paper bag to dry, and label to avoid confusion. Separate the seeds from their dry capsules by rubbing them between the fingers. Sieve the seeds clean of debris and seal them in labeled envelopes. Put them in an airtight container and store in a cool place until sowing.

Seed treatments and germination

Scarify hard-coated seeds by chipping or abrading with fine sand paper, or soak in water for 12–24 hours. Most alpine seed needs exposure to cold before it

SOWING SEED

1 *Fill a pot with a mix of equal parts seed soil mix and perlite or sharp sand. Firm gently to level and remove air pockets.*

2 *Using a clean piece of paper folded in half, tap the seed (here,* Lewisia*) thinly and evenly onto the surface.*

3 *Cover with a fine layer of sieved seed soil mix. Top-dress with ¼–½in (5–10mm) layer of grit. Label and water well.*

4 *Prick out seedlings when they have 2 true leaves (see inset). Lift gently with a widger or spoon, and handle only by the leaves.*

5 *Pot seedlings up singly into pots of equal parts soil-based potting mix and grit. Firm in gently with a dibble.*

6 *Top-dress seedlings with grit and water, and place in light shade. Pot on or plant out seedlings when the roots fill the pot.*

will germinate. The easiest way to effect this is to sow fresh seed in autumn, then plunge the pots in a cold frame in a sheltered site for overwintering. Alternatively, seal the pots in a plastic bag, place in the bottom of a refrigerator for about 3 weeks, then plunge in sand outdoors until germination. A few seeds, such as *Trillium*, need alternating periods of cold and warmth under glass to germinate successfully, while those of primroses and anemones are best sown as soon as ripe and will often germinate within 3–4 weeks.

The speed of germination varies with the age, type, and species of seed, and the time of sowing. Autumn or early spring sowings usually germinate in spring. If they appear before severe weather has passed, move them to a cold frame or cold greenhouse for overwintering. A few seeds, like those of *Ranunculus*, may take several years to germinate, and the slow germinators often do so erratically. In these cases, prick out seedlings as they appear, and keep the pots until more develop.

Softwood and greenwood cuttings
Most rock plants can be raised from these types of cutting. Softwood ones are taken from the tips of non-flowering (vegetative), leafy shoots during active growth or in summer, following shearing back after flowering. Greenwood cuttings are taken in early summer and are slightly riper than softwood ones, but can be treated in the same way.

Cuttings are best taken early in the morning, when shoots are fully turgid. For softwood cuttings, select strong, healthy shoots that are soft and pliable, whereas those just starting to harden at the base suit greenwood cuttings. Cut with a sharp knife and place directly into a plastic bag to conserve moisture and prevent wilting. Prepare and insert cuttings as soon as possible since they will not root well, or at all, if allowed to wilt. Already-prepared pots of 1 part by volume of soil, grit, and peat

Treating cuttings

1 *Remove lower leaves and soft tips (here,* Gypsophila repens*). Dip in hormone rooting powder, then insert in a prepared pot of moist cutting soil mix.*

2 *Water with fungicide, then drain and label. Put pot in a sealed plastic bag and place in good light out of hot sun. Root in a propagator, in a mist propogation unit, or in a closed, plastic bag.*

3 *When well rooted, water and allow to drain. Separate and pot up singly; hold only by the leaves. Top-dress, water in, and label. Return to the propagator. Harden off when new growth appears.*

Basal Cuttings

Taking basal cuttings
In spring, take cuttings 2–3in (5–7cm) long, with new leaves and a short stem. Trim the base, remove lower leaves, and insert to the depth indicated (see inset).

help to reduce their exposure time to open air. Trim to 1–3in (2.5–7cm) long, cutting just below a node. Remove lower leaves and any soft tips, especially if they show signs of wilting. Using a dibble, make a hole in the soil mix and insert cuttings to a depth of up to half their length, with the lower leaves just above the surface. Root with gentle heat from below, in good light, but out of direct sun to avoid overheating.

Inspect daily and remove dead or diseased cuttings with tweezers, since they will infect healthy ones. Watering is seldom required until after rooting. When plants produce new growth, check for rooting by pulling gently. When well rooted, pot up into a mix of equal parts potting soil mix and grit.

Basal cuttings

Some plants, such as *Primula marginata* and its cultivars, can be propagated by basal cuttings. These are taken from young shoots at or just above soil level. Basal cuttings are usually taken in spring. If taken in summer or early autumn, they must be well rooted in time for overwintering. Fill pots with a mix of equal parts commercial cutting soil mix and fine grit. Take 2–3in (5–7cm) cuttings (or ⅘–1⅕in (2–3cm) ones on small alpines), trim the base cleanly below a node, and remove the lower leaves. Dip the base in hormone rooting powder and insert one-half to one-third of the stem (as shown). Keep the leaves clear of the soil and of neighboring cuttings. Water in and root in a cool, shaded propagator or frame. When rooted, after about 3–6 weeks, pot up singly, or line out in a cold frame or nursery bed to grow on.

Semi-ripe and ripewood cuttings

Plants such as *Cassiope* suit semi-ripe cuttings, which are taken from non-flowering shoots of the current year's growth, just as it begins to harden at the base. The shoots should offer slight resistance to pressure when bent gently between fingers and thumb. Semi-ripe material is generally ready for taking between mid- and late summer. Ripewood cuttings are taken from evergreen plants, such as *Salix*, during late summer and autumn when the current season's growth is fully ripened.

Taking cuttings

Depending on the plant concerned and available material, cuttings will be about ⅖–1⅗in (1–4cm) long. Cut them from the parent plant using a sharp knife or pruners. Make a clean cut just below a node and remove soft tips and the lower leaves before dipping the cutting base in hormone rooting powder. Alternatively, take the cutting with a heel of older tissue at the base, and trim it cleanly with a sharp knife. Insert small cuttings, to one-third or one-half

SELECTING CUTTING MATERIAL

1 Semi-ripe (Phlox) *In mid- to late summer, select non-flowering shoots that are just hardening, but not woody at the base. Remove 1¼in (3cm) lengths, trimming to about ⅖in (1cm). Insert to the depth indicated (inset left).*

2 Ripewood (Dryas) *In late summer and autumn, select the current season's shoots and take cuttings about 1in (2.5cm) long. Trim to about ⅖in (1cm) long, below the base of the leaves. Insert to the depth shown (inset left).*

3 Rosette (Saxifraga) *Individual rosettes may be inserted as cuttings during early and mid-summer. With a sharp knife, cut the rosette off at the base, about ⅖in (1cm) below the leaves. Trim cleanly across the base, and insert to the depth shown.*

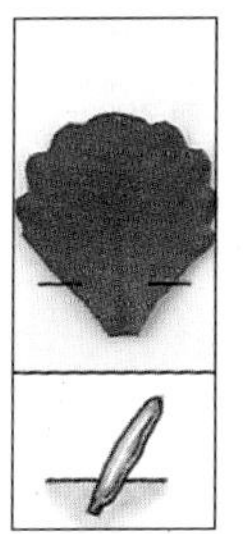

4 Leaf (Sedum) *Throughout the growing season, select young but fully developed leaves that are healthy and undamaged. Cut off and trim cleanly across the base, inserting at an angle of 45 degrees, as shown (insert left).*

of their length, into dibbled holes in pots of cutting soil mix topped with a ⅜in (1cm) layer of fine sand. Label each pot, water with fungicide, and root in a propagator in a cool greenhouse. Alternatively, if large numbers of cuttings are taken, they can be rooted in a prepared cold frame with sharp drainage of rubble or gravel at its base. Dig over the soil at the base of the frame, top with a mix of equal parts peat or commercial cutting soil mix and grit, and finish with a 1in (2.5cm) layer of sharp sand. After inserting the cuttings, close the frame. Ventilate in warm weather, shade from hot sun, and insulate in periods of frosty weather. Check frequently for disease, and remove diseased material and fallen leaves regularly. Water sparingly, keeping the soil mix just moist.

As growth begins, apply a half-strength, balanced liquid fertilizer. The cuttings, whether in a cold frame or propagator, should be well rooted by the following spring. Pot up singly into a mix of equal parts potting soil mix and grit or, when danger of frost has passed, harden off and transfer to a nursery bed. Grow on, keeping the rooted cuttings moist, shaded from hot sun, and apply a balanced liquid fertilizer occasionally during the growing season. Transfer the new plants to their permanent positions in autumn, or the following spring.

Leaf cuttings

Several plants with fleshy leaves, such as *Haberlea*, *Lewisia*, *Ramonda*, or *Sedum* species, are suitable for leaf cuttings. Cut mature young leaves from the parent stem or rosette at their base. Root the cuttings in a mix of equal parts standard cutting soil mix and sharp sand. Trim the leaf base cleanly and insert at an angle of 45°, just deep enough to be held in place in the soil mix. Enclose in a plastic bag. When the new plantlet appears from the leaf base at soil level, pot it up singly and grow on.

Irishman's cuttings

Dianthus and species, and other stem-rooting or creeping species, frequently produce ready-rooted sideshoots. These can be removed from the parent clump and potted up, or transferred to a nursery bed for growing on.

IRISHMAN'S CUTTINGS

1 *Lift the rooted shoots at the margins of the mat, close to the base of the plant (here,* Veronica*) and remove them with a sharp knife. Trim off any sideshoots and straggly roots (see inset).*

2 *Pot up the cuttings individually into a small pot of gritty soil mix. Firm gently, water and top-dress with grit. Grow on in a cold frame and plant out when the root system is well established.*

Division

Many alpines can be propagated by division. The technique is essentially the same as that used for herbaceous border perennials, but on a much smaller scale. The most suitable species are those that are mat-forming with fibrous roots, and clump-forming species that produce clusters of shoots that are easily separated. Division is also used to rejuvenate clump-forming species when they lose vigor or die out at the center.

When to divide

Most plants are best divided in early spring, as new growth begins. Many can also be divided in autumn, and will form a new root system while the soil is still warm. In areas with very cold winters, however, it may be safer to divide in spring, immediately after flowering. Do not divide plants in cold, wet conditions, or in freezing weather. A few plants, like primulas and *Meconopsis*, are divided after flowering when they begin a period of strong vegetative growth.

How to divide

Lift plants, shaking loose soil from the roots. Large clumps can be divided using back-to-back forks or, for smaller-scale plants, back-to-back handforks. Lever the plant into two halves, making sure that each division has a healthy clump of roots and growth buds, then tease out by hand into smaller pieces. For best results, replant immediately into holes that are large enough to accommodate the rootball without restriction. Firm in and water well. Keep the soil moist until the plants are well established.

With small or precious plants, pot up smaller divisions to grow on in a cold frame in shade until they are well established. A mix of soil based potting mix and grit is best for this method, or use an ericaceous mix for lime-hating plants.

If immediate replanting is not possible, wrap the divisions in moist burlap or plastic to prevent them from drying out until they can be dealt with.

Propagating by Division

1 *Fibrous-rooted plants, (here,* Gentiana acaulis*) can be divided to produce new plants. Lift a clump of the parent plant and shake off loose soil.*

2 *Tease the clump apart using back-to-back handforks, then separate into smaller pieces by hand. If necessary, cut through tough roots with a sharp knife.*

3 *Re-plant pieces with a good root system and growth buds, setting directly into their permanent site. Make a hole big enough to accommodate the roots. Firm and water in with a fine nozzle.*

Root cuttings

A limited number of rock plants and alpines, including *Anchusa caespitosa* and *Pulsatilla* species, can be increased by root cuttings. These should be taken when the plants are dormant in late autumn or winter. Select a strong healthy parent and lift it from the soil. Choosing the plumpest healthy roots, cut them off from the parent plant and section them into pieces about 2in (5cm) long. Make a straight cut at the top end (that is, the end nearest the parent crown) and a slanting cut at the bottom end to ensure that they are inserted the right way up. Wash the cuttings in tepid water. Replant the parent. Insert the cuttings in pots at least 4in (10cm) deep. Place a layer of crocks in the bottom of the pot, topped with a 1in (2.5cm) layer of soil-based potting mix, then fill with washed sand and firm. Insert the roots, right way up, into prepared holes around the edge of the pot, aligning the straight-cut edge with the sand surface. Plants with slender or wiry roots should be laid flat on the sand surface. Top-dress with grit, label, and water the cutting in. Place in a cold frame on a layer of grit or gravel, or in a propagator. Keep well ventilated, but close the frames in periods of cold weather. Do not water again until new shoots appear.

When new shoots are showing strong growth, check that they have rooted fully by sliding them very gently out of their pots. If well rooted, pot them up singly in a mix of soil-based potting mix

How to Propagate by Root Cuttings

1 *In late autumn or early winter, use a hand fork to lift a plant with a well-developed root system (here,* Primula denticulata*).*

2 *Wash soil from the roots, then select the thickest healthy roots for cuttings. Cut off with a sharp knife close to the crown of the parent plant.*

3 *Cut into 2in (5cm) sections, with a straight cut at the end closest to the parent plant and a sloping cut at the lower end.*

4 *Over a layer of crocks and soil mix, fill the pot with sharp sand. Insert cuttings with the straight end level with the surface.*

5 *Cover with a ⅖in (1cm) layer of grit, water thoroughly, allow to drain, then place the pot in a propagator.*

and sharp sand. Top-dress the pots with a layer of grit and water well. Set the pots in a sheltered place outdoors, with shade from direct sun, or in an open frame. Grow on until they are well established and the roots fill the pots, then plant out into their permanent flowering site. If they are not ready for planting by late summer, leave them in pots until the following spring.

Scooping rosettes

Robust and rapid-growing species of rosette-forming plants, like *Primula denticulata*, can be propagated by scooping their rosettes in mid-winter. This is essentially a modification of root cuttings that is practiced on plants *in situ*. Some growers consider this technique to be rather risky, since plants *in situ* are exposed to the worst of the weather as well as soil-borne fungi and other pests. Nevertheless, it is a suitable method for increasing robust, hardy species like *P. denticulata*, and is a useful technique for producing a particularly good color form that has appeared in a group of seed-raised plants.

The rosettes are scooped out with a sharp knife to expose the top of the rootstock, thereby stimulating the production of multiple rosettes at their apex. Select strong-growing rosettes and brush the cut top of the root with fungicidal powder to prevent gray mold (*Botrytis*). Cover the cut tops with a thin layer of sharp horticultural sand.

Shoots should soon appear on each root apex. When they reach about 1–2in (2.5–5cm) tall, lift the whole clump and and tease it apart into individual plantlets, with each bearing vigorous, healthy roots and shoots. Use a sharp knife for separating the clump, if necessary, rather than risk damaging the plantlets.

Pot up the young plants into a mix of equal parts soil mix and sharp sand. Water thoroughly, and grow on in a sheltered site outdoors, shaded from direct sun. Keep moist and plant out when the roots have filled the pots.

How to Scoop Rosettes

1 *Scoop out the live crowns of a robust rosette-forming plant (here,* Primula denticulata*) with a sharp knife, so that the tops of the roots are visible (see inset).*

2 *Dust the cut surfaces with fungicide to discourage mold and fungal infections, then cover the exposed surfaces with a thin layer of sharp horticultural sand.*

3 *When new shoots reach 1–2in (2.5–5cm) high, carefully lift the whole clump with a handfork or trowel Separate into individual plants and pot up to grow on.*

ALPINE HOUSES AND FRAMES

For gardeners wishing to grow alpine plants that are unable to withstand the variable conditions of low-altitude, temperate climates, an alpine house provides the ideal solution.

Using the alpine house and frames

An alpine house is a minimally heated, well-ventilated greenhouse used for growing and displaying alpines and bulbs. The alpine house is not designed tö keep plants warm and must always have maximum ventilation. Vents need be closed only during prolonged freezing or foggy, humid conditions in winter.

To reduce temperatures in the hottest months, an alpine house should have a hard floor for damping down and the facility for shading in summer. Electric fans can also help by ensuring good air flow. When used in conjunction with nearby frames (which can be used as an "overspill" area for plants that are not in flower), the alpine house offer cool, fresh air and low temperatures in summer, without the rapid rise in temperatures experienced under glass.

Plants are usually grown in pots plunged in a sand bed on a raised bench to reduce changes in temperature and to keep the roots cool and moist. A plunge bench also allows easy irrigation of plants that dislike overhead watering. Growing alpines in pots ensures that special watering, soil or feeding requirements can be provided for individual plants. Plastic pots can be used, although clay ones stay cool in sand and are more attractive for display.

Soil mixes

All alpines need freely drained soil mix and benefit from a layer of crocks in the bottom of clay pots, or grit in plastic ones. Many will thrive in a mix of equal parts soil-based potting mix and grit; or a mix of equal parts sterilized loam, leaf mold, and grit. High-growing alpines need a less fertile soil mix and prefer to be grown in a mix of equal parts loam and leaf mold, with 2–3 parts grit or stone chips. For acid-loving plants, provide a mix made up of 4 parts lime-free leaf mold, and 1 part each of sharp sand and lime-free loam. Top-dress pots with a layer of grit, or limestone chips for lime-loving plants, and acid, granitic grit on sandstone, or granulated bark for lime-hating plants. Some of the very moisture-sensitive cushion-formers can be propped up with an additional layer of small stones.

CARE OF ALPINES AFTER FLOWERING

Alpines indoors
After flowering, alpines (here, Dionysia*) needing careful watering should be plunged under cover.*

Alpines outdoors
Alpines tolerant of variable summer weather can be plunged in an open frame outdoors after flowering.

Protecting alpines in frames
Alpines grown in frames can be displayed in full flower in the alpine house.

Repotting a Saxifrage

1 When a plant has become pot-bound, transfer it to a larger pot with minimum disturbance to the rootball.

2 Choose a pot that is one size larger than the existing pot. Use crocks and grit at the base to provide drainage.

3 Cover the drainage hole with crocks, then cover the crocks with gravel. This will also prevent soil mix. from blocking the hole.

4 Remove the plant from its pot by tapping gently on the base to loosen the root ball. Tease out the roots carefully.

5 Cover crocks with some soil mix, position the plant with its neck at the same level as in the original pot. Top up with soil mix.

6 Spread grit or rock chips over the surface and tuck it under the collar of the plant to keep it moisture-free.

7 Place the pot up to its neck in a bowl of water and leave it until the surface of the soil mix and gravel appears damp.

8 Remove the pot and place it on a layer of sand in an open frame, where excess moisture can drain away easily.

9 The repotted plant can then be plunged in sand in a plunge frame or bed in the alpine house to re-establish and grow on.

GLOSSARY OF TERMS

Italicized words have their own entry.

ACID [of soil] With a *pH* value of less than 7; see also *alkaline* and *neutral.*

ALKALINE [of soil] With a *pH* value of more than 7; some plants will not tolerate alkaline soils and must be grown in soil that is *neutral* or *acid.*

ALPINE HOUSE An unheated greenhouse, used for the cultivation of mainly alpine plants. An alpine house provides greater ventilation and usually more light than a conventional greenhouse.

ALTERNATE [of leaves] Borne singly at each node, on either side of a *stem.*

AXIL The angle between a leaf and *stem* where an axillary bud develops.

BLOOM 1. A flower or blossom. 2. A fine, waxy, whitish or bluish-white coating found on *stems,* leaves, or fruits.

BRACT A modified leaf at the base of a *flower* or flower cluster. Bracts may resemble normal leaves or can be reduced and scale-like in appearance; they are often large and brightly colored.

BUD A rudimentary or condensed *shoot* containing embryonic leaves or *flowers.*

CALYX (pl. calyces) The outer part of a *flower,* usually small and green but sometimes showy and brightly colored, that encloses the *petals* in *bud* and is formed from the sepals.

CAPSULE A dry fruit that splits open when ripe to release its *seeds.*

COROLLA 1. Collective name for *petals.* 2. Inner *whorl* of *perianth segments* in some monocotyledons.

COTYLEDON A seed leaf; the first leaf or leaves to emerge from the seed after germination.

CROWN The part of the plant at or just below the soil surface from which new shoots are produced and to which they die back in autumn.

CUTTING A section of a plant that is removed and used for propagation. For the various methods, see pp. 168–175.

CULTIVAR (CV) A contraction of "cultivated variety"; a group (or one among such a group) comprising cultivated plants that are clearly distinguished by one or more characteristics which are retained when progagation is performed.

DEADHEAD To remove spent *flower heads* so as to promote further growth or flowering, prevent seeding, or improve appearance.

DECIDUOUS Losing its leaves annually at the end of the growing season.

DIE-BACK Death of the tips of shoots due to cold or disease.

DISC FLORET, DISC FLOWER A small and often individually inconspicuous, usually tubular *flower,* often making the central portion of a composite *flower head,* such as a daisy.

DIVISION A method of propagation by which a clump is divided into several parts during *dormancy.*

DORMANCY The state of temporary cessation of growth and slowing down of other activities in whole plants, usually during winter.

ELLIPTIC [of leaves] Broadening in the center and narrowing toward each end.

ENTIRE [of leaves] With untoothed margins.

EVERGREEN Retaining its leaves at the end of the growing season, but losing some older leaves during the year. **Semi-evergreen** plants retain some leaves or lose older ones only when the new growth is produced.

EYE The center of a *flower,* of particular note if different in color from the *petals.*

FLORET A single *flower* in a head of many flowers.

FLOWER The part of the plant containing the reproductive organs usally surrounded by sepals and *petals.*

FLOWER HEAD A mass of small *flowers* or *florets* that, together, appear to form a single flower.

GENUS (pl. genera) A category in plant classification, consisting of a group of related *species.*

HABIT The characteristic growth or general appearance of a plant.

HARDY Able to withstand year-round climatic conditions without protection.

HERBACEOUS Dying down at the end of the growing season.

HYBRID The offspring of genetically different parents, usually produced accidentally or artificially in cultivation, but occasionally arising in the wild.

LAYERING A propagation method whereby a *stem* is induced to root by being pegged down in the soil while still attached to the parent plant.

LEAFMOLD Fibrous, flaky material derived from decomposed leaves, used as a soil improver.

LIME Compounds of calcium, the amount of lime in the soil determines whether it is *acid*, *neutral*, or *alkaline*.

LINEAR [of leaves] Very narrow with parallel sides.

LOAM Well-structured, fertile soil that is moisture-retentive but free-draining.

MULCH A layer of organic matter applied to the soil over or around a plant to conserve moisture, protect the *roots* from cold, reduce the growth of weeds, and enrich the soil.

NATURALIZE To establish and grow as if in the wild.

NEUTRAL [of soil] With a *pH* value of 7, the point at which soil is neither *acid* nor *alkaline*.

PERENNIAL Living for at least 3 seasons. A woody-based perennial dies down only partially, leaving a woody stem at the base.

PERIANTH The outer part of the *flower* comprising the calyx and the corolla. Often used when the *calyx* and the *corolla* are very similar in form.

PERIANTH SEGMENT One portion of the *perianth*, resembling a *petal* and sometimes known as a tepal.

PETAL One portion of the usually showy and colored part of the *corolla*.

PETIOLE The stalk of a leaf.

pH The scale by which the acidity or alkalinity of soil is measured. See also *acid*, *alkaline*, and *neutral*.

PROSTRATE With *stems* growing along the ground.

RAY PETAL The *petal* or fused petals, often showy, of a *ray flower*.

RECURVED Applied to *petals* of *flowers* and florets that curve backward.

REFLEXED Applied to *petals* that are bent backwards at an angle of more than 90°. Also referred to as fully reflexed.

ROOT The part of a plant, normally underground, that functions as anchorage and through which water and nutrients are absorbed.

ROSETTE A group of leaves that radiate from about the same point, often borne at ground level at the base of a very short *stem*.

RUNNER A horizontally spreading, usually slender *stem*, that forms *roots* at each *node*, often confused with *stolon*.

SCALE A reduced or modified leaf.

SEED The ripened, fertilized ovule containing a dormant embryo capable of developing into an adult plant.

SEEDHEAD Any usually dry fruit that contains ripe seeds.

SEEDLING A young plant that has developed from a *seed*.

SELF-SEED To produce *seedlings* around the parent plant.

SEPAL Part of a *calyx*, usually insignificant, but sometimes showy and *petal*-like.

SHOOT The aerial part of a plant which bears leaves.

SIMPLE [of leaves] Not divided into leaflets.

SINGLE A flower with the normal number of petals or tepals for the species, arranged in a single whorl. Also applied to (composite) flower heads that have a single row of outer ray florets with the center filled with disc florets.

SOLITARY Flower borne singly rather than in an inflorescence.

SPATHE One, or sometimes two, large *bracts* that surround a flower cluster or individual *bud*.

SPECIES A category in plant classification, the rank below *genus*, containing closely related, very similar individual plants.

SPRAY A group of *flowers* or *flower heads* on a single, branching stem.

SPUR A hollow projection from a *petal*, that often produces nectar.

STAMEN The male reproductive organ in a plant, comprising the *anther* and usually its *filament* or *stalk*.

STEM The main axis of a plant, usually above ground and supporting leaves, *flowers*, and fruits. Sometimes referred to as a stalk.

STERILE Infertile, not bearing spores, pollen, or *seeds*.

STIGMA The part of the female portion of the *flower*, borne at the tip of the *style*, that receives pollen.

STOLON A horizontally spreading or arching *stem*, usually above ground, which roots at its tip to produce a new plant.

STYLE The part of the *flower* on which the *stigma* is borne.

SUB-SHRUB A plant that is woody at the base although the terminal shoots die back in winter.

TOOTH A small, marginal, often pointed lobe on a *leaf*, *calyx*, or *corolla*.

TENDER Of a plant that is vulnerable to cold damage.

TRUE [of seedlings] Retaining the distinctive characteristics of the parent when raised from *seed*.

UPRIGHT [of habit] With vertical or semi-vertical main branches.

WHORL The arrangement of 3 or more organs arising from one point.

INDEX

Each genus name is shown in **bold** type, followed by a brief description. Species, varieties and subspecies are given in *italics;* cultivars are in roman type with single quotes. Common names appear in parentheses.

A

B

H

I

J

V

Y

ACKNOWLEDGMENTS

Key: t=top; b=bottom; r=right; l=left; c=center; cra=center right above; cla=center left above; crb=center right below; clb=center left below

The publishers would like to thank the following for their kind permission to reproduce the photographs:

Alpine Garden Society 29, 52tr, 99br, 117tl, 139bl, 147cr; **A-Z Botanical Collection** 32br, 44l, 83t, 100br, 138tr,/ **Derek Gould** 135crb/**Jiri Loun** 113l, **J Malcolm Smith** 51bl; **Gillian Beckett** 25tr, 84tl, 94tr, 97b, 98cr, 102tr & bl, 124cl, 126bl, 127br, 132tl; **Kenneth A Beckett** 76bl, 84bl; **Deni Bown** 46br; **Neil Campbell-Sharpe** 2; **Eric Crichton** 10, 41tl, 54br, 56br, 87tl, 103bl, 127tr, 128tl, 143tr; **Geoff Dann** 15tr; **Garden Matters** 81bl; **Garden Picture Library** 14, / **Brian Carter** 120cr,/**David England** 7,/**Vaughan Fleming** 74tl,/ **Jerry Pavia** 123br; **John Glover** 88, 135tr, 147tl; **Derek Gould** 22tl, 141tr; **Chris Grey-Wilson** 50tl, 53, 95br, 100tl, 146br; **Jerry Harpur** 13; **Muriel Hodgman** 131bl; **Mike Ireland** 77r, 145br; **Andrew Lawson** 28l, 30tl, 72bl, 104tl, 135bl, 145tl; **Photos Horticultural** 27, 33tr, 47cr, 56bl, 58bl, 59l, 68bl, 91, 128tr, 154bl; **Howard Rice** 47br; **Eric Sawford** 144br; **Harry Smith Collection** 28tr, 30tr, 33bl, 38tl & r, 49bl, 51r, 54tl, 61bl, 63tl, 65tl, 67bl, 74bl & br, 85bl, 87br, 90tl & br, 92bl, 94tl, 95tr, 105tr, 110bl, 118cr, 119cr, 123cr, 124t & bl, 125tr, 127tl, 128bl, 135tl, 141br, 147cl, 148bl, 153r; **Elizabeth Whiting & Associates** 11.

Special photography Howard Rice

In addition to the above, the publishers would also like to thank the staff of the Royal Horticultural Society Publications.

Abbreviations

C	centigrade	in	inch, inches
cm	centimeter	m	meter
cv.	cultivar	mm	millimeter
F	Fahrenheit	oz	ounce
f.	forma	sp.	species
ft	foot, feet	subsp.	subspecies
g	gram	var.	variant

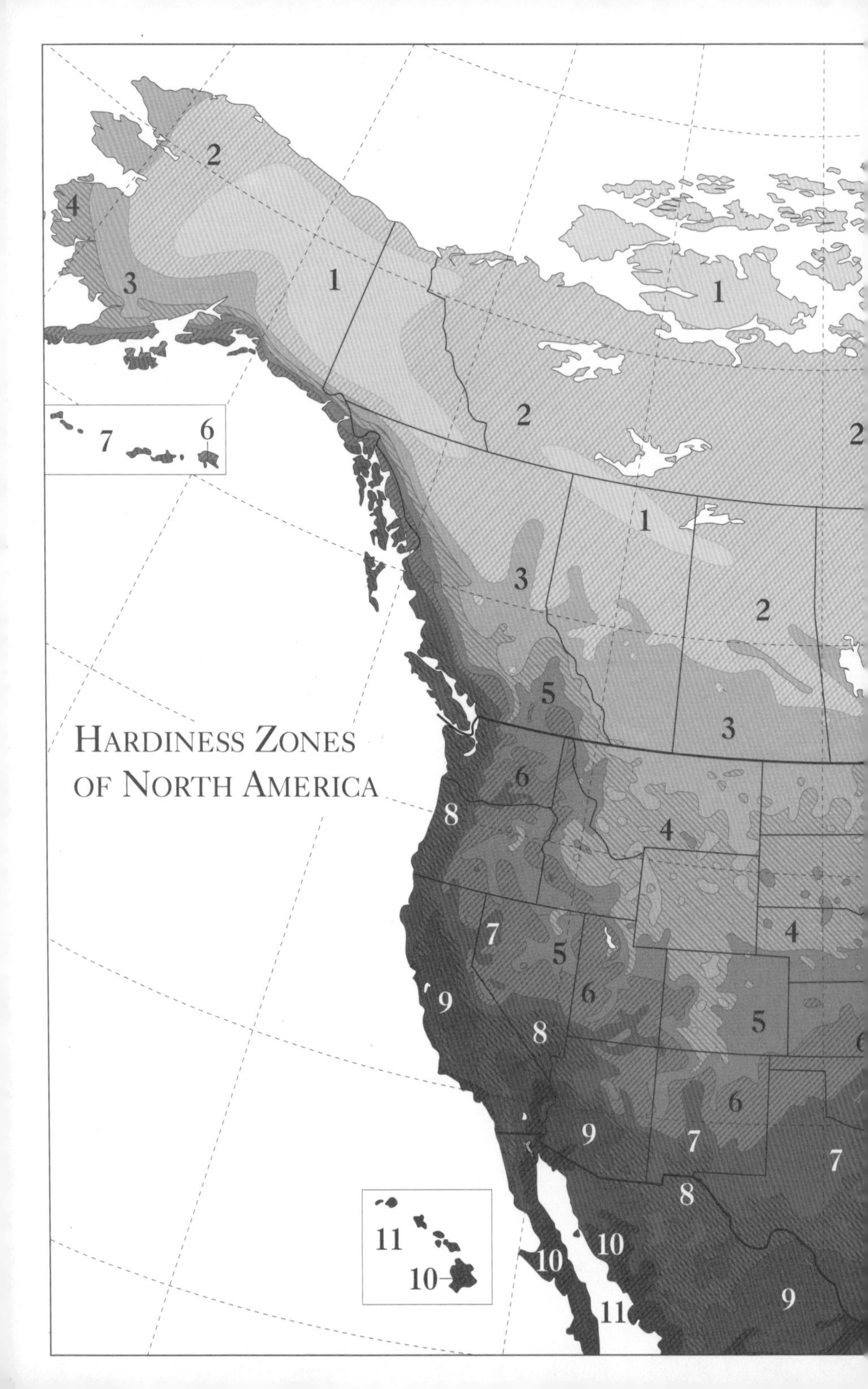
HARDINESS ZONES
OF NORTH AMERICA
1
2
3
4
5
6
7
8
9
10
11